SO CLOSE TO FREEDOM

SO CLOSE TO FREEDOM

FREEDOM

A WORLD WAR II STORY OF PERIL AND BETRAYAL IN THE PYRENEES

JEAN-LUC E. CARTRON

Foreword by ROGER STANTON

Potomac Books

AN IMPRINT OF THE UNIVERSITY OF NEBRASKA PRESS

Library of Congress Cataloging-in-Publication Data
Names: Cartron, Jean-Luc E., author. | Stanton, Roger, writer
of foreword.
Title: So close to freedom: a World War II story of peril and
betrayal in the Pyrenees / Jean-Luc E. Cartron; foreword by
Roger Stanton.
Description: Lincoln: Potomac Books, an imprint of the
University of Nebraska Press, [2019] | Includes bibliographical
references and index.
Identifiers: LCCN 2018040943
ISBN 9781640121027 (cloth: alk. paper)
ISBN 9781640121751 (epub)
ISBN 9781640121768 (mobi)
ISBN 9781640121775 (pdf)
Subjects: LCSH: World War, 1939–1945—Prisoners and prisons,
German. | Escapes—Pyrenees.
Classification: LCC D805.G C3525 2019 |
DDC 940.54/72430922—dc23
LC record available at https://lccn.loc.gov/2018040943

Set in Sabon Next LT Pro by E. Cuddy.

CONTENTS

ILLUSTRATIONS

22. James F. Fowler crew, 427th Bomber Squadron
23. Saint-Laurent/Saint-Paul railroad station during the 1940s
24. Superbagnères Plateau overlooking the
Lys Valley to the south
25. HM submarine *Splendid* crew, 1943
26. Edmond "Eddie" Luff, 1945
27. One-peseta note signed by three of the evaders

FOREWORD

ROGER STANTON

Many years ago while serving in the British Army, I was involved with the Army POW Escaping Club (APOWEC) and the RAF Escaping Society (RAFES). Members of both organizations had tremendous personal stories to tell but they always gave precedence to the deeds of another group—their "helpers." Without those people, many of the escapers and evaders would not have survived the rigors of being alone and "on the run" in occupied territory. If they did not perish while attempting escape over treacherous mountain routes, the fates awaiting solo escapers and evaders often included capture, torture, or even execution for being mistaken as a spy. They would have most certainly ended up in a POW camp or, in some cases, a concentration camp.

In the years following my meetings with the APOWEC and the RAFES, I began to research the helpers and their selfless exploits to aid the Allied cause of freedom from tyranny, who were always forefront in the accounts of the escapers and evaders. Together with like-minded researchers, these stories were followed up, and we traced helpers and their "parcels" and the routes they had taken, piecing together their stories. In 1988 the escapers, evaders, and helpers, together with their families, researchers, historians, and supporters were gathered into one commemorative organization called the Escape Lines Reunion which, over the years, evolved into the World War II Escape Lines Memorial Society (or ELMS). The society, now a registered charity, includes helpers, veterans, families, students, researchers, and other supporters intent on maintaining the memory of seldom-broadcast selfless acts of courage.

In the dark days of 1940 when, on mainland Europe, all seemed lost to the might of the German army, the helpers came forward at great risk to themselves and their families, to assist fleeing Allied soldiers and airmen and other fugitives to make a "Home Run" and return home safely to England to continue the fight against a common enemy. The helpers hid, clothed, nursed, and fed their charges; they escorted them across occupied Europe to neutral countries, or over dangerous, forbidding borders into Spain or Andorra, then onward to Gibraltar or Lisbon. The helpers were given no training, were not armed, received no payment, and if caught were subjected to harsh treatment by the Gestapo: they were tortured; many were executed; and those who survived interrogation were thrown into concentration camps, where many died owing to the harsh conditions. Life expectancy on an escape line could be as low as three months before capture. Many believe that for every escaper or evader who made it home, four escape line helpers died or suffered in a concentration camp.

"Helpers" came from all walks of life: the rich and the poor, farmers, lawyers, nurses and doctors, teachers, train drivers, priests, police and criminals, even boy scouts and girl guides. Many adopted professions that allowed them to avoid curfews, enabling them to "legitimately" pursue their work at night. Anonymous people gave money and produced passes and permits. Farmers provided food. Doctors treated the injured and asked no questions. Many, mainly young girls, acted as couriers. Tough mountain guides took their "parcels" over the dangerous mountain routes, while at home their wives often provided a safe house for the next group to cross. Regardless of nationality, communication was not a major barrier. Helpers all played their part in ensuring that more than 3,500 British and colonial Allied servicemen and more than 3,400 Americans returned home from occupied Europe to Great Britain to fight again.

Women played a key role in the work of the escape lines, as many men from mainland Europe had escaped to England to join their countrymen in the free forces of European nations. Others had taken to the hills to join Resistance forces in the mountains and wooded areas. Many others had been deported to Germany under the German Todt organization to work in factories or in farming. So it fell to the women to not only run the safe houses but also to take on the roles of couriers moving messages, supplies, and evaders both locally and on the dangerous intercity routes.

Wartime life on mainland Europe was particularly hard. To enhance their supplies the enemy requisitioned or stole food, water, fuel, vehicles, and animals from their occupied territories and local populations. Factories making clothing and shoes ceased operations. Households practiced frugality and improvisation, so a helper giving food and clothing to a stranger who had suddenly appeared and did not speak the language would cause much hardship to a family who were rationing and hardly had sufficient food and supplies for their own needs.

Most people today have not been personally touched by total war, but in Great Britain in the 1950s and 1960s nearly every family had a World War II connection, and almost all had been affected by the war. Today few people are aware of the courage, physical hardship, and endurance that the World War II generation experienced. How can we possibly imagine what it would be like to be in charge of a Lancaster Bomber on a night operation over enemy territory, targeted by enemy night fighters and anti-aircraft guns and illuminated by searchlights—at only twenty-one years of age, and commanding a crew possibly younger than that? Nor do we know what it would be like to storm ashore on a Normandy beach under withering enemy machine gun fire, an artillery barrage, and an air attack from enemy fighters—when only eighteen years of age! Or to be in a convoy to Murmansk in Arctic waters, pursued by enemy submarines! And what was it like to suddenly find yourself alone, possibly injured, in a foreign country, knowing that enemy forces were all around you?

In all the Allied nations young men and women, barely out of school, volunteered to fight for their freedom. Within the occupied territories many young people came forward to fight with Resistance forces, overtly carrying out sabotage attacks, while others covertly collected Allied escapers, evaders, and other fugitives. For the Allied serviceman, particularly aircrew, the knowledge that there were people on the ground in the occupied territories who could help them return home to England was the best morale booster they could receive as they embarked on their operations.

Most countries are bounded by natural borders such as mountains, rivers, or seas. These were the obstacles placed before the escapers and evaders; some were more surmountable than others. Fast Royal Navy motor gunboats (MGBS) or motor torpedo boats (MTBS) from isolated beaches on the Brittany coast provided an extraction route across the English Channel. Small fishing boats from Denmark took their charges to Sweden. Norwegian fishing boats transported their evaders to the Shetland Isles and Newcastle. For many their fates rested on the expertise and knowledge of the *passeurs*: the French, Spanish, Basque, and Catalonian mountain guides of the Pyrenean routes. Dutch routes initially ran to Switzerland before changing to the Pyrenees. There were the *contadini* of the Italian mountains and countryside; the Cretan and Greek guides; the Polish and Norwegian mountain guides who often worked in subzero temperatures. The guides were prepared not only to risk their lives against the enemy, but also against harsh nature and the elements abounding in the mountains and in the seas, to assist their brother combatants and achieve a common goal.

Escapers and evaders from all branches of the services knew their options were bleak if captured in civilian clothing. When apprehended, many who could prove their identity as airmen or soldiers were entitled to be treated as prisoners of war. Others were treated more harshly; some were shot, especially if they were evading in Germany. Eventually most were sent to, or returned to, a POW camp. Some of the least fortunate were directed to concentration camps.

But what about the helpers? To be caught with evaders was, in most cases, a death sentence for men and a concentration camp for women, but not before harsh interrogation by the Gestapo prior to their sentencing. In many cases complete families suffered the same fate, regardless of their knowledge or complicity—for strange though it sounds, many helpers went about their work without the awareness of their families, although often it was a "family business." That dreaded knock on the door in the middle of the night has haunted many helpers for the rest of their lives. Instead of a "friend in need" it could have been the enemy, the

Gestapo or English-speaking Germans posing as escapers. Right or wrong, a decision had to be taken and a response made!

As a guest at a safe house, evaders shouldered a tremendous responsibility toward their hosts in order not to compromise them. Life at the safe house had to appear normal to the locals and not attract attention: why is madame buying so many provisions? The light was on way after madame's bedtime! There is men's clothing on the washing line but madame lives alone! Did we hear the toilet flush when madame was out? Suspicions and rumors led to betrayal.

Today there is often talk of "man's inhumanity toward man," but the helpers demonstrated "man's humanity toward man" in the most practical of ways. In the United Kingdom there existed the spirit of "pulling together," uniting communities, supporting neighbors, and welcoming strangers. A different story unfolded in continental Europe and other occupied areas, where the enemy and collaborators were all around and communities were often unsure who was in their midst. Every stranger was suspect, and many helpers were often betrayed by their own people. In any occupied country the enemy seeks clues; local knowledge is vital to their intelligence gathering, and those best equipped to supply it are local collaborators, many often collaborating solely for their own survival or gain rather than for any political ideology. No one knew whom they could trust, yet the helpers took a risk, seeking out Allied strangers in need and offering assistance.

Militarily there is a distinction between escapers and evaders, and this presented consequences for those "on the run"; in some instances an escaper had earned his enemies' respect for his skills and benefited from a "blindeye," but the Axis troops took evaders into custody! An escaper is defined as one who has managed to escape from "secure enemy custody," whether it be a prison, POW camp, prison train, or from guards on the ground. Once free, he then has to turn to the tactics of evasion. Escapers were mainly army personnel. An evader has not been captured and has, with luck, managed to retain some of his escape kit and equipment—his task is to remain undetected, outwit the enemy, and stay free from capture in order to return to his unit.

An evader holds the advantage. World War II evaders tended to be mainly aircrew or Special Forces.

An escaper has different priorities from the evader, which begin at the moment that he is apprehended. The best time to escape is immediately upon capture. At that point he is probably in open ground, aware of his location, probably still has most of his kit, and is guarded by relatively few enemy. However, luck and opportunity diminish once blindfolded and transported through the front-line units to the rear echelons to a heavily guarded prison miles behind the enemy front line, then relieved of his kit and boots to reduce the gamble of an escape.

A successful evader utilizes the close link between evasion tactics and survival techniques. Appropriate kit, the ability to use it effectively, and relative fitness play their part, but the key ingredient of survival is mental ability—the fight against loneliness and the will to survive against the odds when everything is stacked against you. The other ingredient is "luck"—the luck of knocking on the right door, trusting the right person, working in the right weather, and remaining healthy and uninjured. And then there are the principal rules of remaining undetected: walk by night, sleep by day; cycle on the correct side of the road; observe local curfews; do not draw attention to yourself; and above all, stay calm.

At the end of the European war, escapers and evaders sought out their helpers with a view to expressing their gratitude more fully. Many helpers were untraceable, disappeared into the "fog of war." Some had "just got on with their lives" and started a new chapter. Some had used assumed identities, others had moved home, some had died under interrogation or been executed, and many had been sent to the camps, where they died in the harsh conditions. Some helpers had disappeared into the dark world of the camps under Hitler's *Nacht und Nabel* (NN) (Night and fog) order. Some survivors did return from the disease-ridden camps, from Mauthausen, Dachau, and Ravensbrück (the principal camps to which escape-line helpers were dispatched), ill and emaciated, resembling skeletons dressed in striped rags. But it was from these camps that brave and courageous people emerged, perhaps slowly and unsteadily, but with heads held high. They had been up against possibly the best intelligence organization in the world. They had fought a lonely war in the cause of freedom, and won.

The story that follows tells of the trials and tribulations of a group of evaders, Resistance fighters and *Engelandvaarders* whose destinies converged on Toulouse, where they were gathered in by the helpers of the "Françoise" organization to begin their route to freedom over the high Pyrenees and into Spain. The experiences of the fugitives and their guides as they combined forces to battle the elements, yet were trusting of no one, although unique to each group were far from uncommon. It took courage, determination, a focus on the ultimate goal, and luck!

PREFACE

"We must have passed it," I said, stopping to pull out the map. My son Matthieu and I were hiking along the northern slopes of the Superbagnères mountain in search of the "black shed." Or rather, what was left of it. Earlier in the day, we had met with French mountain guide André Sacome—a bit of a local celebrity—at his cabin in Gourron. Because he was due to return to the town of Luchon, he could not accompany us on our hike. But he had his own ideas about the possible location of the black shed, which nearly seventy-five years ago had served as a secret resting place for downed Allied airmen headed for the Spanish border. Most compelling were the ruins of a small building in the forest, about one thousand feet in elevation below what had once been the rack-and-pinion railroad leading up to Superbagnères. According to Sacome, no one in the area knew the purpose of that building. "Certainly not a sheep barn," he told us, "not with it being located in the forest." And it was not one of the small train stations built along the rack railroad.

So far, the map drawn by Sacome had proven very reliable. From the tiny village of Gourron (once known as the "Granges de Gourron"), we had crossed a small stream and hiked to a dam before leaving the main trail and climbing a faint path that zigzagged up into a forest of silver firs. We had reached another main trail and followed it downslope, with the trees on both sides closing in above and obscuring much of the sunlight. Somewhere along the trail were the ruins mentioned by the guide, but we had yet to find them.

Months earlier, I had talked on the phone with André Crampé, Charbonnier's last surviving (mountain guide and people smuggler). In the spring of 1944, he and his brother Pierre made one of the two teams—with Jean Ferret and Jean-Louis Pène in the other—smuggling downed airmen and other fugitives over the last mountain pass before Spain. "From the black shed," André Crampé repeated several times, "we followed the rack railroad then dropped down into the Lys Valley heading for the Ravi Bridge." "After that, we climbed in the direction of the inn Hospice de France and the mountain pass just below the Col du Portillon." Although there was no helper file in his name in Washington, I trusted André Crampé completely. He had brought up an incident that took place on March 27, 1944, as a group of evaders struggled to climb the last mountain before Spain. The same incident was mentioned in a letter written by Dutchman Sam Timmers Verhoeven after the war. Crampé could not possibly have known had he not been one of the *passeurs*.

André Crampé had since passed away, but upon hearing us describe what we knew of the black shed, Sacome told us the passeurs logically must have followed the rack railroad between Artigue-Ardoune and the Fountain of Broucas just below the plateau of Superbagnères. Given the interest of Sacome and several of the other locals I talked to—the mayor of Saint-Aventin, among others—I might have wondered yet again how the story had never been told in France, where it all took place. But since our earlier visit with Christian Ferret, Jean Ferret's son, I knew one of the main reasons. French historian Emilienne Eychenne had no doubt come closest to telling that story. In one passage of her book, published in 1984, she alluded to a betrayal that led to the capture of a group of fugitives in April 1944 near Luchon. The traitor, she even wrote, was said to have confessed on his deathbed.

In her time, Emilienne Eychenne (now also deceased) likely did not have access to key legal proceeding files; these were released only recently. During her research, however, she had also contacted Jean Ferret. In his apartment along the Allées d'Etigny in Luchon, Christian Ferret (the son) explained to us that like many others, his father had returned from Germany's concentration and slave labor camps a changed man. He remained kind and honorable, but he had also become obstinate and occasionally disillusioned with society, showing no interest in receiving the usual distinctions for members of the French Resistance. He had done his duty, he would repeat to others, no less, no more. And when Eychenne came to see him many years after the war, he would not open up to her. "If I told you, you simply would not believe me," he had said to her.

Matthieu and I were now retracing some of our steps in the forest below Superbagnères. On our left, among the ferns that blanketed the forest floor, something else now stood out. Not a wall nor even a wall section, but instead a few piles of bricks and stones. We stepped off the trail and reached the ruins. We could see the dark gray stone foundations standing just above the ground and covered with lichen. At 3,500 feet in this subalpine forest, time and humidity had clearly taken their toll. We combed through the area and found a few rusty nails and an old can of food. "Were these the ruins of the black shed?" we asked ourselves. Was this the place where, on April 21, 1944, the Germans caught up with a group of thirty-five Allied evaders and other fugitives bound for Spain? One of the American airmen had later written about a "large barn" on a "heavily forested side," and of not being able to see the Germans above and below them because of all the trees. Another American, the P-51 fighter pilot in the group, spoke of the trail making a ninety-degree turn to the right at the cabin. We could see, perhaps, the path the group would have followed to reach our location: not along our trail, but instead straight up the mountainside among the trees. If so, then the trail in the direction of Superbagnères would have appeared to make that right turn at a ninety-degree angle.

We left Luchon that evening, unsure about the significance of the ruins we had found. But I had gained a sense of scale and direction I had been lacking before. Many of the valleys in the region—the lower Larboust Valley, the Valley of Luchon, and especially the Lys Valley—were narrow and steep-sided. I tried to imagine what it must have been like to climb the Pyrenees to reach freedom, penned in by abrupt mountains and thick forests. Not for the thrill of adventure, not by choice, but because one must. All I felt was renewed admiration for those who had made the attempt, often without the appropriate footwear and with no prior experience in the mountains. They were truly men (and women) of courage and grit.

ACKNOWLEDGMENTS

So Close to Freedom was initially not intended to be a book-length project. I had just completed the biography of my grandfather Marcel Chichery and dug up information on several of his companions of misfortune in Germany, including Belgian Roger Bureau. Just hours before their deaths, all twelve men had managed to send news to their families through a French prisoner of war. It was that story I set out to write, with just an opening chapter on the capture of Roger Bureau in the Pyrenees. With the wonderful assistance of the Bureau family (grandson James, daughter-in-law Janet, and son Jack), the story of Roger Bureau—one of the many unsung heroes of World War II—took on a life of its own. Fr. Pierre Tritz and Aurore Darnet of the Catholic congregation Fils de la Charité (Sons of Charity) made another important, early contribution with priest Paul Louis's World War II memoirs and letters. The stories of two American evaders captured under very similar circumstances as Paul Louis and Roger Bureau were available through www.evasioncomete.org, an association dedicated to the history of the Comet line. Researcher Philippe Connart, whom I contacted, was at once convinced the stories of the two American evaders and of Roger Bureau and Paul Louis were linked. It became increasingly clear that Roger Bureau and Paul Louis had attempted to climb over the Pyrenees with a large group of evaders, mostly American, British, Canadian, and Australian airmen. In their riveting volume, *The Long Road: Trials and Tribulations of Airmen Prisoners from Bankau to Berlin, June 1944–May 1945*, Oliver Clutton-Brock and Ray Crompton dedicated a few pages to the story of that attempt. In the Fils de la Charité archive collection, a letter written not by Paul Louis but by his friend Raymond

Krugell, also present in the Pyrenees, suggested that the group of evaders had been betrayed by someone with intimate knowledge of who they were. With the escape and evasion reports available from the National Archives and Records Administration, and the autobiographical story of Sam Timmers Verhoeven translated from Dutch to English for me by Katelijne (Kat) Flies, all of those early sources form the origin of this book's concept.

In addition to the individuals and organizations listed above, I am deeply grateful to the Luff family (David, Peter, and, especially, Christopher) for Eddie Luff's World War II memoirs; Dave and Rick Drollinger for the World War II memoirs of their father, 2LT Lynn H. Drollinger; Joe Sutphin, ILT Joseph E. Sutphin's son, for information regarding his father's life during and after World War II; Harry Cammish, who at the age of ninety-three kindly answered my questions regarding his adventures during the war; André Crampé, one of Charbonnier's passeur, whom I interviewed on the phone on two occasions, and who drilled into my head the road followed by Charbonnier's men from the Valley of Barousse toward the Spanish border; and the family of Blanche Fontagnères (daughter Lorraine Moucheboeuf Guingand and granddaughter Michèle Guingand in France; niece Delphine Fontagnères in the United States) for details of Blanche and Lorraine's life in the Valley of Barousse during the German occupation. Christian Ferret—son of Jean Ferret, another passeur—agreed to discuss at length his father's arrest and deportation to Germany; Jeannine Heib, daughter of Mr. and Mrs. Floerchinger, spoke to me over the phone regarding local Resistance leader Robert Durand in Mazerulles. Jacques Lautman was always willing to answer questions and send me materials regarding his father, Albert Lautman, of the "Françoise" organization, as well as his uncle Jules. Angus McGeoch, the son of Vice Admiral Sir Ian Lachlan Mackay McGeoch, emailed me a report typed by his father regarding his capture and subsequent escape, as well as a photograph of the HM submarine *Splendid* crew. Raymond Krugell and his son Jacques—nephew and great-nephew of Raymond Krugell, respectively—provided the photograph of their uncle/great-uncle.

Special thanks go to Claudie Dussert, Laurine Forest, and Anne Grandjean of the Entraide Généalogique du Midi Toulousain, who digitized for me a large number of documents from the Archives Départementales de la Haute-Garonne in Toulouse, in particular all the files pertaining to the December 1944 ruling and proceedings in the case against Michel Pautot. Suzanne Zoumbaris of the National Archives at College Park, Maryland, was also a wonderful help, locating and digitizing copies of reports on helpers and escape lines. Oliver Clutton-Brock, Marie-Laure Le Foulon, Philippe Connart, Noemí Riudor i Garcia, and especially Michael Leblanc provided expert advice and assistance, in addition to sharing files on some of the escape lines and evaders mentioned in this book. Michael Leblanc also introduced me to the story of Maddy De Deken. Jackie Mansas was an important source of information regarding the secret life of Resistance fighters in the Valley of Barousse and surrounding area.

I am indebted to Lora Beth Barlow Wright for the memoirs and photograph of Archie Barlow Jr.; Gary L. Moncur and www .303rdbg.com for the photograph of the James F. Fowler crew, 427th BS; Philippe Sugg for the photograph of John Acthim and for excerpts of the airman's diary; Alexandra Matagne and Sylvie Vander Elst, directorate-general war victims of Belgium's Federal Public Service Social Security, for documents about Belgian victims of the Gardelegen massacre and Roger Bureau's photograph; Christophe Cathelain for the postcard featuring the Saint-Laurent/Saint-Paul railroad station during the 1940s; Lionel Fontaine for sending me his copy of Jean-Marie Chirol's rare and long-out-of-print book, *Sur les Chemins de l'Enfer*; Amand Collard for the text of his article on the crew of the B-17G Flying Fortress downed on March 2, 1944; Jean-Guy Rens for the transcript of the interview he conducted with his aunt regarding his uncle, Jacques Rens; Rose Fischer Touret for information on her father, Charles de Hepcée and the timeline of his arrest in the Pyrenees; Guy-Pierre Souverville for his article on the death of Jean-Louis Bazerque in Larroque; Jeanne Hyvrard for sharing information on the life of Jacques Liddell; Lynda Wright for all the materials regarding her father, Harry Cammish; Léo Capcarrère for information regarding his father, Georges; Pauline L. van Till for sharing a letter sent by Sam Timmers Verhoeven in 1991 and for translating some of its contents; Herman van Rens for the notes he took during his interview of Dr. Max Rens; wo Xavier Van Tilborg (DGHR-HRA--E/N/Arch) for Roger Bureau's military record; wo Ronny Wierinckx and Kathleen Van Acker (Historical Documentation Center of Belgium's Ministry of Defense, SGRS-S-CA) for Roger Bureau's Secret Army file; Martine and Bernard Corbineau, daughter and son of Jacqueline Houry, for sharing letters written by their mother, and for information on their grandfather Gérard Houry; Sophie Barthès-Marcilly and the Musée Départemental de la Résistance et de la Déportation for the deposition of Jean Ferret in the legal proceedings against Karl Dethlefs; Michiel Wilmink (Institute for War, Holocaust and Genocide Studies [NIOD] in Amsterdam) for the text of Sam Timmers Verhoeven's adventures in the Pyrenees; Gaëlle Avan and the Direction des Archives Départementales de la Haute-Garonne for the photograph of Marie-Louise Dissard; and Mike Sutphin and Julia Smith for putting me in touch with ILT Joseph E. Sutphin's son, Joe.

My thanks extend to many in my family and circle of friends, especially my parents Claude and Jacqueline, always willing to assist me in all aspects of my research and through their visits to the French military archives in Vincennes (SHD); my father-in-law and professional photographer Bob Nugent for cleaning and restoring some of the photos illustrating the book; Ryan Trollinger for the maps; my wife Dominique and our son Matthieu for reading draft chapters of the book; and Michael Shane Thompson, who came to the rescue when my computer misbehaved.

Finally, I am grateful to Evelyn Le Chêne, Oliver Clutton-Brock, and Ryan and Mandi Trollinger, for reviewing the complete manuscript; Tom Swanson (Potomac Books) and the editorial board at the University of Nebraska Press for their interest in publishing *So Close to Freedom*; Walt Evans for his copyediting; Ann Baker for overseeing the production of the book; and Roger Stanton, who did me the great honor of writing the foreword.

AUTHOR'S NOTE

Throughout *So Close to Freedom* I have attempted to strike a balance between easy readability and detail, between providing historical context—following the main flow of events—and bringing to light personal stories and memories. Such a balancing act has been difficult, owing in part to the large and complex cast of characters. That cast ranges from American, British, and British Commonwealth escapers and evaders to *Engelandvaarders* and members of the French Resistance on the run, from the heads of escape-line organizations to simple helpers, from *passeurs* to infiltrators and informants. The main narrative thread is the story of thirty-five men who attempted to reach Spain by climbing over the high mountains of the central Pyrenees in April 1944. Who were those men and what were their reasons for wanting to escape from France? What happened to them during the attempt and afterward? How did the Germans discover their presence in the mountains near the town of Luchon? In answering the last question the book is also an investigative narrative, a retracing of several interrelated historical strands to explore what or who may have alerted the Germans. The reader will discover, for example, that the Nazis placed spies in some of the Spanish border towns and that they seemingly received the help of the Guardia Civil. Two important escape organizations—Dutch-Paris and Françoise—operated in Toulouse during the early months of 1944. Their functioning was complex yet always precarious and under the constant threat of betrayal or infiltration. With the help of one medical student and a network of passeurs, both organizations sent groups of fugitives from Toulouse to the central Pyrenees for passage to Spain. The group that followed the Pyrenees escape route around Luchon in April 1944 was mainly assembled by Françoise but it also included fugitives funneled through Toulouse by Dutch-Paris. The book includes five appendixes, in addition to maps, a time line, and source notes; I encourage the reader to examine all for additional information on escape lines, escapes over the central Pyrenees, and other events related to the story. It is my hope that readers will gain or deepen their appreciation of the courage of Allied evaders and other fugitives determined to reach freedom under the most daunting circumstances and the commitment of those who risked their lives to help them.

ABBREVIATIONS

BBC: British Broadcasting Corporation
BEL: Belgium
CPO: chief petty officer (RN)
CPT: captain
FLT: flight lieutenant (RAF, RAAF, RCAF, RNZAF)
FO: flying officer (RAF, RAAF, RCAF, RNZAF) or flight officer (USAAF)
FSG: flight sergeant (RAF, RAAF, RCAF, RNZAF)
FR: France
FUS: fusilier
GNR: gunner
LT: lieutenant
LCDR: lieutenant commander
LTC: lieutenant colonel
MAJ: major
MIS: Military Intelligence Service (U.S.)
MI9: British Directorate of Military Intelligence Section 9
NCO: noncommissioned officer
NL: Netherlands
NZEF: New Zealand Expeditionary Force
PO: pilot officer
POW: prisoner of war
PTE: private (other than U.S. Army)
PVT: private (U.S. Army)
RAF: Royal Air Force
RAAF: Royal Australian Air Force
RCAF: Royal Canadian Air Force
RN: Royal Navy

RNVR: Royal Naval Volunteer Reserve

RNZAF: Royal New Zealand Air Force

SAAF: South African Air Force

SD: Sicherheitsdienst des Reichsführers–ss (Security Service of the Reichsführer–ss)

SSG: staff sergeant

SGT: sergeant

SiPo: Sicherheitspolizei (Security Police)

SOE: Special Operations Executive

STO: Service du Travail Obligatoire (Compulsory Work Service)

TSG: technical sergeant

USAAF: U.S. Army Air Force

WO: warrant officer

1LT: first lieutenant

2LT: second lieutenant

SO CLOSE TO FREEDOM

ONE

A Perilous Hide-and-Seek

On February 6, 1944, Belgian Roger Bureau made it as far as the mountain pass known as the Portet d'Aspet with a group of fugitives led by *passeurs* Palo Treillet ("Pierre") and Henri Marrot ("Mireille"). After twenty hours of arduous climbing in heavy snowfall, the exhausted men rested for two hours inside a mountain cabin on the other side of the Portet d'Aspet. With two more mountain passes to cross before reaching Canéjan in Spain, they set out again, but not for long. Unbeknownst to Pierre and Mireille, the group had been spotted two days earlier, before they had even started on their climb from Arbas in the foothills of the Pyrenees. Just beyond the cabin, six German mountain troopers lay in ambush, armed with rifles and accompanied by dogs.[1] Pierre had gone ahead of the party to scout. He saw the ears of one of the dogs jutting out from above a rock. He turned and signaled to the rest of the party to run. The Germans opened fire and two bullets flew by Pierre as the passeur ran for cover. Led by Mireille, Roger Bureau and several other climbers ran as far as they could up a wooded slope and, catching their breaths, hid in bushes. Still too exhausted from their climb, the rest of the men simply returned inside the cabin and soon found themselves surrounded. Mireille went back in search of the other passeur. Circling around a hill, he attempted to lead the mountain troopers away. He was captured, however, and the Germans immediately seized his papers and a stash of Spanish money he carried. Meanwhile, Pierre stumbled upon the tracks left by the men in Roger Bureau's group and followed them up that same slope. He found the group still huddled under the cover of bushes. Together, they fled to safety, back toward the foothills on the French side of the Pyrenees.[2]

Roger Bureau followed passeur Pierre to Saint-Girons, at the confluence of the Salat and Lez rivers, and from then on to Cazères, about forty miles southwest of Toulouse. By then, only seven men besides Roger Bureau and Pierre remained of the original climbing party—Dutchman Chris van Oosterzee, RAF FSG George L. Watts, Australian PO John Geoffrey McLaughlin, and four U.S. airmen: TSG Nicholas Mandell, SGT Norman Elkin, 2LT Campbell C. Brigman Jr, and SGT Walter R. Snyder.[3] Two other Dutchmen had also managed to slip away from the Germans, Sam Timmers Verhoeven and Gijs den Besten, but instead of turning back with the others, the two men had decided to remain on the mountain and look for some other passage to Spain. In Cazères, Pierre's group stayed in a temporarily unoccupied home, where they were soon reunited with Mireille, the second passeur.[4] Mireille had escaped his captors while still at the Portet d'Aspet, before a bus came up the road to the mountain pass to collect all the prisoners. He had faked a sudden illness, and after one soldier had left to retrieve a stretcher, Mireille had punched the other German who guarded him, sending him tumbling down a slope. The Portet d'Aspet was now too dangerous, Mireille told them, as the Germans were bound to keep a close watch on it.

The group left Cazères on the morning of February 15. They returned to Toulouse, where less than two weeks earlier the Dutch-Paris escape network had brought them on the train from Paris. They spent the night in a room belonging to one of Mireille's friends, and the next day, Dutch-Paris operative Salomon Chait (aka Edmond Moreau) came to see them. There are few known details of his visit, but the Dutchman told the group they were leaving that same day back toward the Pyrenees. Other than Roger Bureau, who then remained in Toulouse, most or all of the others took a train to Montréjeau on the afternoon of the sixteenth. The stationmaster in Montréjeau had ties with a local *maquis*, and he arranged for the transfer of the group to the foothills. It was passeur Jean-Louis Bazerque ("Charbonnier"), described by McLaughlin as an "elderly guide," and "Frisco," a tall, blonde, and tough-looking member of the maquis, who came to collect them. Accompanied by an escort of maquis fighters armed with Sten guns, they all drove to a shepherd's hut at an elevation of about three thousand feet. Here the evaders had to bide their time for several weeks, as heavy snow in the mountains prevented any new attempt to reach Spain. Second Lieutenant Brigman's foot became infected during that time. He was taken to a suburb of Saint-Gaudens to see a French doctor trusted by the maquis. When he returned with a healed foot, the number of men waiting for passage across the Pyrenees had increased considerably. With armed guides from the maquis led by Charbonnier, thirty-eight evaders left Ardon in the Valley of Barousse and for three days climbed in a wide arc around Bagnères-de-Luchon, regional headquarters of the Zollgrenzschutz (ZGS), the German Customs frontier police. On March 19, having made only two stops along the way, Van Oosterzee, Mandell, Elkin, Brigman, Snyder, McLaughlin, and Watts all reached Bossòst in the Aran Valley of Catalonia, Spain.

Less than ten days later, another group of fugitives crossed the border with Spain and it, too, arrived in the Aran Valley. As many as twelve Dutchmen were in this second group, among them Vic Lemmens, Han Langeler, and Sam Timmers Verhoeven. After their capture at the Portet d'Aspet in February, Lemmens and Langeler had been detained in Saint-Michel's prison in Toulouse but later escaped by jumping out of a truck during a prisoner transport. Along with Gijs den Besten, Sam Timmers Verhoeven had fled the Portet d'Aspet, but without a compass and unable to read the stars, the two men had become lost. Exhausted, they found a hut nearly buried in snow where they intended to rest. Inside, however, it was so cold that they could not sleep. The men put their frozen shoes back on and started out again. In the hope that they had arrived in Spain, they went down into a valley and reached the tiny village of Autrech, south of the Portet d'Aspet but still well shy of the border. A farmer's family took them in and gave them food. Den Besten suffered from severe frostbite on his feet. His condition only got worse, and in the end local Frenchmen transported him in a horse cart to the hospital of Saint-Girons to receive medical help.[5] After staying two more weeks in Autrech, Sam Timmers returned to Toulouse by bus and then by train.[6] He found the restaurant Chez Emile he remembered from his previous stay in the city, and by chance, there he was reunited with his two friends Lemmens and Langeler, who, having just escaped, were enjoying a quiet meal.

With other Dutchmen, Timmers, Lemmens, and Langeler had a long layover, during which they stayed in a house on the outskirts of Toulouse, playing chess and bridge to break the monotony of their days. In the early afternoon of March 25, they boarded a train at Toulouse's railroad station, Matabiau, and traveled in the direction of Tarbes. At 5:30 that afternoon, the train pulled up in the small station of Saint-Laurent / Saint-Paul west of Saint-Gaudens. The train doors opened and out stepped this large group of evaders, mostly American, and the twelve Dutch.[7] The group walked to an unoccupied building to eat. All the fugitives were then transported onboard two cars up a mountain road while receiving the protection of fifteen armed maquis members who had joined them. Starting on foot from a lumber mill, they followed a stream up toward a mountain pass. After spending the night in the hay inside a hut, they continued on toward the south throughout the day of March 26. The weather was on their side as they crossed a glacier and climbed a steep mountain, at times trudging through waist-deep snow. They changed guides, hiked parallel to a "very slanted mountain," and during the middle of the night arrived at a storage shed below Superbagnères, west of Luchon. On the twenty-seventh the climbing party continued to bypass the town of Luchon. After crossing a rack railway and a road flanked by a stream, the climbers approached the last mountain separating them from Spain. Here they encountered difficulties as the American airmen in the group could no longer follow. LT René Van der Stock, a Belgian officer who had spent three years in a POW camp, was also having problems breathing.[8] Inch by inch the fugitives climbed, and once they had to retrace their steps after getting lost. According to Sam Timmers, matters even threatened to get out of hand when some in the group rebelled against having to help their weaker companions. Pierre Crampé, one of the two guides, pointed his rifle at one of the Americans who refused to keep climbing. "We can't leave you behind," the guide told him, "you either get going or I have to kill you."[9] In total the ascent lasted seven and a half hours. Stopping every twenty minutes to rest, the party reached the mountain pass marking the border with Spain shortly before dawn. To their left the climbers could see the flickering lights of Luchon, to their right the shadows of the Spanish Pyrenees. As the guides turned around to head home, the fugitives shook hands with them gratefully, then went down the mountain yelling in glee. As they reached the bottom of the Aran Valley in Spain, they fell asleep on a grass field in the sun.

THE GERMANS HAD SHUT down the route through the Portet d'Aspet in February 1944. By the end of March 1944, they were already closing in on Charbonnier's route through the mountains near Luchon, and the Spaniards seemed to be actively helping them, as indicated by the American, British, and British Commonwealth airmen who were arrested by the Guardia Civil upon their arrival in Bossòst on March 19.[10] Second Lieutenant Brigman's debriefing report shows that on that day, all of the airmen were interrogated by the Spaniards but on the whole were treated well, then put up at a hotel for the night. The following day, March 20, they boarded a bus to Viella, and having arrived in that town were interrogated again. On March 21 they reportedly walked thirty miles to catch a bus to Sort, where they again spent the night in a hotel. Next they traveled south to Lleida, and here they were questioned more roughly by the Guardia Civil, which accused them of being Russian communists.[11] The men spent two weeks in a hotel in Lleida before the Spanish Air Force transferred them to Alhama de Aragón, along the road between Zaragoza and Madrid. A representative of the American Military Attaché came to see them in Alhama. After two weeks, the American airmen were finally released from Spanish custody, and the American Military Attaché took them to Madrid and from there on to Gibraltar, where they arrived on April 24. Two days later they left by air to the UK.

The interrogations conducted by the Guardia Civil aimed at discovering the route followed by the airmen to reach Spain, as reported by RAAF PO John G. McLaughlin:

After our arrest we were interrogated by the frontier police at Bossòst. They asked our route, but we said we did not know it. They tried to get out of me particularly how we knew we had crossed the frontier, but I said I did not know and had asked a de Gaullist [sic] on the other side where the frontier was. I was also asked political questions, such as "Who started the last war and this war?" and what I was fighting for. In reply to the latter question I said I was in the war for adventure, which seemed to satisfy them. At Viella a Czech who spoke Spanish and myself—I speak some French—acted as interpreters at the interrogation of two Americans (Finney and Carson). The Americans were asked about helpers, and we gave camouflaged answers. I was asked here to show our route on the map, but refused. The Spaniards had a wall map on which was marked a route corresponding pretty closely to ours. In answer to questions about places through which we had passed, I said we had been near Luchon, but the Spaniards did not know on which side of that town we had passed. We had circled Luchon, but had not stopped there, and Luchon was not a center of the organization which got us through.[12]

According to SGT Norman Elkin, it was the two Czechs in the party who had drawn the route marked on the Spaniards' map. But Elkin was also critical of McLaughlin, stating that in Viella the Australian had not just told the Spanish police about Luchon being the last French town along their route. McLaughlin had insisted on going along with SSG Kenneth Carson and SSG Robert Finney, whose turn it was to be interrogated. "I want no welts raised on my back," the Australian had told some of the American airmen, "I want to see my parents."[13] For his part, SGT Walter R. Snyder had seen with his own eyes the Czechs draw a detailed map of the last mountain pass before Spain for an individual in civilian clothes in Bossòst.[14] By the time Staff Sergeant Finney reached the UK in May 1944, he had learned of the capture of the group that followed their route a month later, and he himself drew a connection with the information volunteered to the Spaniards by members of his own party.

The hotels in the border towns in the Aran Valley, Bossòst

and Viella, were by all appearances dens of German spies. Sometime around the first day of April, members of the two parties of evaders that had just reached the valley met up in Lleida. 2LT Victor Ferrari of the first party seems to have had contacts with a "very tall blonde" Dutchman—presumably Han Langeler—who arrived with the second group. The Dutchman had managed twice to break out of a labor camp in Germany, and he was one of the men who had been caught in the round-up in February but had escaped from the Germans later, after being incarcerated in Saint-Michel's prison in Toulouse. When he finally reached the hotel in Viella, Langeler recognized one of the guests in the hotel as the German officer in charge of the soldiers at the Portet d'Aspet. The German was wearing civilian clothes and was fraternizing with the evaders, using an English-speaking girl as his interpreter. The tall, blonde Dutchman had revealed to the Americans who the German really was.

Spain might have declared itself nonbelligerent early on during the war, and even neutral in early February 1944, but it never ceased helping the Germans gather intelligence. Not only did the Spanish government collaborate with the Sicherheitsdienst des Reichsführers–ss (sd), the intelligence branch of the ss, the Gestapo maintained a permanent presence in Spain and effectively had an office in Barcelona. Belgian LT René Van der Stock crossed the Spanish border at the end of March 1944 with Sam Timmers and Han Langeler, and later received false ID papers and other help from the British consulate in Barcelona. He decided to make for the Portuguese border but was arrested on the train between Barcelona and Madrid. Van der Stock remained in the custody of the Spanish Dirección General de Seguridad (DGS) for five weeks, from April 8 through May 14. "In Madrid I was interrogated by members of the German Gestapo in uniform," he wrote afterward. "During my arrest, I had told them that I purchased my ID papers in France. [The Gestapo agents] laughed, 'You should have turned to the British for your papers. They would have issued them to you for nothing. We know them, they always use the same ones!'" The Germans evidently were well informed, at least on the Spanish side of the Pyrenees.[15]

TWO

For King and Country

Nearly four years had passed since Roger Bureau had last seen his Scottish-born wife Helen and their three sons. In the early days of May 1940, with German forces massed on the Belgian border and poised to attack, he had been recalled to his artillery unit. Bureau had bid his family goodbye, giving his eldest son Peter his watch and telling him, "You are the man of the family now." The family had made contingency plans should Belgium be overrun by Germany. And when it happened, Helen fled across the country's border with France, her three sons in tow. They intended at first to reach Brittany, but instead found themselves traveling to Calais on a train. By the time they arrived, Calais was already under direct threat from the rapidly advancing German armies. Helen and her children spent a harrowing night in the cellar of a boarding house, listening to bombs exploding over their heads as German planes pounded the city. Feeling desperate, Helen left the boarding house before daybreak, in search of the British consulate. There, she heard that a British warship was to leave the harbor at dawn. She rushed back to the boarding house and woke up her sons. All four of them then hurried to the harbor. As luck would have it, the warship had not yet left. They were allowed to climb onboard and safely made their way to England.

Belgium's armies were defeated in just eighteen days, and on the twenty-eighth of May the king of Belgium, Leopold III, surrendered unconditionally to Hitler's Germany. More than two hundred thousand captured Belgian soldiers were taken to Germany as prisoners of war.[1] An "exemplary" noncommissioned officer during the Battle of Belgium, Roger Bureau avoided being captured, and by then he must have known—or at least been reasonably confident—that his wife and children had reached safety on the other side of the English Channel.² Perhaps he was tempted to follow them, but from all appearances he felt it his duty to remain in Belgium. He joined the Belgian Resistance and took part in the work of "escape lines," helping downed Allied airmen hide from the Nazis and return to England. After the war, Roger Bureau's sons would learn of their father's "motorcycling around the country collecting British airmen as pillion passengers, to take them to the sea routes home."³

A handsome and lively man, Roger Bureau worked in his father's raw materials brokerage house, where his charm, energy, and honesty earned him success. His main claim to fame, however, lay elsewhere: "In an age where professionalism had yet to emerge seriously in most sports, he swam brilliantly, cycled ferociously, ran like a hare and skated for Belgium for about ten years—both as an Olympic speed-skater and as a member of the Belgian ice-hockey team."⁴ The list of Roger Bureau's accomplishments in the world of sports was nothing short of impressive, beginning in 1926, when he competed in the European Speed-Skating Championship held in Chamonix in France.⁵ Also in 1926, he made his debut on the Belgian national hockey team in the opening game of the European Ice Hockey Championship in Davos, Switzerland.⁶ During that game, a 5–0 rout of Spain, Bureau, who played as a defenseman, scored one of the goals for his country. A month later, Belgium hosted a game against the newly crowned European champions Switzerland in Antwerp in front of two thousand spectators. Belgium won 3–0 and Roger Bureau scored again. In 1927 he and the national Belgian team won second place in the European Ice Hockey Championship in Vienna, Austria.⁷ Sports historians would later remember Roger Bureau for having participated in two winter Olympic Games, in 1928 in St. Moritz, Switzerland, and in 1936 in Garmisch-Partenkirchen, Germany. He was, however, only a spectator when he and Helen attended the Olympic Games in Berlin in August 1936. For those summer Olympics, Hitler's regime attempted to project the image of a peaceful and tolerant Germany. With no inkling of what was yet to come, Roger and Helen Bureau sat within thirty yards of the Nazi dictator.

There can be no doubt that the lengthy, forced separation from his family weighed heavily on Roger Bureau. He was both a loving husband and a devoted father. "Whatever other pressures existed on his life," his son Jack later recalled, "he made time—and frequently—to fly kites, make and build big model gliders which we then flew with him, construct and run a model o-gauge electric train in the attic, run, swim, and play with us." A close family, the Bureaus lived in a somewhat austere and unpretentious house in Berchem, a middle-class Antwerp suburb. In the spring and summer, the rooms were awash in light from the large windows, which provided a view of Berchem's bustling main thoroughfare, the tramway track, horses and carts, cyclists, motorists, and pedestrians. In contrast to the busy world outside the front of the house, the family's backyard was a quiet oasis, where in the winter Roger Bureau brought the magic of outdoor ice-skating to his children.

> When the temperature was cold enough, my resourceful father flooded the open centre of the back garden with the garden hose, waited for the water to freeze, and taught us to skate over the small impromptu rink. As much of his own spare time was involved in playing ice-hockey, the creation of a rink was perhaps nothing to be surprised at. To the three children it seemed like a special variety of those miracles that adults seemed always to be able to conjure up. My father was particularly magical in what he could create to entertain us.[8]

Roger Bureau seemed to have boundless energy, and his exuberance was on display during family vacations. Although the Bureaus did not own a car, they often escaped outside the city. They most likely traveled by train, as did many Belgian families, especially after workers were granted several days of paid annual leave in 1936. The Bureaus took camping trips through the Belgian countryside. They also enjoyed time on the beach at the seaside resorts of Le Zoute (Knokke) and Middelkerke along the North Sea coast.

> [Here were] the mile-long beaches, broken only by breakwaters, long stone barriers drifting out to sea, in which were embedded

stubby wood blocks covered with green goat-beards of slimy sea-weed. Often there was a sharp sea-wind, when grains of sand would be whipped up a foot off the ground, lashing our ankles with needle-pricks of pain. The sea-wind blew frequently, even on sun-filled days. If you lost a beach ball in such a wind you might have to run a mile before you could catch it. Because he was a fast runner, my father seemed to feel it was his job to chase errant beach-balls, and he was forever retrieving other people's, as they lurched out of control or were wrenched out of small hands, racing away in huge bounds, hysterically driven by the wind along the beach, pursued by the cries of children and the curses of their parents.[9]

A native French speaker, Roger Bureau was also fluent in several other languages, a distinctive, though not unique, trait among people of his generation in World War II Belgium. Dutch enjoyed official status in all of Belgium's Flemish region, including Roger Bureau's native Antwerp. At home Bureau and his wife spoke French with their children but communicated with the house maid and the cook through Flemish. Roger Bureau also spoke and understood German, as shown later in the grimmest of circumstances, and he was fluent in English. At the onset of World War I, aged only nine, he had been evacuated to England and had stayed with his cousins, the Lamonds, Helen's family.[10] The two families had remained in touch and held reunions after the war. Roger and Helen had grown closer and were married on January 14, 1925, at Saint-Joseph Church in Antwerp, in a double ceremony that also saw his sister Marthe wed James R. Lamond, Helen's older brother.

Of Roger Bureau's involvement in the Belgian Resistance, few additional details have survived. Postwar documents from the Belgian Defense Ministry office reveal that beginning in early 1943, Bureau worked for UCL 55, a Secret Army unit founded in August 1940 by Professor Norbert Laude, the director of Antwerp's Colonial University. UCL 55 agents gathered intelligence on German defenses in and around the harbor and the Scheldt estuary. Under the very nose of the Gestapo, UCL 55 also operated an escape line with the use of forged passports and fake deafness certificates. The

Colonial University had resumed its teaching mission in October 1940 but now also served as a front operation for the Belgian
Resistance. Young Belgians eligible for the mandatory labor service masqueraded as students while Allied secret service agents,
downed airmen, and Resistance fighters on the run were kept in
hiding on university premises or elsewhere, including in vaults
at a nearby cemetery.[11] A member of UCL 55, Roger Bureau was
also apparently the head of his own organization. According to
official Secret Army documents, he was personally involved in
intelligence gathering activities in 1943. He also looked for and
rescued downed airmen, whom he or his organization brought
to Brussels. Bureau must have had contacts with some of the
larger and better known escape networks, particularly Dutch-
Paris. A letter written after the war by his mother suggests that
Roger Bureau came to the rescue of some seventy downed airmen, "each time risking his life."

Escape lines or networks arguably played an important role in
the fight of the Allies against Nazi Germany, but with the large
number of helpers involved, they were particularly vulnerable to
betrayal and infiltration by enemy agents. In late January 1944,
the Gestapo came searching for Roger Bureau at his sister's house.
They did not find him though he was there, hiding on the house's
flat roof. Belgium had become too dangerous for him. On February 1 Bureau left Antwerp. With help from Dutch-Paris, he crossed
the French border and made his way to Paris, then to the south of
France, arriving in Toulouse on the fourth of February.

After his arrival in the UK in April 1944, Australian PO John
Geoffrey McLaughlin remembered first meeting Roger Bureau
on February 3 at the train station in Paris. Also present on the
train platform was a guide introduced to McLaughlin as Mr.
Jacques, "aged 29–32, about 5 ft. 10 in. in height, fair, and expen-
sively dressed." He understood Jacques to be the head of the Toulouse section of Dutch-Paris. "Bureau told me that Jacques had
done a lot of work for the organization," McLaughlin stated, and
"that he was very reliable, a good organizer, and could hold the
organization together." McLaughlin would have been referring
to Dutchman Jacques Rens, one of Jean Weidner's chief lieuten-

ants in the Dutch-Paris network.[12] Roger Bureau thus seemed to have been familiar with the functioning of Dutch-Paris and known Jacques Rens personally.[13]

THANKS TO THE DUTCH-PARIS organization, which would have covered his living expenses, the thirty-nine-year-old Roger Bureau had stayed put in Toulouse from the time of his return from the Portet d'Aspet in mid-February through the end of March. In early April, however, he almost certainly made another attempt to reach Spain, only to fail again. On April 8, two groups of fugitives met on the slopes of the Pyrenees above Saint-Girons, and in the larger of the two groups was a Belgian. He had arrived at a hillside farm two days earlier, accompanied by three Frenchmen and U.S. 2LT Michael L. Smith, the five men sharing the bus ride between Montsaunès and Saint-Girons.[14] With the ten men already waiting at the farm, the group totaled fifteen as it started off into the mountains on the night of April 7. Among the seven fugitives in the other, smaller party were RAF FSG Art J. "Dick" Holden and RCAF FSG Wilfred M. Gorman from the same Lancaster III bomber crew. The weather was cold and the wind was roaring. After the climbers of the now combined parties found themselves trudging through snow up to their hips, Holden nearly collapsed of physical exhaustion and he had to be left behind at a house. The remaining party reached a mountain pass the next day, but as they started down on the other side, a storm engulfed them. They descended into a valley and took shelter in a cave, where they spent the night. By then Canadian Wilfred Gorman knew he could no longer continue.

> I was wearing a kind of dress boot. On the third day of the journey, the boots just fell apart. There was not a thing at all I could borrow to wear so I took off my coat and tore some of the fabric into strips and I wrapped those around my feet. That wasn't much help with all the snow. I suffered damage to my feet. [...] We had to scale one more mountain to get to Spain. I remember the rocks in the valley and that it was just killing me to walk over them. I made up my mind over that night that I would not attempt another mountain.[15]

To make matters worse, one of the two guides went missing during the night. The following morning, as Gorman was not the only one who wished to turn around, the men decided that the party would break up into two groups. The Belgian and a Frenchman by the name of Valentin were to take Gorman and several others back to Saint-Girons. Accompanied by the remaining guide, Second Lieutenant Smith would go on climbing with six other evaders, U.S. SSG Lowell Creason, U.S. SSG Arnold O. Pederson, U.S. ILT Neil H. Lathrop, RCAF FLT David Goldberg, RAF PO William Edward Watkins, and FO Robert Gordon Crosby.

On April 9 Second Lieutenant Smith and his group reached Spain, having crossed a high mountain pass just north of the Puerto de Salau. Climbing down the other side, they arrived in the Noguera Pallaresa river valley. The men spent the night of April 9 in a barn that belonged to a Spanish friend of the guide who had just brought them across the border, then continued on south along the Noguera Pallaresa River to Esterri d'Àneu. After a change of guide, they pushed on farther south still, to the small village of Escaló. They spent several days in that village before finally making their way to Barcelona, where the British consulate took them under its protection. Meanwhile, the other group, which included Gorman and the Belgian, had returned to the foothills of the French Pyrenees. They came to the bank of a river deep and swift enough that they dared not cross it. A bridge in a nearby village was guarded by German soldiers. The group decided to attempt the crossing farther downstream and in pairs. Gorman and a "Frenchman" drew straws to decide who between them would go first. They both made it to the other side, but later learned that the others had been captured. The villagers were afraid to help the two fugitives. In the surrounding hills, however, a man gave them food and shelter for the night, and even provided Gorman with a pair of shoes. The next day he took them to a bus stop and paid their fares for them to return to Toulouse.

THE STORY OF WILFRED GORMAN'S World War II adventures was published in April 1995 by a Canadian newspaper, the *Mira-*

michi Leader. Mid-upper gunner Gorman and radio operator Dick Holden had flown twenty-seven night-bombing pathfinder missions as members of the same seven-man crew. They were on their third mission under a new pilot when their Lancaster III bomber was attacked and damaged by a German JU 88 night fighter on September 27, 1943, near Brunswick, Germany.[16] The pilot attempted to fly the aircraft back to England, but the damaged starboard inner engine caught fire over the Netherlands and all seven men had to bail out. Having landed in a field near the Dutch city of Groningen, Gorman buried his parachute and his Mae West life jacket. Because he could already see German military vehicles approaching on a nearby road, he headed out in the opposite direction and stumbled into Dick Holden. The two crewmen decided to stay together and evade capture for as long as they could. Fortunately for them, a farmer's family took them in and later the Dutch Resistance arrived to take charge. During the following eight months, Gorman and Holden were assisted by Fiat-Libertas, EVA, and Charles Gueulette's Felix line, all the while making their way south first to Brussels, then Tourcoing in northern France, Paris, and Bordeaux. In Brussels EVA turned them over to the Felix line, but long delays ensued. Gorman and Holden stayed in Tourcoing for six weeks and in Paris for more than two months. "Complained about delay," Holden stated in May 1945 during a debriefing, "but was told it was due to lack of financial support from England." In March 1944, Gorman and Holden finally reached Bordeaux. They were to be smuggled into Spain from Bayonne, a town in the foothills of the western (Atlantic) Pyrenees. There were more delays, however, and instead of heading south to the Pyrenees, Gorman and Holden traveled back north to reach Pons in the Charente Maritime. There they stayed for three weeks. At the time, they learned that the Felix line "had fallen into Gestapo hands." But Gorman and Holden got a break when they were able to make contact with "Françoise," the organization that arranged their journey from Toulouse to Saint-Girons and beyond.

"Holden and I made a habit of not knowing the names of the people helping us," Gorman is quoted as saying in the *Miramichi Leader* article. "In the event we were captured," he explains, "if we didn't know their names, we couldn't say who they were."[17] Gorman was telling his story fifty years after the events took place, when some of the details including names may have faded from his memory. Other than Dick Holden, no other names are mentioned, not even those of other evaders with whom he crossed paths or traveled. The identity of the "French" evader who went back to Toulouse with him after they crossed the river together remains a mystery, perhaps even more so because Gorman makes no mention of a Belgian climbing companion in the Pyrenees. That last piece of information instead came from Second Lieutenant Smith's debriefing in early May 1944. Perhaps the English-speaking Gorman assumed that all those who spoke French in his group were French, when they were not. Perhaps others from Gorman's group managed to get past the German patrols after crossing the river. Could the Belgian have evaded capture and, like Gorman, returned to Toulouse? The Belgian's actions, perhaps, point to someone with leadership experience, someone familiar with the region. Belgian or not, could a newcomer to the Pyrenees guide a party of fugitives from the high mountains back toward Saint-Girons?

BEFORE SECOND LIEUTENANT SMITH and his group reached the border on April 9, a Belgian aviator, CPT Charles de Hepcée, departed from the Spanish village of Son just west of Esterri d'Àneu, headed for France. De Hepcée had been biding his time at the Casa Moreu, a boardinghouse, waiting for the arrival of passeur Jaume Soldevila. Unexpectedly, another guest checked into the Casa Moreu, a local Franquist priest. For fear of being found out and denounced by the priest, De Hepcée left early, accompanied by Soldevila's brother Ricardo and by a young passeur named Jean Fauré. The three likely headed north along the Noguera Pallaresa river valley and, having crossed into France, followed the Salat River to Salau. During the night of April 12, Jean Fauré left de Hepcée near Couflens along the Salat River, still inside the Forbidden Zone on the French side of the Pyrenees. At four in the morning the Belgian was captured by the Zollgrenzschutz at a village called Pont de la Taule, seemingly the result of his passeur betraying him to the Germans.

Captain de Hepcée had crossed the Pyrenees a dozen times prior to his capture. Having left London on March 1 and transited through Lisbon then Barcelona, he was on a special mission to establish a new escape line from Belgium through occupied France to Spain. As directed by the Belgian State Security Service in London, the new escape line was to be used for the exfiltration of secret agents and important figures of the Resistance, but it had to be tried and tested first. A career officer in the Belgian Air Force before the war, the thirty-three-year-old de Hepcée had become a veteran in the work of escape lines, having left Belgium for France in 1941 and created the escape network "Rose-Claire" (after the names of his two young daughters) with his friend Anselme Vierneuwe. The two men had later become the trusted lieutenants of William Ugeux within the Poste de Courrier Belge (PCB) and helped operate a lumber mill in the western Pyrenees. The organization had secretly installed a cable crossing over the Iraty, a mountain stream marking the border between Spain and France. For eighteen months, the cable allowed the smuggling of mail, goods, and fugitives across the border.[18]

BECAUSE CHARLES DE HEPCÉE was still in Spain on April 6, he could not have been the Belgian first seen by 2LT Michael L. Smith on that day in Montsaunès in France. But de Hepcée's last border crossing is tied to the story of the two groups of climbers who started out from Saint-Girons and, having traveled together toward Spain, took shelter in a cave. RCAF FLT David Goldberg narrated what happened on the evening of April 8, before the combined party decided to split up again into two groups. "Our guide was lost (he actually told us we were already in Spain which Gordon Crosby as a geologist knew was wrong). We waited in a large cave while our guide went to seek his bearings and get assistance. Many of the escapers were extremely weak. Some had been ambushed in a previous attempt to cross the Pyrenees. The crews of two downed bombers argued bitterly over who was responsible for their crashes." The guide who left and never returned was the older and more experienced of the two passeur. U.S. Second Lieutenant Smith described the remaining passeur as the "organization's guide," "making the trip for the first time so as to learn the way." Although Smith did not mention his name, the younger passeur was none other than Jaime (Jaume) Soldevila.[19]

If all had gone according to plan, he would have joined Charles de Hepcée in Son and then returned to Saint-Girons accompanied by the Belgian officer. Born on April 26, 1906, in Escart near Escaló, in the Spanish county (*comarca*) of Pallars Sobirà, Jaume Soldevila lived in Toulouse with his wife Generosa Cortina, having immigrated to France in 1931. His two brothers Ricardo and Joan, however, still lived in the Pallars Sobirà in Spain. What better team of passeurs than three brothers living on either side of the border? Unfortunately, the presence of the Franquist priest in Son—Generosa Cortina's native village—had thwarted their efforts to ensure Charles de Hepcée's safe passage to France.[20]

IF THE MYSTERIOUS BELGIAN mentioned by Second Lieutenant Smith was not Charles de Hepcée, then who was he? Not Charles Gueulette either, though the head of the Felix line did cross the Spanish border on April 10, 1944, just not in the central Pyrenees but farther west, near Oloron-Sainte-Marie.[21] There are clues pointing to Roger Bureau instead. With Montsaunès located along the Toulouse–Pau railroad line, the appearance of the Belgian in that town suggests that just like Smith, he had traveled earlier on the train from Toulouse—where Bureau had been staying since his return from the Portet d'Aspet and Cazères. Smith provided another important clue about the Belgian who joined him on the bus from Montsaunès to Saint-Girons. That Belgian, he said, spoke "many languages." And what about RCAF FLT David Goldberg mentioning that some of the fugitives arrived at the cave had being ambushed during a previous attempt to cross the Pyrenees? He could only be referring to the ambush at the Portet d'Aspet, and of those who had escaped the Germans there, only two were still in France, den Besten, hospitalized in Saint-Girons, and Roger Bureau. . . . Was Roger Bureau experienced enough to guide a group of exhausted fugitives back down the mountain to Saint-Girons? He had, after all, already made that return journey two months earlier. And after the war, his mother wrote that she had received news of her son's involvement with a French maquis. In a letter she even stated that during that time, her son had saved "his group" on several occasions.

NOT ONCE, BUT TWICE, Roger Bureau had been forced to turn back before reaching the border. In two weeks' time, he was to make a third attempt, accompanied this time by an even larger group of fugitives and by Charbonnier. In the Frenchman, he could not have dreamed of a more reliable , for Charbonnier had the reputation of having never failed.

THREE

The Route Past Luchon

Four months or so before the German ambush at the Portet d'Aspet, the French passeur—people smuggler—known as "Charbonnier" returned to Toulouse, having been gone for three weeks. He made his way to Saint Cyprien's district along the Garonne River. Along the south side of the hospital complex, on *Rue Réclusane*, he hid behind a gate and waited. Across the street from him was a side entrance to the hospital, a passageway used by prostitutes who sought treatment for venereal diseases at the dispensary. Charbonnier had spotted a police truck parked along the street, and by remaining hidden from view he was being cautious, though generally he also seemed fond of making sudden, unexpected appearances. After a while his friend Gabriel Nahas, aka Georges Brantès, emerged from the passageway. As Nahas climbed on his bicycle, Charbonnier left his hiding place and hurried across the street toward him, his hobnail shoes clattering against the pavement.[1]

With his wild hair, thick stubble, and weather-beaten face, Charbonnier looked the part of the smuggler, especially when wearing his black cape and scarf during his travels. He was short and stocky, and his aquiline features stood out sharply, as did the thick eyebrows over his piercing dark eyes. Despite Australian PO John Geoffrey McLaughlin describing him as an elderly guide, he was only in his late thirties, but his hair was beginning to turn gray and his teeth, crooked, were stained yellow from years of smoking. According to Nahas's later recollections, Charbonnier also had the colorful, larger-than-life personality to match his singular looks and garb. Six years earlier, Charbonnier had sat on the benches of lecture halls, a pre-med student who was popular and well-liked, and not just for his chatty nature and bawdy humor. His real name was Jean-Louis Bazerque, but fellow students referred to him then as "Brother Jean des Entommeures," a fictional character borrowed from the writings of Rabelais, a cheerful, humorous monk who alone answered the call to action and won the day with his moral integrity.[2] Those were the days of the Spanish Civil War, however, and Charbonnier neglected his studies, choosing instead to help Spanish refugees. He failed his medical school entrance exam and, having served in the French military during the Battle of France in 1940, then escaping from a POW camp a few months later, he embraced the dangerous life of a passeur.

The two men greeted each other happily. Charbonnier, who on that occasion sported a wrinkled jacket, announced with a big smile the success of his last expedition to the Pyrenees, having taken yet another group of fugitives across the Spanish border.

"I must say," Charbonnier said, "that your American aviators slowed us down. They don't like walking."

"What do you expect?" Nahas responded in jest, "They prefer flying."

As the two men walked side by side, Nahas pushing his bicycle, Charbonnier's tone became more serious. The problem, he explained, was that the Americans did not have the right footwear for climbing mountains and for hiking through snow and ice. Nahas knew the problem all too well, but hiking boots large enough to fit the typically taller Americans were in short supply. Every week, Nahas's cobbler found him one or two pairs of large boots through the black market, just not enough to accommodate the needs of every American airman.

STANDING AT FIVE FEET, six inches tall, medical intern Gabriel Nahas was a young man imbued with a strong sense of purpose in life. Born in 1920 to a Syrian father and a French mother, he had spent the first eight years of his life in Alexandria, Egypt. It was there, perhaps, that he had found his calling for medicine. Walking through the streets of Alexandria with his father Bishara, he had noticed the ragged, lethargic beggars and their shuffling gait.

"Papa," he had asked, "What's wrong with them?"

"Hashish is what's wrong with them," his father had replied.

After Bishara himself fell ill and developed multiple sclerosis, the family had resettled in France in the hope that Parisian doctors could stop the disease. In just two years' time, however, Bishara Nahas had succumbed to his illness. Now facing the prospect of poverty, Gabriel's family had moved to Auch, a town in the heart of Gascony fifty miles west of Toulouse. Through it all, Gabriel's mother had remained a model of strength and courage for both her son and her daughter Hélène. An independent-minded woman and loving mother, "she demanded the best of us," Nahas would later say of her.[3]

BUILT ON TERRACED STEPS up a hillside and along the west bank of the Gers River, Auch afforded distant views of the snow-capped Pyrenees. As a teenager, Gabriel Nahas might have found himself already drawn to the mountain range that forms a natural border between France and Spain. Later, having moved to Toulouse and now a first-year medical student, he spent his vacations climbing many of the Pyrenees' peaks. No doubt Nahas learned much then about the contour lines of the Pyrenees—their peaks, valleys, and the mountain passes along the old trade routes—all valuable knowledge that he would later put to good use. At the age of eighteen, he also opted to become French. When Marshal Philippe Petain rose to power in 1940, Nahas at first felt ambivalent about the new French regime, but in February 1941 he joined the French Resistance with a few other students, and together they started the clandestine newspaper *Vive la Liberté*.[4] With only a typewriter at the disposal of the organization, the newspaper had a circulation of only about twenty copies, not enough for any meaningful impact. It was also short-lived. In November 1941 two of Nahas's friends were arrested by the Vichy police, and one of them carried with him a notebook with the names of all organization members. The Vichy police raided Nahas's apartment at dawn, finding incriminating evidence in the form of pamphlets. Accused of being a terrorist and a communist, Nahas was interrogated and beaten all day. As he would later recall, he was even subjected to torture, strapped in a dental chair while a Vichy police agent started to hammer a nail through the back of his skull.

Nahas lost consciousness, and when he came to, he found himself locked up in Saint-Michel's prison. Fortunately, he received help from some of Toulouse's prominent public figures. All charges against Nahas were dismissed and the young medical student was set free. More determined than ever to play a role in the Resistance, Nahas learned two lessons from his ordeal. From now on he would leave all the propaganda work up to London, and to evade any future police raid, he would no longer spend the night in his own apartment.

IN THE SPRING OF 1942, Nahas went to see Charbonnier in Varilhes, a village south of Toulouse in the Ariège department. According to Nahas, Charbonnier had already begun to smuggle fugitives across the Spanish border. They agreed to work together, and after some scouting in the mountains chose a route through a region of the central Pyrenees known as the Couserans, around the towns of Saint-Girons and Couflens. Before the war, Charbonnier had been involved in the world of politics, and his many relations now proved important as he established contact first with the underground network Combat and later with Libérer-Fédérer.[5] Nahas himself smuggled the first group of fugitives over the Pyrenees in June 1942, and for four or five months, the pace of crossings over the Pyrenees remained manageable for the two men. It all changed in November 1942, after the launch of Operation Torch—the Allied landings in French North Africa—and Nazi Germany's response, the invasion of France's Free Zone. Already, the rounding up of Jews had intensified in France since the summer of 1942. In September a law requiring all able-bodied men aged eighteen to fifty "be subject to do any work that the Government deems necessary" had also been signed into law by Marshall Petain. In response to the German demand that 250,000 more Frenchmen be enlisted for work in Germany, Prime Minister Pierre Laval instituted the Compulsory Work Service (Service du Travail Obligatoire, or STO in French) in February 1943. The tide of public opinion was turning against the Vichy government. Tens of thousands of young Frenchmen went into hiding to evade the STO, many of them joining the Resistance or heading to North

Africa to enlist in De Gaulle's Free French Forces. Fugitives bound for Spain flocked to Toulouse and the surrounding region, requiring Nahas and Charbonnier to step up their efforts. Nahas was in charge of gathering fugitives into the fold of the organization—even collecting them from nearby maquis—and also of logistics in Toulouse. Charbonnier established new routes and hired guides for the crossing of the Pyrenees. He himself took charge of fugitives in towns with easy access to the Valley of Barousse, including at Barbazan along the Garonne River. From there he guided them south toward Luchon in the direction of the border. Charbonnier also operated the route through Aspet in the Couserans.

CHARBONNIER WAS KEPT QUITE busy, no more so perhaps than on July 27, 1943, when he sent one group of fugitives over the Pyrenees from Siradan, then left with another group from the main part of the Valley of Barousse. Each group followed its own route and made it safely to Spain. Frenchman André Castex, a teacher in Boulogne-sur-Gesse, was a member of the first group, and he left Toulouse on July 27 on the afternoon train to Montréjeau. Having changed trains, he continued on toward Luchon, but got off early in Siradan, where he had been instructed to contact Gesse and Charbonnier. "There were no formal introductions," he stated, "but I knew the activities of both men. If I remember correctly, there were 24 of us ready to go, plus our three guides." The group set out in the late afternoon and during the night followed the Ourse River upstream in the Valley of Barousse. Their route took them first to Peyrahitte and Jurvielle, and continuing south, they reached Gouaux-de-Larboust, where they rested. From Gouaux-de-Larboust they left at night with passeurs Jean Sans and Joseph Arnauduc, reaching Spain after following the route of Esquirry, Sadagouaux, Spijoles, and Port d'Oô.

A member of the second group that left on the same day, Eugène Bèze—a judge in Mont-de-Marsan—told the story of his journey over the Pyrenees with Charbonnier as their passeur.

At nightfall on July 27, 1943, ten of us left from Ferrère [in the Valley of Barousse]. We [went] through Granges de Crouhens and arrive[d] at sunrise on the Plateau of Monné. There, a German plane lurking overhead forced us to hide for a long time behind some boulders. We had been reported. We veered off toward Mayrègne [in the Oueil Valley], where we rested in a barn. At midnight, we left behind us the [Col de] Peyresourde, south of Garin, between two German patrols. I still remember the small light that flashed on and off to warn us. Cabanes d'Astau, Oô Lake, Espingo [Lake], the climb to Gourgs Blancs in knee-deep snow. At Espingo, we wanted to send three Germans who were fishing to the bottom of the lake. We were armed. Charbonnier deterred us from doing it, and he was right. We arrived at the top of the mountain at [9,700 ft.], and there we slept in a cave that was bitterly cold. Police dogs farther down the mountain were barking, searching for us. At dawn, Charbonnier started on his way back by himself. He refused to accept any [money]. Poor devil! We climbed down to Benasque, where we were taken prisoner [by the Spanish].[6]

JUST BEFORE THE ESTABLISHMENT of the Forbidden Zone in February 1943, Nahas and Charbonnier had taken charge of a group of forty people, including some "servicemen in uniform." In early 1943 STO evaders, Jewish refugees, and other civilians would have represented the vast majority of people to be smuggled across the border, but not so during the latter part of 1943 or in 1944.[7] The ever-increasing Allied air supremacy over occupied Europe meant more bombing raids by American and British planes. The number of airmen shot down and in need of repatriation rose steadily through early 1944.[8] At first, according to Nahas, they arrived somewhat haphazardly in the region, and local Resistance organizations reported them only after they had found shelter in the homes of families in the towns of Lannemezan, Saint-Gaudens, Saint-Girons, Foix, and Toulouse. Later, Allied airmen came accompanied by escape network helpers, and Nahas would receive news of their impending arrival from radio broadcasts or through a liaison agent. Nahas had met Jean Weidner in June 1943 and with the help of Simone Calmels, Andrée Moulonguet, and Anita Boucoiran—all of three of them students like him—he assisted Dutch-Paris in looking after fugitives bound for Spain. Those fugitives arrived in Toulouse on the overnight train from Paris, often accompanied by Dutch-Paris courier Jacqueline Houry. Nahas or one of the three other students collected them outside the train station. And later they escorted them by rail to Saint-Gaudens or other towns near the foothills of the Pyrenees. The fugitives were instructed to step off the train not on the platform, but on the track side, to go meet Charbonnier and his guides in a nearby field.

Nahas and Charbonnier did not yet work with—and later for—the "Françoise" organization headed by Marie-Louise Dissard. That association would not begin until later, in December 1943, taking its final form in February 1944. By then Charbonnier's Luchon route (or variations of it, most or all beginning in the Valley of Barousse and extending south to the Larboust Valley) had likely already been used countless times. As one of Charbonnier's men would once tell TSG Nicholas Mandell in March 1944, it was the highest and the most difficult of the organization's routes over the Pyrenees. It was also supposed to be the safest.[9]

TUCKED BETWEEN THE VALLEY of Nistos to the northwest, the Pique River valley to the east, and Mount Né to the southwest, the Valley of Barousse rises from north to south toward the high mountain pass known as the Port de Balès, gateway to the Valley of Oueil. Here, far removed from the hustle and bustle of city life, creeks tumble over rocks and plunge in cascading waterfalls, their soft banks shaded by the lush foliage of ash trees and by alder trees that quiver in the breeze. Like a giant fortress, the towering silhouette of Mount Las in the midst of the upper valley stands guard over the two forks of the Ourse River, which meet at Mauléon-Barousse. To the north, the Ourse River races past picturesque villages and immutable pastoral scenes before flowing into the Garonne at Loures-Barousse.

A few World War II tales have survived from the Valley of Barousse.[10] One story mentions the two French priests, one from Mauléon, the other one from Sost, who sheltered Allied servicemen escaping to Spain. Once, in November 1943, a group of servicemen hid in the rectory in Mauléon while a parade organized by the French Milice took place in the village, under the watchful eyes of a ss-Sturmbannführer. The two priests took a less than enthusiastic part in the parade. Going back to the rectory afterward, they were told that the servicemen were safe, still hiding behind bundles of wood in the shed. In fact, the servant announced, they had woken up in great spirits and had eaten with a hearty appetite. They had arrived only the night before, after a long and tiresome trek through the woods, guided by a passeur whose name has long been forgotten. Another story involves a doctor from Loures-Barousse known for his outspokenness and his large, imposing presence. The good doctor made house calls on his motorcycle while at the same time organizing safe passage for fugitives bound for Spain—*clandestins*, as they were called by the local population. Through the end of October 1943, the Pyrenees Hotel in Loures-Barousse often served as a rest stop just before the climb over the mountains. On the evening of November 8, the ss stormed the hotel, no doubt tipped off by an informant. The innkeepers were arrested, but not the group of men the ss were looking for. Alerted by the doctor, they left the hotel just in time and fled along the canal. A young servant also escaped, the innkeepers quickly pushing her out the door. She walked all night, following the river and going across fields, and in the morning she arrived safely in her native village. Several passeurs picked up their "clients" at the Pyrenees Hotel for the trip over the Pyrenees, Louis Bordes on October 26—less than two weeks before the ss raid on the hotel—Charbonnier or one of his associates the week before.[11]

IN THE 1960S A French newspaper published a letter written by a Frenchwoman whose name it did not disclose but introduced as someone living abroad and forced by circumstances to spend the years of the war in the small village of Izaourt in the Valley of Barousse.

A French expatriate living in the U.S., I happened to be visiting my family when war broke out. From 1940 to 1942, I experienced the same worries and the same hardships as everyone. In March 1942 [sic], my twenty-year-old son was requisitioned for the Compulsory Work Service (STO) [in Germany]. He refused to leave. With three friends, he escaped to Spain, whereupon he was jailed. From that moment on, many young people from all corners of France decided they wanted to join the Free French Forces (FFL).

From March through October, life was unbearable at home. I no longer felt safe. It was at that time that Vinal and Barrère from Loures-Barousse asked me to find a hideout where groups of young people bound for Spain could be sheltered—sort of a reception and screening center—for all the roads in the Barousse were being watched by the Germans. Our meeting place was Soca's car repair garage in Loures-Barousse. I knew Barrère well. Born in the U.S. to a French father, he had returned to France at the age of 17 or 18. We met from time to time; being able to speak English with me made him happy.

I had a little house in the mountain, more like a cabin, four walls, a roof, a cement floor. Beginning in October 1942, I lived there with my daughter. Nearly every week, young folks arrived, occasionally thirty at a time. I gave them shelter, which did not prevent me from continuing with my work: the raising of a small herd of sheep, which served as my cover and often saved our lives. None of the people nearby suspected anything. The villagers did see young people come to my house. No doubt they thought it was all for a reason having nothing to do with wanting to escape to Spain. I was careful not to reveal anything. Once, however, a complaint was lodged at the Kommandantur in Luchon. The Gestapo came to the mountain. Perhaps they had been misinformed. They went the wrong way and ended up at the cemetery (!) then left. [...]

We would buy our food at two nearby farms. During winter, with the snow, we would hide the young men at the farms of Puysségur and Pouyfourcat, at the town hall, at the school. The latter burned one day, probably as a result of carelessness. [...]

All those who transited through my house arrived sound and safe, with the exception of a young Serb who died in the mountain in December.[12]

Both U.S. ssg Orville G. Greene and U.S. tsg Bertil E. Erickson stayed with the Frenchwoman, born Blanche Fontagnères, and her daughter Lorraine in December 1943, just before an "especially rough" crossing of the Pyrenees. ssg Greene later remembered her as an "American woman," about forty years old, who spoke French and whose husband was in the United States. In truth Blanche Fontagnères was originally from the village of Ilheu, only three miles to the south of Izaourt. It was only sometime between the two wars that she immigrated to the United States with several of her siblings. Having married, she settled down in Illinois, where her son François (Frank) and her daughter Lorraine were born. Following her separation from her husband, she returned to France with her two children and bought a home on the edge of Izaourt. There she gave shelter to fugitives and Jewish refugees. Decades later, Lorraine still remembered their reclusive life during the war. The men they sheltered were told to make as little noise as possible as Blanche and Lorraine had neighbors, and two German soldiers would occasionally stand watch nearby. The men slept in the loft above the sheep and helped with some of the chores, but mostly they played cards to kill time. And they could not go out except at night, and only to stretch their legs.

The route over the Pyrenees from the Valley of Barousse past Luchon was seemingly always grueling—as was to be the case for the large party of American evaders and Dutch patriots in late March 1944. U.S. ssg Orville G. Greene afterward related the story of his own crossing of the Pyrenees in December 1943 using that route:

> Four Europeans with us had to drop out completely. I had some wooden soled shoes, and my feet were pretty sore, but I managed to carry on. It was a tough trail. For a long distance we walked in deep snow. When a man fell down in the snow, we were all so exhausted there was little we could do for him. A couple of men had a bottle of what seemed to be pure alcohol; I was awfully thirsty and drank too much of it. It almost knocked me out, and I was pretty sick and miserable. Some sugar was the only thing I had to eat. I was getting more and more thirsty and started eating snow; once

I started I could not stop. The snow made me very sick afterward. [...] I took a benzedrine tablet, the last thing I had left from my escape kit, and it seemed to give me strength to go on. About 15 minutes from the frontier one man just gave out, moaning sadly, "Ça ne va pas." I kept telling him, "Pas rester ici," but he just lay there paying no attention to me. Later, however, he finally did get across. I heard that it was only 10 minutes farther to the frontier, and then I knew that somehow I was going to make it, but it was a climb which I would hate to repeat.[13]

FOUR

On the Run

On November 6, 1943, the Gestapo came looking for French priest Paul Louis inside the convent of Saint-Vincent-de-Paul in the Paris suburb of Clichy. He was getting dressed when another priest came running up the stairs to his quarters: "Hurry, father Louis, run, the Gestapo is here!" Upon hearing that Gestapo agents were waiting for him inside the vicarage, in the sacristy, and by the door to the church, Paul Louis took the time to destroy a few compromising papers and photographs, then got hold of his prayer book and his beret. On his way out, he calmly greeted the two Germans who now guarded the bottom of the stairs, acting as though their presence was of no concern to him. Gestapo agents were nearly everywhere inside the convent, but they had left a small courtyard and an outside gate unguarded. Waving goodbye to his fellow clergymen, Paul Louis found his way to the gate. Once outside, he closed the gate behind him and, putting on his beret, walked off down the street.[1]

Born in 1906 in a small town in Brittany, France, and ordained in 1934, Paul Louis was no ordinary priest. A member of the Resistance organization "Vengeance," he had created his own underground network, which gathered intelligence for the Allies and helped funnel Allied servicemen out of France. Even during the early days of German occupation, before joining the Resistance, he would listen to the BBC's *London Radio* broadcast operated by the Free French, then pass on any new information to the members of his parish in Argenteuil. Out of concern for his safety, his superiors had decided to transfer him from Argenteuil to Clichy in 1941. The convent of Saint-Vincent-de-Paul had become his base of operation, all until the raid by the Gestapo. "Beware of the Gestapo," a German officer and friend of Paul Louis had once told him, "its agents are very clever." "No matter," the priest had responded, "the French can outsmart them." Paul Louis might have won the first round against the Gestapo, but he was now a man on the run.

In the weeks and months that followed, Paul Louis remained in hiding, while also continuing some of his activities in the Resistance. He altered his physical appearance, changed identity papers three times, and kept moving from one safe house to the next. He also tried to arrange for his own passage to Britain. In January 1944 Resistance workers helped prepare for his departure, notably MAJ Emile Ginas, military commander of the *Armée Secrète*—the Secret Army—in Paris and national leader of the large Resistance movement Ceux de la Libération. When, however, Ginas was arrested on January 19, 1944, the opportunity to flee to Britain had passed.

At the time, Paul Louis might have been staying in Paris, sharing a room with a friend and member of his network, LT Raymond Krugell, who had just returned from Brittany. Krugell had been similarly unlucky in his attempts to leave France. Twice he had been given a rendezvous point for a sea evacuation. In November 1943 he had guided downed Allied airmen from Paris to the port city of Douarnenez along the coast of Brittany. But the submarine that was to transport all of them to Britain never arrived. Then, on Christmas Eve, he waited with some thirty airmen and a few French partisans on the docks at Tréboul. The escape line Bourgogne (Burgundy) had brought many of these fugitives, and a man by the name of Yves Vourc'h had made the necessary arrangements for the journey. Despite anonymous threats and rumors that the Germans had been tipped off, Bourgogne operatives pushed for the evacuation to go forward. During the night, the fugitives came on board the fishing vessel *Jeanne*. With still no signs of the Germans, the crew was preparing to refuel the boat when it detected acts of sabotage. A padlock on a valve could not be removed, so the operation had to be aborted. The fugitives disembarked, and with an American evader in tow, Krugell walked nearly twenty miles back to his base of operation in Quimper.[2]

A teacher by profession, Raymond Krugell was also a French army reserve officer. He had been called up for active duty in August 1939, fought during the German invasion of France, and been captured with his entire infantry unit in the Vosges Mountains on June 21, 1940. After several months of captivity, first in France and then in Germany, he had been transferred to a repatriation camp in Offenburg. Born in 1906 in Strasbourg, Raymond Krugell had ancestral roots in Alsace, a French province annexed by Germany in 1871 and returned to France only at the end of the First World War. In the camp in Offenburg, all Alsatian officers were offered their freedom back, provided they sign a statement, "I want to become German!" Krugell refused, and for this he was sent to another POW camp. There, he managed to bribe a German guard and organized the escape of several fellow officers. He was caught and sent to a correctional camp in Lübeck, Oflag x-c. "So, you're not a friend of Germany and you spread enemy propaganda," the commanding officer, a "Colonel von Wachtmeister," told him upon his arrival in the camp in June 1942. "Heavens, I hope it doesn't happen here. Otherwise it could cost you dearly. Watch out, we have machine guns placed on all of the watch towers, and trigger happy guards to boot!" Undaunted by the warning, the French reserve officer found a way to escape from the camp in December 1942.

After overcoming many obstacles, Krugell made it out of Germany, and in Paris he joined the French Resistance. His first mission took him to Montmaur Castle in the Alps. LT Antoine Mauduit, a fellow ex-POW, rented the castle, using it as a safe house for French STO evaders. For some time, Krugell assisted Mauduit by operating an underground printing press to produce false papers for the evaders. But Krugell now wanted to join the Free French Forces in North Africa. In July 1943 he crossed the Swiss border illegally, having learned of a direct air liaison between Switzerland and Portugal, both of them neutral countries. He was arrested then later released when he accepted work as an intelligence-gathering agent for the Allies. He climbed over a wall and slipped back into France without being seen by German border patrols. Over the next several months, he operated over a vast territory—the Alps, the Rhône Valley, the greater Paris area, and Brittany. Some of the intelligence data he gathered was for Priest Paul Louis.

By the early spring of 1944, Paul Louis and Lieutenant Krugell appeared to be running out of options for arranging their escape from France. On April 13, however, the two men left Paris together on the express train to Toulouse. With the help of a French patriot named Gérard Houry (Dutch-Paris courier Jacqueline Houry's father), they had linked up with an escape line in Toulouse and were now headed for the Pyrenees. Their plan was to cross into Spain and then make their way to North Africa, where Priest Paul Louis would, "God willing," enlist as chaplain in Free France's navy.

In the early afternoon on April 18, 1944, Paul Louis and Raymond Krugell found themselves waiting together at the Matabiau train station, having spent five days in Toulouse, and booked seats on the slow train to Tarbes. Their official destination was Capvern, but while they were waiting on the train platform a stranger instructed Paul Louis to get off earlier, at Saint-Laurent / Saint-Paul instead. The two men were not alone. Four Americans and two Canadians had just been entrusted to Paul Louis, while Krugell now served as guide for six other Allied servicemen. Unbeknownst to them, more groups of fugitives were waiting on the train platform with their respective escorts.

HARRISON (HARRY) STANLEY CAMMISH was not quite sixteen when war broke out. His father, a World War I veteran who had fought at Passchendaele in 1917, managed a confectionary shop in Scarborough, a coastal resort in Yorkshire, England. At the age of fourteen, Harry left school to become a carpenter's apprentice and learn the house-building trade. In the early days of the war, however, there were greater public needs than building new houses. "We mainly worked on blackout screens and shutters," Cammish later remembered. "Scarborough felt the heat of the German bombing raids and was hit by a lot of incendiary bombs. Trawlers and small fishing boats were often the target for machine gun fire. Repair work kept us pretty busy."[3]

To face the threat of a German invasion, the British government set up a force soon to be called the Home Guard, made up of volunteers aged seventeen to sixty-five. Cammish joined and, having been fitted "with a rifle, 40 rounds of ammunition and a bayonet, [was] sent out to patrol the beaches and protect essential services such as the gas and electricity works." In 1942, having now turned eighteen, he enlisted in the Royal Air Force and served in 50 Squadron as a "fill-in" flight engineer on board Lancaster bombers, flying with crews of mixed nationalities. With its graceful lines, the Lancaster bomber was by all accounts a beautiful aircraft, "the queen of the skies" to Cammish's mind. It was manned by a standard crew of seven, and as flight engineer, Cammish sat next to the pilot on a drop-down seat in the front cockpit, keeping an eye on all of the instruments. "All crews had a feel about them," Cammish said after the war. "The pilot especially set the tone. Some were smooth and relaxed, others stiff and jerky perhaps with nerves. Some left the throttles to me, others shared control as a pair."

On August 29, 1943, Lancaster III VN-A carrying Cammish and six other crew crashed on take-off from Skellingthorpe Airfield, 50 Squadron's base of operation just west of the city of Lincoln.[4] The aircraft was fully loaded with bombs and fuel for a mission to Hamburg, Germany. Its Merlin engines often pulled to the left and when it happened again, the pilot overcompensated while attempting to bring the aircraft back around. The aircraft was not yet airborne when it struck a hangar, then broke into two pieces and burst into flames. With the fire spreading through the wreckage, Cammish and the others were rescued in time before the aircraft exploded, and were taken to a military hospital. Cammish was the first to be discharged from the hospital and return to his squadron. The commanding officer ordered him to fly immediately again to regain his confidence. The prescription worked to good effect, and Cammish went on to complete another twelve bombing missions. Crews thought themselves invincible, Cammish later recalled, and despite his earlier brush with death, "[he] never had time to be nervous when getting ready for a mission, as there was too much preparation to do and no mistake could be allowed."

For his sixteenth bombing mission, Cammish joined the crew of VN-Q (serial LL791) under PO William Herbert Taylor, an Englishman. The crew included two more Englishmen, navigator SGT Kenneth Edric Gilson and rear gunner SGT Thomas James Taylor. Two of the remaining crew members were Australian, wireless operator FSG John Ansell and bomb aimer and front gunner FSG David Thomas Balmanno, a "big chap" according to Cammish. SGT John Acthim, a Canadian, completed the crew as mid-upper gunner. Cammish had never before flown with any of the others.

At 6:30 p.m. on February 25, 1944, Lancaster bomber VN-Q took off from Skellingthorpe. As part of a one-two punch against Nazi Germany, the U.S. Eighth Air Force had bombed the Augsburg Messerschmitt works earlier that day, and it was now the RAF's turn to attack the German city during a night mission involving nearly six hundred aircraft. Around 11 p.m., two German fighters attacked VN-Q ten miles west of Strasbourg. "A shower of cannon shells" hit the rear fuselage and one engine caught on fire. As the fire spread in the aircraft, rear gunner Sergeant Taylor "saw a wall of flames shooting upward between the mid-upper turret and the bulkhead door." Shaking like straw in the wind, the aircraft went into a nosedive. The controls were by now unresponsive, and the pilot ordered the crew to bail out.[5]

Balmanno had to throw himself onto the front hatch to get it open, and Cammish followed the Australian the same way out of the aircraft. The rest of the crew also bailed out, although navigator Sergeant Gilson was last seen by Pilot Officer Taylor holding a flashlight and looking around his table for what must have been his parachute pack. In all likelihood the delayed jump cost him his life. Gilson was later found dead on the ground. His parachute had deployed but probably too close to the ground. The others all came down safely in northeastern France just a few miles from the German border.

Cammish landed softly in two feet of snow. He heard the whistle of a train nearby and, having buried his parachute, found the embankment of a railroad. More trains rolled by, too fast for him to attempt climbing on board one of them. He had hurt his ankle during the bailout but for now was still able to walk. Cammish set out along the railroad track and after "quite some time" reached the small train station of Emberménil. He heard voices. Two men were talking in what sounded like French. Peeking through the window of the station, Cammish saw a man at his desk wearing a railroad uniform. He remembered the mission briefings during which crews were told many French railroad workers belonged to the Resistance. With his ankle now swollen, he knew that he could not go any farther. He tried his luck and walked into the station. The railroad worker did not speak English, but Cammish pointed to England on a map on the wall and the Frenchman understood. "*Chut, les Boches,*" he said to Cammish, placing a finger in front of his mouth, urging him not to talk, as there could be Germans nearby. He then took Cammish to his house, a single-story cottage in the local village. The railroad worker was married, and his wife was at first bewildered at the sight of Cammish. When she recovered from her shock, she asked whether Cammish had hidden his parachute. Like her husband Georges, she did not know much English. Much of the communication between Cammish and his two helpers took place in sign language. "George[s] mimed, "time to sleep" and took me to their bedroom and to a great big feather bed. I'd never seen anything like it, but I was a bit stunned when both Monsieur and Madame climbed in with me after offering me the privacy of the "psst" china pot that hid behind a curtain in the corner of the room. Madame even demonstrated a man peeing into the pot. I got the idea quick enough."[6]

In the morning, Cammish received new clothes to wear, a railroad luggage carrier uniform two inches too short in the legs, together with black leather shoes. A member of the local Resistance stopped by to ask him not just his name, serial number, and squadron, but also the names of his crewmates. Other than the navigator wearing the inscription "Gilly" on his helmet, Cammish remembered very little about them. To make matters worse he also had difficulties explaining what a stand-in crewman was. As the man left, Cammish worried that the Resistance might think he was a German spy posing as an English evader. A day or two later, however, word came that Cammish's story had been accepted as genuine, probably after radio contacts with London. He was moved about ten miles to Lunéville, where he stayed for twenty-four hours with an older couple and received his ID papers. Harry

Cammish, despite wearing his railroad luggage carrier uniform, was to assume the identity of Louis Blanc, a painter.

FEBRUARY 25, 1944, MARKED the end of "Big Week" for the American Eighth and Fifteenth Air Forces, with six days of uninterrupted bombing over industrial targets in Augsburg and other German cities. American bomber losses stood at more than one hundred for the week, and only hours before Cammish and his crew had bailed out of their Lancaster bomber, an American B-17F bomber also on its way to Augsburg had crashed northeast of Thionville, about fifty miles north of Nancy. Several of the crew had had time to jump out, including 2LT James L. Liles.

> After our number three engine and the electrical system had been knocked out we were forced to drop out of formation. Six fighters were pounding away at us and we had to bail out. As I cleared the plane I pulled the ripcord, remembering too late that I should have made a delayed jump. A [Focke-Wulf] peeled away from the fighters to swing by me. I thought he was going to fire, so I pulled the shrouds to slip the chute, but he only waggled his wings and departed.[7]

Liles came down in a small woodland. As he fell through the top of a large tree, his parachute caught on some of the top branches and he was left with his feet dangling a few inches from the ground. He managed to free himself from his parachute but then could not pull it loose from the tree. He threw his Mae West life jacket and flight boots under an embankment and ran, using his compass and trying to put as much distance between himself and his all too visible parachute. Liles heard trucks go by on a nearby road. A car stopped and there were voices. He kept to the wood and paused every few minutes to listen for any more signs of a German search party. Once, four Germans did come within 150 yards of him, armed with what might have been Schmeisser MP40 machine-pistols, but somehow they did not see him.[8] He next ran into a group of French woodcutters. Liles could not understand what they were saying to him, but as they kept pointing in one direction, he turned and headed off that way. Soon, he "found a small stream and crawled under an embankment that jutted out over the water." He remained several hours in his hiding place, while listening to the Germans as they searched noisily through the area.

After they had gone, Liles pulled himself from under the embankment and started off again. He came to the edge of the wood and, using scattered trees for cover, crossed a main road. It was now nighttime and in the dark, exhausted, he kept running into trees and falling into ditches and streams. At about the same time that Cammish had gone to bed in Emberménil, Liles was still on his own and now struggling through vineyards. He followed the sounds of a church bell ringing in the distance, and stumbled upon an empty *Blockhaus*, in which he rested and ate food he carried in his aids box. He left the Blockhaus at dawn and decided he must now go to the first house he found. It was around 6:30 a.m. when he knocked on the back door of a large dwelling, more like a *château* than a house. At first the Frenchwoman who opened the door would not let him in. He kept knocking, however, and when she opened the door again he stuck his foot through the opening. The Frenchwoman called her brother. Liles showed him the Adjutant General's Office (AGO) card he carried with him, proving he was American. In the end, the two siblings allowed Liles in but told him that a local Nazi official occupied another wing of the house. They took him to a room upstairs, fed him, and gave him new clothes. He slept until dark, and by the time he awoke another man had arrived. The man would serve as Liles's guide and escort to Thionville.

Cammish had landed in northeastern France near the German border, but in Thionville Liles found himself in an area now annexed to Germany. The French Resistance in Thionville gave Liles shelter and told him that three of his crewmates had been captured by the Germans, and another "wounded badly." A Frenchman by the name of René Lebrun took him to Nancy across the French border on a train. Lebrun was married, and as his wife's name could be female or male, Liles borrowed her travel documents and became René Lebrun's brother for the time of the journey. Lebrun had also told him to play the part of a deaf man during the German security check. Otherwise the American ran the risk of showing himself unable to understand questions in French. Liles played his role to perfection and at first ignored the Nazi official who asked for his papers. Lebrun shook him just as the German was running out of patience. When Liles handed him his papers, however, the official hardly glanced at them.

In Nancy Liles remained with René Lebrun and his wife for three days, then went to the home of Daniel Charton over a café and beer parlor on Rue Saint-Lambert. Meanwhile, Sergeant Cammish had gone from Lunéville to Nancy, guided by a high-ranking police officer who boasted of having the key to the German armory and whose favorite prank was to call out, "*arrête*, stop!" while pulling his gun out. After spending several days in Nancy, Cammish had moved again on March 6, this time to a farm in nearby Mazerulles. The owner of the farm was Robert Durand, the head of a local Resistance group. "He had a wardrobe full of weapons and hand grenades supplied by parachute drops from England. To see the way that they handled Mills grenades scared me stiff. The Germans called regularly for milk and eggs while I stood behind the curtain and watched them. He told me he would never be taken alive and I believed him."[9]

While in Mazerulles, Cammish had been reunited with three of his crewmates, PO William (Bill) Taylor, rear gunner SGT Thomas (Tilly) Taylor, and wireless operator FSG John Ansell. An American airman, 2LT James J. McMahon from New Jersey, also arrived at Robert Durand's farm at that time, and together the five men took the train to Nancy for what would be Cammish's second stay there. Liles witnessed their arrival in Charton's home. They were soon followed by Acthim and Balmanno, the other two survivors of Cammish's crew, in addition to American 2LT Robert Lindstrom, whose aircraft had also been shot down on February 25, and FSG Charles William Jackson, sole survivor of a Halifax crew downed during a mission to Stuttgart during the night of March 1–2, 1944.

In Nancy Charton had established contact with the organization "Jean-Marie," and two of its operatives came by one day. Jean was a short, paunchy man with brown eyes, a double chin, and puffy cheeks. Mickey, who did not speak English, was a little taller than Jean and heavyset, with a broad face, dark brown hair, and brown eyes. During the two men's visit to Charton's apartment, Jean agreed to organize the transfer of the airmen to Paris. It took his organization longer than expected, but on the evening of April 11, Jean was back. With him this time was a tall, slender man with curly blonde hair, who was to accompany Liles and nine other evaders on the trip to Paris.

Charton was looking to make arrangements with another escape network for more evaders who had arrived.[10] Liles does not mention the names of the nine who left with him, but based in part on the timeline, his travel companions almost certainly consisted of U.S. 2LT Robert Lindstrom, U.S. 2LT James J. McMahon, and RAF Flight Sergeant Jackson, in addition to Cammish and his five crewmates.[11] With their escort, the slender, blonde man, they all took the overnight train to Paris. When they arrived early in the morning the next day, no one was there to meet them at the train station. The blonde man made several phone calls but failed to reach any of his contacts. They all left the station on foot, the airmen following the Frenchman at a distance. They traveled on the subway and later walked into a crowded bar. The blonde man brought them beer, then left the group to go find help. He was gone for what seemed an eternity to the airmen. Feeling exposed to the scrutiny of all the other customers, they just sat and stared while waiting. When the helper finally returned, he was accompanied by a "Jean-Marie" operative who spoke English, having lived in Los Angeles for fourteen years.

Liles met the head of the network "Jean-Marie"—known as "Donkeyman" in London. After three days in Paris, he was taken to a house along Boulevard-du-Montparnasse, a beautiful mansion inside and out, according to Liles, set back from the street and guarded by a wrought-iron fence. The American airman never found out the name of his host, architect Henri Frager, a man he described as being about fifty years old and having the "sharpest gray green eyes, iron gray hair, [and] a vivid personality."[12] Henri Frager lived together under the same roof with his brother, a chemist who owned or used to own a factory, and his sister, an agent of the network. Frager told his guest that he had just returned from

London after crossing the English Channel by boat. In all likelihood, the Frenchman, code names "Paul" and "Jean-Marie," left out the nature of the mission he had just been assigned by the Special Operations Executive (SOE) in London, to organize maquis groups in the Yonne River valley and along the Côte d'Azur. Liles nonetheless understood that there had been a serious incident on the day that Frager flew out to London. As later told by Hugo Bleicher of the Abwehr, the incident involved Henri Frager, his lieutenant Roger Bardet, and Henri Déricourt, aka "Gilbert," a man trusted in London but now suspected by Frager to be a double agent. As he described the incident to Liles, Frager did not know that he had thrown his lot with the wrong man. When it was time for the airmen under the care of "Jean-Marie" to leave for Toulouse, Henri Frager went to the Paris-Austerlitz train station to see them off. Four months later, he was to be betrayed by Roger Bardet and arrested by Hugo Bleicher. Having shipped Frager to Buchenwald concentration camp, the Germans would end up executing him.[13]

Liles, Cammish, Balmanno, Acthim, Ansell, Bill Taylor, Tillie Taylor, Lindstrom, Jackson, and McMahon left the French capital in the early afternoon on April 17, 1944. Upon their arrival in Toulouse, they were passed on to Marie-Louise Dissard's "Françoise" organization. But the ten evaders hardly got a glimpse of the city, known even then for its dark pink buildings and its violets. After a layover of only a few hours, they prepared to embark on the last leg of their journey to the Pyrenees. On the train platform at Matabiau, Canadian John Acthim joined the group of evaders entrusted to Paul Louis. The priest's group included another Canadian, SGT Wilfred Gorman, rescued in Toulouse by the Françoise organization after his first, failed attempt to climb over the Pyrenees ten days earlier.

FIVE

Too Many

Marie-Louise Dissard ("Françoise") likely had her hands full on Tuesday, April 18, 1944. Not just one but two large groups of Allied evaders had arrived from Paris, one sent to her by "Jean-Marie," the other by "Marie-Odile," the escape line run by Frenchwoman Pauline Gabrielle Barré de Saint-Venant (known as "Marie-Odile Laroche"). Françoise's operative René Lamy ("Copain") had also just returned from Périgueux, northeast of Bordeaux, and brought back with him two American airmen, ILT Joseph E. Sutphin and SGT Melvin Porter.[1] And to make matters even more complicated, Marie-Louise Dissard was also looking to evacuate several civilians to Spain, including a Frenchman traveling under the name of Julien Leclair, in reality the younger brother of Françoise's trusted lieutenant, Albert Lautman. Only three months earlier, Françoise would have arranged for all those fugitives to then travel east to Perpignan, and from there to cross the eastern Pyrenees into Spain. She now relied instead on the escape routes over the central Pyrenees set up by Gabriel Nahas ("Georges Brantès") and Jean-Louis Bazerque ("Charbonnier"). From Toulouse the fugitives would first journey southwest by rail to one of the towns overlooking the Garonne River in the area of Saint-Gaudens, within easy reach of the Valley of Barousse in the foothills of the Pyrenees. Charbonnier would be on hand with his team of passeurs, ready to take charge of the evaders as they stepped off the train.

IN HER EARLY SIXTIES and suffering from rheumatism, Marie-Louise Dissard looked more like any ordinary, elderly spinster than the indomitable Resistance leader that she was. Hunched over and walking with the help of a cane, she was a petite, rather austere-looking woman dressed in black, with sharp gray eyes peering out from behind wire-rimmed glasses, her hair braided in a crown around her head. Besides her cat Mifouf, her other constant companion was the cigarette holder she seemed to keep in her mouth at all times. Her strong sense of patriotism aside, nothing, it seems, predisposed her to playing a decisive role in rescuing downed Allied airmen during World War II. As a teen, Dissard had shown natural talent for sewing and embroidery, and many years later, she opened her own dressmaker shop on Rue de la Pomme in Toulouse. In between those times, she had been a teacher and a school inspector, gaining the affection of her colleagues and her students for her cheerfulness, exuberance, and kindness. Despite her age and frail appearance, however, her voice carried loud and strong, and those who met her were all struck by her prodigious energy.[2]

Following France's defeat, Marie-Louise Dissard wasted no time joining the fight against both the German Occupation and the collaborationist Vichy régime. Every night she ventured out on the streets and covered city walls with inscriptions calling for resistance. Later, she distributed pamphlets titled "Liberation" and "Combat," while also collaborating with Pierre Bertaux's intelligence-gathering network, already in radio contact with London. In mid-December 1941, Pierre Bertaux and several of his comrades were arrested and incarcerated at Furgole, Toulouse's military prison. For nine months, Marie-Louise Dissard visited the prison, bringing food parcels for the prisoners two or three times a week. And it was on one of her errands to secure food for them that she met Paul Ulmann in early July 1942. Ulmann, who worked for the Pat O'Leary escape line, confided in Marie-Louise Dissard that he was harboring British and American airmen in his home. The Frenchwoman was then introduced to other members of the escape line, and at their request she rented a villa on Rue Pierre Cazeneuve in Toulouse for the organization. From then on, the villa served as a safe house for airmen, and Marie-Louise Dissard brought them meals two to three times a week. On December 13, 1942, Pat O'Leary—whose real name was Albert Guérisse—came to thank her personally and asked her to now rent an apartment for him. That apartment ended up not being available until the end of January 1943, and in the meantime Marie-Louise Dissard's home became Pat O'Leary's headquarters. At times, it also sheltered airmen when no other lodgings were available. By then Marie-Louise Dissard had become a member of the escape line and chosen to become "Françoise."

Pat O'Leary was betrayed by Roger le Neveu ("Roger le Legionnaire"), an undercover German agent, and arrested on March 2, 1943, in Toulouse. The other members of the organization faced the risk of now being arrested, as already, on the day of Pat O'Leary's capture, several homes were searched by the Germans. At 3:00 a.m. on March 3, Françoise fled the city with three airmen in her charge and went into hiding in Bergerac. While there, she learned that the entire organization in Paris had been dismantled through a series of new arrests. She assumed command of what was left of the Pat O'Leary organization and left for Cahors, then traveled through much of France to rally around her those in the organization who had evaded capture. On June 3–4 Françoise went to the France-Switzerland border region to reestablish contact with the British intelligence services in Geneva and obtain funding for her new organization, which she simply named after her own code name. Less than two weeks later, on July 15, she rented the Villa Pamplemousse in Toulouse, where airmen entrusted to her could now be sheltered. The work of the escape line resumed.

Jean Brégi ("Philippe"), a member of the Pat O'Leary organization arrested and jailed after a sabotage mission, went to work for "Françoise" after his release from prison in October 1943. Starting in November, he and Françoise traveled all the time, and according to Brégi the Frenchwoman's energy was nothing short of tremendous. Françoise spent around twenty-five nights out of every month riding trains, whether collecting airmen and bringing them to Toulouse, or escorting them to Perpignan and handing them over to passeurs for the journey over the Pyrenees. Philippe had seen her jump over the barbed wire marking the Swiss border in Annemasse. And once, she had not hesitated to drag two frightened men across that same border.[3] Françoise was also a master of disguise and ingenuity. When the Germans cordoned off Saint-Georges' district in Toulouse, she managed to get past the checkpoint masquerading as a drunk, wearing a dirty cooking apron, with a wine bottle sticking out of her errand bag. She called out to the soldiers loudly and walked up to one of them, before proceeding to examine the material of his uniform. "Quite nice," she said with a slur in her voice, before the soldier shoved her back, past the checkpoint.[4]

Françoise was no stranger to being arrested. During her early days in the Resistance, she was detained three times briefly for anti-Nazi propaganda and for aid given to Gaullist prisoners. And later, as the leader of "Françoise," she was apprehended by the Gestapo twice. The first time, she was traveling by rail, returning from a trip to Lyon. Her hands tied by the Germans for the remainder of the ride, she asked to use the restroom before they reached their destination. When Gestapo agents untied her hands but followed her, she admonished them for not giving her any privacy. The Germans finally turned their backs on her and, before they could stop her, she jumped off the train, managing to avoid injury. In late 1943 she was arrested again, this time between Narbonne and Perpignan while convoying four airmen. And again she escaped from the train. At that point, however, she realized she could no longer escort airmen herself to Perpignan.[5]

Françoise turned to Gabriel Nahas for help in December 1943 and for the first time asked him to organize the next several convoys of airmen from Toulouse to Spain over the Pyrenees. Then, in January 1944, the British consulate in Barcelona sent her a new operative known as "Sherry." He was to resume the convoys of airmen to Perpignan on behalf of Françoise. But after a Gestapo agent posed as an American airman and infiltrated the line, Sherry was arrested. In his possession, he had a notebook with the address of the "Villa Pamplemousse," where airmen were being looked after by Françoise and one of her operatives, Olga Baudot de Rouville, code name "Thérèse Martin." Françoise later recalled how she first learned of the incident. "Philippe and I found out [about it] from one of Sherry's guides, on January 31 in Brive, while we were on our way to go pick up airmen who were hiding with the maquis of Terrasson. We had to hurry back to Toulouse to evacuate the Villa. On Tuesday, February 1 we abandoned [it]. [. . .] I left for Annemasse to let "Uncle François" know about the disaster."[6] Just before Olga Baudot de Rouville was sent to safety in Marseille, she heard Marie-Louise Dissard acknowledge that "the workload was too heavy for her." "We had to return to Georges (Gabriel Nahas) for the subsequent departures," Baudot de Rouville also recalled.[7]

Whereas until that point Gabriel Nahas had not kept any lists of the fugitives he helped reach Spain, Marie-Louise Dissard had all Allied airmen answer questionnaires asking for full name, rank, and a physical description (hair and eye color, height, and other distinctive traits). Next came some questions written in poor English, such as, "Give names of rest of crew and state of they" or "why your machine is happened?" After the war Françoise compiled the names of Allied evaders handed over to her, arranging them chronologically by their date of departure from Toulouse. The list for April 18, 1944, is neither complete nor entirely accurate, but even without the names of the civilians who joined the party of evaders, it is quite a long one.[8] Later, Lieutenant Liles would state that the party leaving for the Pyrenees had been too large. That feeling was echoed by several other Allied evaders.

2LT LYNN H. DROLLINGER sent frequent letters to his parents from England, where he was stationed with the 357th Fighter Group. In those letters, which he signed with his middle name "Howard," Drollinger urged them not to worry about him. "I'm in no more danger over here than I would be if I were at home instead," he wrote to them on February 16, 1944. And he often commented on the rain and the bad weather he was becoming accustomed to. "The weather today was rather funny," he wrote in another letter.

It first rained, then snowed, hail and sleet finally the wind really blew. [...] Now it's nice, but muddy."

Trained as a P-51B mustang fighter pilot, Lynn Drollinger had gone into combat for the first time around the middle of January 1944. Having moved to a new base near the North Sea coast, a "mud hole" according to Drollinger, the 357th Fighter Group now flew daytime fighter escort for the bombers of the Eighth Air Force. Drollinger had already flown three missions to Berlin, in addition to several more over France, the Netherlands, and the North Sea. And when no missions were planned, or when they were scrubbed owing to fog in England or poor weather over the target, Drollinger and the other pilots were assigned more menial tasks. "I had to censor mail today," Drollinger wrote on February 10 to his parents. "Boy what a job. Some of the GIs can sure write good love letters." But the life of a fighter pilot also had its perks. "We had a snack bar in our pilot's ready room," Drollinger would later recall, "and we hired our own cook." On any normal day, the pilots could count on their standard fare of pancakes and eggs for breakfast.

On March 28, 1944, the day Lynn Drollinger went missing in action, the pilots of the 357th Fighter Group were awakened at 5:00. They ate an early breakfast, then went to a 5:30 briefing. "The sun doesn't come up until about 6:30 or 7:00," Drollinger wrote in his memoirs, "and the fighter pilot is one of those guys who likes to lay in bed and take it easy while the bombers are out there getting in formation and taking off for Germany." Their takeoff time that day was scheduled for around 9:30 or 10:00, giving them more than enough time to catch up with the bombers. "This was going to be another Berlin mission," Drollinger went on, "and we didn't get too excited about these missions anymore." But then the mission was cancelled as a result of bad weather over Germany, and the 357th Fighter Group pilots were instead called to another briefing.

We were going to escort a box of bombers, which is about sixty or eighty bombers in a box. They were going to go to Dijon, France, which is a town right on the border of Germany and France. They had a big airfield with a lot of German airplanes on this field and the bombers were going to bomb this field. This was the first time we had permission that after we got done escorting the bombers to the base and back to the P38s who would pick them up and escort then back home, we were released from the bombers and then could go down and strafe targets of opportunity. So we were all pretty excited, this was the first time we had permission to go down and do any strafing.[9]

At 11:00, the forty-eight P-51B mustangs from the three squadrons took off from the runway. They flew over the English Channel and, as they caught up with the bombers, Drollinger's squadron took up its position in the front of the whole formation. The weather was now beautiful, and all was going well, Drollinger flying as wingman to squadron leader LTC Hubert I. Egnes. "Radar command called us up," Drollinger remembered, "and said there was a bunch of German fighters coming up from the south to meet us." But even before the German fighters appeared, Drollinger's aircraft was hit by flak and its engine began to let loose a stream of coolant. Drollinger radioed to Lieutenant Colonel Egnes that he was forced to turn around, and on his squadron leader's instructions, another P-51B peeled off from the formation to escort him back.

Drollinger did not go far, as the engine of his fighter plane overheated and then stopped. He announced over the radio that he was going to have to bail out. "Don't forget to brush your teeth," he heard back on the radio from a pilot in his squadron headed for the target. "Be good to the French women," another pilot's voice added. Rolling his plane upside down, Drollinger unfastened his seat belt and out he went.

As the ground came up at him, Drollinger observed a farmhouse directly below and, less than a mile away, a German soldier on a motorcycle. Two Frenchwomen—a mother and her daughter—watched as he landed near them and the farmhouse. He picked himself up and hid his parachute near the bottom of a haystack, and as he walked toward the two women, they gestured for him to go hide in the barn. The German soldier was already approaching on his motorcycle. From inside the barn, Drollinger took a quick peek outside and saw the two women signal to the German and point down the road. The soldier must have believed them. He continued down the road past the farmhouse and disappeared from view.

The two women came to see him in the barn and gestured for him to climb up into the hayloft. Having retrieved his parachute, he spent the whole afternoon there, and in the evening, several Frenchmen stopped by the barn to give him a loaf of bread, white cheese, and wine. The following morning, three or four Germans arrived at the farm in a command car. From the top of the hayloft, Drollinger watched them talk to the farmers, but the Germans never thought of searching the barn. The day whiled away without any new signs of a German search party, and after dark, a man came to take Drollinger away. The Germans had established a perimeter around the general area where they thought the American had landed. To slip past that perimeter, the Frenchman had them both crawl down an embankment, then across a railroad track, and up the other side. Later, during the middle of the night, they arrived at the Frenchman's home, and there they ate and slept.

Until that point, Drollinger had not been able to understand much of what he was told, even with the help of a French-English dictionary from his escape kit. The Frenchman he had followed the night before did not speak a word of English, but his associate Lucien Sée did. The associate arrived in the morning and spoke to Drollinger in good English. He explained that his deceased father Léon Sée had been a world-renowned prizefighter manager, while his mother was English.[10] Through Lucien Sée, Drollinger discovered that he had landed some sixty miles east of Paris. The other Frenchman had wanted to show Drollinger a small room in his house the night before. Drollinger had seen the red dots on the wall, but now Lucien explained to him that they were bloodstains. The Germans had found out about the other man's brother picking up British parachute bundles of guns and ammunitions, which were then stored in a cistern underneath the house. And they had beaten him to death in that little room.

Lucien Sée and the other Frenchman lived off the black market in Paris. They visited farms in the region and obtained eggs, meat, and cheese. They packaged all those goods inside tin containers, which they then loaded onto their bicycle luggage carriers. They rode their bicycles to Paris and sold the black market food to restaurants around the city. Lucien Sée offered to take Drollinger to Paris, but asked that the American help them transport about fifty pounds of the day's load. Drollinger traded his flying suit for an old French army shirt, an old brown suit coat, a pair of women's slacks too large for him, and a blue French beret. He kept his army shoes on but "scuffed them up quite a bit and got them dirty" so they no longer stood out.

They set off toward Paris on bicycles, Drollinger following three hundred feet behind the two Frenchmen in the event of a German security checkpoint. The front tire of Drollinger's bicycle had no inner tube, and instead the Frenchmen had stuffed it with corks from wine bottles. "After a while," Drollinger recalled, "the wine corks would start to break up and you'd get a flat spot in your tire." Before reaching Paris the airman found it too difficult to keep up with the two Frenchmen. As a result, the three men went the rest of the way on a bus, Drollinger keeping his load of black-market food between his legs. They arrived safely in the French capital and, after making stops at restaurants along their route, the two Frenchmen took Drollinger to a hotel on Rue d'Amsterdam where Lucien Sée's sister Pauline worked. Sée left to find contacts with the French underground, and after he returned they walked together to A la Fortune du Pot, a café a few blocks away, at the corner of Rue de Douai and Rue de Bruxelles. They entered from the back and went down to the cellar, where Drollinger met a blonde woman named Gabbie, a member of the French escape network "Marie Odile." Lucien Sée and his associate left, but another Frenchman later stopped by to ask Drollinger questions, not just his name but also his place of birth and details on his childhood. The American remained in the cellar and later, Gabbie came back, accompanied this time by Simone Rossenu, "a nice looking brunette about twenty-two or twenty-three." Gabbie instructed Drollinger to follow Simone, who took him to her parents' home. There, Drollinger met another American evader, six-foot-three TSG Archie R. Barlow Jr. "He had learned a lot of French and could speak pretty well," Drollinger explained in his memoirs, "so he did a lot of interpreting for me." The apartment was now quite crowded. "The area [we] stayed in had three rooms. We stayed in the parents' room most of the time where they ate and lived. The next room up had been Simone's room with her husband, but he was dead, and the top room was Simone's sister (Paulette). The parents slept in the first room, Archie and I slept in the second and the girls took the top room." During the day, Simone worked as a waitress, Paulette as a secretary. In their absence, Drollinger and Barlow kept themselves busy as best they could. Drollinger found books in English and read Charles Dickens's *David Copperfield*. The two men also played cards, and naturally they must have told each other their story. Barlow in particular had already had enough adventures to last him a lifetime.

IN PARIS TECHNICAL SERGEANT Barlow was hoping to return to the Pyrenees for his second attempt to cross into Spain. In early March his climbing party with other Allied airmen had started off from Montgaillard, south of Tarbes and west of Montréjeau. During the first night, he and his companions had climbed for ten hours to reach a mountain cabin where they could rest. Barlow, however, was wearing boots too small for his feet. Feeling sick and exhausted, he could not follow the pace and fell behind. One of the Basque guides stayed with him and kept him going for a while. Barlow's condition worsened. He lost consciousness several times and when he grew delirious, the guide abandoned him, though not without first taking his watch and the money he carried. Barlow passed out again but when he came to this time, he felt better. He found enough strength to follow the footprints in the snow and reach the cabin where the rest of his group was now resting. Given his weakened condition, he decided not to confront the guide who had abandoned him. Barlow, the guides now also argued, was endangering the progress of the group. U.S. MAJ Leon W. Blythe, the senior officer in the climbing party, ordered Barlow to stay behind and remain in the cabin for several days, long enough to give his companions a chance to cross into Spain. Afterward, Barlow was free to go back to Montgaillard, where he would have to decide what to do next.

Sergeant Barlow had served as the top turret gunner of a B-24

Liberator brought down over the Pas-de-Calais in northern France by Messerschmitt fighters on January 21, 1944. While flying over the target, the aircraft piloted by ILT Hartwell R. Howington had been attacked by enemy planes:

> We had just been cautioned by the pilot to hold our fire until the German fighters were in range. At the exact instant I pressed the gun switches of my turret's twin fifties, the explosion occurred. It felt like several sticks of dynamite had exploded right in my face. Stunned momentarily, I can remember keeping pressure on the switches and wondering why the guns weren't firing. Simultaneously with the explosion, I felt stinging sensations in my left chest and upper arm. It took a few seconds to realize that my guns were useless and the terrible buffeting my head was taking was due to the plastic turret dome having been blown off, leaving me to receive the full effect of a 180 mph wind blast head-on.[11]

Struck in the arm and the leg by fragments of 20mm shells, his hair and ear singed by the explosion, Barlow saw the radio operator, TSG Alvin A. Rosenblatt, motion for him to bail out. "As I jumped," Barlow later remembered," I saw sheets of flame roll out of the bomb-bay." During his training, he had been told to delay opening his parachute if ever he bailed out of an aircraft under attack by enemy fighters. The delayed opening of the chute could well save his life, because it reduced the risk of being targeted by enemy planes. But he now discovered that a free fall went against all his survival instincts and he could not resist pulling the ripcord. Luck was on his side, however, and no aircraft opened fire on him. Instead, he landed safely in a field at the edge of a village. His landing hardly went unnoticed. All the villagers, or so it seemed, came running out of their homes to watch. From the crowd gathered at the scene came a shout, "Boche!" and Barlow realized they might mistake him for a German in his dark overalls without any insignia. After he repeated several times "No Boche, no Boche" and "American," the villagers finally stepped forward to greet him warmly with handshakes, pats on the back, and even "the customary French embrace complete with kisses on both cheeks." Some of the villagers had gotten ahold of Barlow's parachute and they now ran back toward the village to hide it. A middle-aged Frenchwoman gestured for Barlow to follow her. He had sprained an ankle when he hit the ground and he limped, rather than ran, behind the woman as she took him to a nearby forest. Waist gunner Charles W. Blakley happened to be hiding in the forest along their path and he called out to them. Later, around 2:00 p.m., the Frenchwoman left them by a large oak tree, where they would have to wait.

Barlow and Blakley heard the sound of heavy vehicles from the direction of the village. Without any warning," Barlow remembered, "Blakley shoved me to the ground from my sitting position and motioned for quiet." They remained flat on the ground on their stomachs as German soldiers walked by on a nearby path on their way back toward the village. A man finally came around 10:00 p.m. and led them to a farmhouse, where radio operator TSG Alvin A. Rosenblatt and waist gunner SGT Alfred M. Klein had already arrived. The four were overjoyed to be reunited, but by then Barlow also kept cringing at the thought of his parents receiving the telegram notifying them he had gone missing.

> When I had enlisted in late October 1942 it was with my parents' reluctant blessings, and only after I had convinced them that I had been guaranteed training and duty as an airplane mechanic, a fairly safe job. Several months later, and just prior to completing that training, I had told them I had been ordered to next attend aerial gunnery school and that there was nothing I could do to get out of it or the combat flying duties that would follow. This was an absolute lie of course. I had actually volunteered for gunnery school because it meant faster promotion and more adventure.

More adventure was indeed to be found, in Paris and later, when the four airmen traveled together to the Pyrenees, with Andorra then Spain as their intended destination. After Barlow made it to the cabin and Major Blythe ordered him to remain behind, it was Rosenblatt who gave his crewmate most of his food and money, enough to return to Paris.[12] And in the French capital, Sergeant Barlow was able to find help again. He stayed in an apartment on Molin Street, where one day in early April Simone Rossenu returned, accompanied by Second Lieutenant Drollinger.

JUST OVER SIX MONTHS had passed since SSG Lepkowski had bailed out of a burning B-17 G Flying Fortress during a bombing mission to Münster, Germany. Looking back on it, the entire crew of ten must have shared the same sense of apprehension and fore-boding on takeoff that day. Meeting at the plane before board-ing, the pilot, 2LT Earle Verrill, had greeted the others with those words, "Don't expect to be home for dinner tonight." And while the plane picked up speed on the runway, they had all remained silent, including Lepkowski, who normally would strike up the "Clarinet Polka," the others soon joining in and humming over the interphone. After their first ever combat experience on Septem-ber 27, 1943, it had only taken a week for them to have their first narrow brush with death. During a bombing mission to Frank-furt, their formation had run into what, to them, seemed like the "entire German air force." On board their B-17 F, Stan Lepkowski and the rest of the crew had sprung into action. In the ensuing melee some of the enemy planes had come within thirty feet of them, and above the ball turret, Lepkowski and the other waist gunner had fired their machine guns, defending against attacks from the left and the right. The aircraft had been hit by enemy fire and the oxygen supply had been damaged, resulting in sev-eral of the crewmen passing out, but somehow they made it back to Britain. Their aircraft was beyond repair, however, "a complete wreck with parts blown off . . . [and] a gaping hole right behind the bulkhead." The crew had been assigned to another aircraft, a nearly new B-17G-10-DL Fortress baptized *Tennessee Toddy*. And on the first bombing mission, not only had the aircraft barely gotten off the ground on takeoff, but the engines had also overheated over the Baltic Sea. The pilot had made the decision to turn around, abandoning the formation and aborting the mission. Back on the base, Verrill was lectured by the squadron commanding officer, who insisted that overheating engines were no reason to abort a mission. He had left Verrill with little doubt that on their next mission, there should be no repeat of what had just happened.

On October 10, all 236 of the U.S. Eighth Air Force's B-17 Flying Fortress bombers attacked Münster, causing heavy damage on the German city. P-47 Thunderbolt fighters, 216 in total, provided the flying cover for the fifteen-mile-long formation. The Luftwaffe committed 350 fighters to the defense of Münster. The bombing raid came with a heavy price for the Eighth Air Force, which on that day lost thirty bombers, with another 105 sustaining heavy damage. After a hair-raising takeoff—the aircraft barely cleared utility poles at the end of the runway—the *Tennessee Toddy* had managed to climb and take its place in the bombing formation. It dropped its two one-thousand-pound bombs on the target but was hit by flak and lost its left outboard engine. Verrill had had a difficult time with the aircraft on the way out, but now, as the formation turned around and headed home, *Tennessee Toddy* could no longer keep up. And when a second engine failed, it started losing altitude. The last two engines also showing signs of overheating, Verrill finally ordered the crew to bail out. Lepkowski did not hear him, because he was busy helping the ball-gunner.

[The ball-gunner] hollered out that he couldn't breathe, so I unplugged my oxygen mask and went to him with the portable walk-around bottle of oxygen he needed to breathe until he switched to the general oxygen system.

He pointed to show there were fighters around, then pointed to the waist gunner, Loorman, who was putting on his chute and then he began putting on his own parachute and I helped him.

After getting it on, he headed for the little hatch at the rear of the plane. That is when I knew we were bailing out. I had difficulty with the release on the waist compartment door but it finally loosened and I kicked out the door. Loorman went out the waist door hatch and I followed him. [...]

As I bailed out the waist compartment door my oxygen mask ripped off my face. I didn't use the bail-out bottle because it was empty. The guys in the hangar had not filled it. I couldn't breathe for what seemed like a long time. Because I figured I might pass out, I pulled the rip-cord too soon and barely missed the tail when my chute popped open.

Lepkowski landed safely in a pine tree near Markelo in the Netherlands, some thirty miles from the border with Germany. In a nearby field he ran into several Dutch civilians, who told him to hide in the wood where he had just landed. There Lepkowski found the tail gunner from his crew, SGT Robert D. Deghetto. The Dutch people had left but soon returned with a bag of civilian clothes. After the two Americans changed out of their flight suits, their rescuers took them to two different farmhouses. Over the next few weeks, Lepkowski hid in safe houses then one day took a train to Brussels accompanied by a helper, a girl no older than nineteen. He had not been given any ID papers or money and worried that he would be arrested. Most of all, he feared for the safety of his helper and asked her not to sit next to him. During a stop at a railroad station near the Belgian border, two German guards boarded the train. They began to inspect the papers of every passenger. Lepkowski told his helper not to worry about him and to take care of herself. He then stepped outside and, after one last hesitation, jumped off the train, landing safely alongside the track. His only request to his guide had been that she make sure their contact in Belgium would wait for him. Having let the train roll past him and disappear into the distance, Lepkowski walked the rest of the way to the Belgian border. In the border town he managed to find his contact, a man who approached him from across the street and simply asked him, "American?"

Shortly thereafter, Lepkowski arrived in Brussels, where he was first helped by Service EVA operatives then handed over to the escape line Comet. He spent about a month in the apartment of Anne Brusselmans and her husband, Julien. In early November he left Brussels with a Comet Line guide and crossed the French border on foot at Hertain with U.S. TSG Theodore R. Kellers and two other American airmen.[13] The four servicemen took a bus to Lille, then traveled to Paris by train with another Comet Line guide, a young woman known as "Diane" (Amanda Stassart). For the next five months, Lepkowski and Kellers lived in Gentilly on the southern outskirts of Paris, in the apartment of Emile Chassagne, a World War I French veteran and Possum escape line helper. Chassagne complained of suffering from the lingering effects of a gas attack during the previous war. How much of his moaning and groaning was genuine, however, Lepkowski could never be sure. The Frenchman played the part of the wounded veteran, especially when they were out on errands. The cane that he had no use for inside his apartment became a much-needed accessory then.

On April 17, 1944, a plainclothes *gendarme*—and member of the Marie-Odile escape network—took Lepkowski and Technical Sergeant Kellers to a bus station in Clamart, a southwestern suburb of Paris. There they joined two other American servicemen and their woman escort, and together the six of them made their way to the Gare d'Austerlitz in Paris. When the four Americans boarded the overnight train to Toulouse, they found their compartment already occupied by several other fugitives. The group now totaled seven American servicemen and two Frenchmen, in addition to the woman serving as their guide. One of the two Frenchmen was twenty-three or twenty-four years old, the other a doctor by the name of Marcel Hulin, a member of the French Resistance from Vinzier, near the Swiss border. He and his family had fled their village in October 1943 after the French Milice found out about a parachute drop involving containers of rifles, grenades, and ammunition.[14] A container landed beyond the drop zone, near a school and not far from the home of a known member of the Milice. The local Resistance retrieved all the other containers, emptied them of their weapons, and afterward threw them in the nearby lake. But the Milice man had seen children play with the missing container. The schoolteacher pleaded with him to not say anything, to no avail. The French Milice and the Gestapo raided the village, set homes on fire, and arrested Resistance members. Together with the Hulins, the local teacher René Barrut and his family also managed to escape.

Among the Americans on board the overnight train to Toulouse were SSG William B. Hendrickson and SGT Paul C. Pearce. The two servicemen belonged to the same crew of a B-26 Marauder hit by flak two months earlier, on February 5, 1944, and they had parachuted down into a field just north of Hestrus in Pas-de-Calais in northern France. The other Americans were 2LT Lynn H. Drollinger and TSG Archie Barlow, in addition to TSG Curtis

Finley, whose B-17G bomber had been shot down by fighters on a mission to Frankfurt on January 29, 1944.

ON APRIL 18, 1944, disaster nearly struck for some of the fugitives arriving in Toulouse with Staff Sergeant Lepkowski, Second Lieutenant Drollinger, and Technical Sergeant Barlow on the overnight train from Paris. Lepkowski barely escaped capture.

> At Toulouse, we got off the train, split up and went to different homes in the area. I, with a few other people, went to the home of an old lady who fed us and gave us bread in paper sacks before we headed back to the train station to board again for the trip to the Pyrenees.
>
> I again stated to the woman helper that there were too many people in the group. We weren't in the station more than five minutes when a Mercedes pulled up and a man in an expensive suit got out, someone yelled "Gestapo" and Germans started to come in.
>
> We ran in all directions. I ran across the street through the front door of a house and ran through the house out the backdoor. If that door had been locked, I would have been nailed to it. From there I went to other streets and after a while, [a] woman and a few of the group came about and gathered the group for the remainder of the trip.[15]

"After the war," Lepkowski reported, "I heard the old lady who gave us the bread for the trip was killed." He might have been misinformed, however, as the "old lady" was probably none other than Marie-Louise Dissard herself and the head of the Françoise organization made it thought the war unscathed.[16] After his earlier scare, Lepkowski made it back safely to Matabiau Station, and with Drollinger, Barlow, Kellers, Pearce, Finley, and Hendrickson, he boarded the slow train to Tarbes.[17] The train pulled out of the station and left Toulouse to follow the Garonne River upstream. It rolled on across a landscape of picturesque villages, vineyards, and fields, and made frequent stops along the way to take on a few more passengers. All the while, the tall peaks of the Pyrenees loomed larger and larger on the southern horizon, the last obstacle standing between the fugitives and Spain.

SIX

April Attempt

A s the slow train pulled to a stop in the small station of Saint-Laurent / Saint-Paul, Priest Paul Louis got up from his seat and stepped into the car's corridor, heading for the exit. The other six passengers in his compartment followed suit. One was a distinguished-looking man who had sat opposite Paul Louis reading his scientific magazine and exchanging a few words with the priest. The other five had dozed off or watched the countryside roll by their window, all the while remaining silent. They were deaf-mute, at least according to their papers.

Stepping onto the train platform, the seven men took in their desolate surroundings. There was no town or village in sight, just a gravel road and a few farmhouses in the distance. They huddled near the tracks and waited for the train station to empty. To nearly everyone's surprise, other groups of disembarked passengers remained on the train platform. A tense silence hung over the crowd of travelers as they all eyed one another nervously, until finally an American airman whispered that he recognized a member of his own squadron in one of the other groups. By then, the last of the other passengers had left the station. It had become safe to talk. Whispers grew into a loud murmur, and as more of the travelers recognized others or became acquainted, they realized they were among friends.

The scene that unfolded at Saint-Laurent / Saint-Paul followed a familiar script. On someone's signal, they all walked to the unoccupied inn behind the station. There they ate and met Charbonnier and the other two passeurs who were to guide them over the mountains. A man in his early thirties from Loures-Barousse pulled up to the inn in his truck. Known simply as "Frisco," he drove the fugitives up through the Valley of Barousse and into the mountains several at a time, dropping them off at a barn. Frisco made a strong impression on many of his passengers, who were packed like sardines for the ride. As later told by TSG Archie Barlow, Frisco was quite the fast driver, taking hairpin curves at such high speed that the truck kept swerving from side to side on the road:

> A skid very close to [the] road's edge and a sheer cliff caused one of our riders to exclaim, "Where in the world did this guy learn to drive?" The driver, who hadn't said a word until then, responded in good English but with a definite French accent. "Oh, I learned right here, but I drove a cab in San Francisco for six years before the war." As the laughter died down he went on to explain that he had returned to join the French Army just before the German occupation.[1]

In reality, Joseph (Joe) Barrère, aka Frisco, was a California native, born in Oakland in 1913. And considering that he had moved to France at the age of seventeen or eighteen, he could scarcely have been a taxi driver in San Francisco. But the Englishman Eddie Luff similarly remembered Frisco as a driver "who hardly ever used the brake pedal and approached hairpin bends with the panache of a Nuvolari." Luff likely guessed the real reason for Frisco's fast driving. Night was about to fall, and Frisco had to hurry because he still had more fugitives to pick up at the inn at Saint-Laurent / Saint-Paul.[2] Frisco was already taking considerable risks transporting the fugitives in his truck. Eddie Luff remembered that during the ride, he and the rest of his group had been handed *Sten* guns and told, "If we hit a roadblock, we won't get away by showing our papers since we're entering a forbidden zone. We'll have to shoot it out."

And thus it was that after nightfall, thirty-five fugitives and three passeurs gathered at a barn in the mountains. With twenty-one American, English, Australian, and Canadian servicemen, the priest and the doctor among the Frenchmen, Belgian Roger Bureau, and two Dutchmen, they made quite the motley crew. The American Barlow, the Canadian Gorman, and Roger Bureau were all returning to the Pyrenees. Their earlier attempts to cross the border had failed, but at least they knew now what to expect: the cold and unpredictable weather, the steep climbs, the sheer drops, and the deep snow. The others could not have been fully prepared for the challenge ahead. During his second stay in Paris, Archie Barlow had pushed himself to exercise. "Push-ups, sit ups, and running in place were orders of the day," Barlow recalled, "and I did them religiously." But there were those who had been on the run for months, enduring long periods of inactivity, skipping meals or living on a diet of turnips and potatoes. After the war, Second Lieutenant Drollinger even remembered one member of the party as this small, French Jewish refugee who weighed only about one hundred pounds. Who knew what hardships he had already lived through?

There had been a last-minute addition to the group. Nineteen-year-old Frenchman Jacques Lartigue of the Françoise organization was now to make the climb over the Pyrenees with the other thirty-four. After accompanying many Allied airmen from Toulouse to the foothills of the Pyrenees, it was his turn to leave for Spain. Only two days earlier, he had escaped from the Gestapo by throwing himself in front of a cable car in Toulouse.

On Friday, 14 April 1944, I left for Tarbes to carry out a liaison mission. In the train I was arrested by the Gestapo which, having searched me, found the papers that I was carrying concerning the destruction of [some] railroad lines. I was first interrogated while still on the train. They took me to Biarritz where I was tortured. Under torture, I decided to talk, and [revealed to them the name of] my boss. I gave a very detailed description, but false and the [...] rendez-vous spot [was also false]. Escorted by five Gestapo agents, I arrived in Toulouse Saturday morning 15 April. The rendez-vous was at 13 hrs Place Esquirol. At 13 hrs the Germans placed me under the clock at the Place Esquirol. At 13 hrs 15, my boss, naturally not being there, they took me to the St Michel prison [but heeding] my advice, decided to return the next day, Sunday. [Thus], Sunday 16, they took me back to Place Esquirol. At 1 hr 15, nobody. They began to understand that I had lied. We waited for the tram [cable car] to return to the prison. At the moment of getting into the tram, I succeeded in escaping. The Germans [fired] two shots at me with a revolver. I wasn't hit, and thus succeeded in escaping. I took refuge on the roof of a house where I stayed for 3 hours then I went to the Law School, to the house of Paul [Jourdan], whence I notified my boss. Knowing that an Anglo-American convoy was to cross the [border], I decided to leave in order to enlist in North Africa.[3]

Most of the thirty-five fugitives had been assisted by the Françoise organization in Toulouse. Three "Englishmen" had arrived together through another escape line, and Eddie Luff, who was one of them, later recalled that while standing around the barn, they were yet to reach their final destination for the night.

> It was a very dark night. We could hardly see each other. The only audible sounds were the whispered congenial greetings of kinsmen and the rushing of a mountain torrent. We got a briefing on the program: first we had to reach higher ground, rest there a few hours and then start for the big journey across three mountain ranges at an altitude averaging 9,000 feet. This would take about two days.
>
> We set off. A guide would climb first and, when high up on the slope, would swing a petrol lamp to show us the way. Keeping an eye constantly fixed on the swaying light, we climbed mostly on all fours. This system was repeated several times, until we arrived at the hut, where we bedded down in the hay, exhausted.[4]

The group set off at dawn the next day—April 19—and walked and climbed all through the morning, before stopping to eat lunch inside a mountain cabin. Despite many of them only wearing street clothes and lacking proper boots, the mood was confident and cheerful. Charbonnier impressed the evaders with his experience, and he told Priest Paul Louis that he had taken three thousand fugitives across the Pyrenees to Spain. He and the other two guides were armed with Sten guns, and after lunch they engaged in target practice outside, shooting at a bottle.[5]

In the afternoon, the climb became more difficult. With no ropes and no hiking sticks, they all found themselves struggling through knee-deep snow, each of them stepping into the footprints of the man directly in front, lest one sink deeper. They had now reached 7,500 feet in elevation.

We traveled above the tree line in the snow. In order to cover our tracks, we walked in creeks, in the ice-cold water whenever we could. We stopped several times to rest and to take off our socks and wring them out but that was worse than leaving them on. We walked along a ledge, high up the mountain, where there was just enough room for your feet to make the crossing and looking down, buildings looked like toys.[6]

When they reached the first mountain pass, there were shouts of joy, as for a moment some men thought they had already arrived in Spain. Climbing down, they reached the Valley of Oueil in the evening and broke into an abandoned farmhouse and its barn. There they built a fire to dry their clothes and to bake potatoes. Paul Louis went to bed early, but some of the men in the group stayed up and exchanged stories. By the end of the evening, most fugitives—and the passeurs—would have learned something of the identities of the others. "During our conversations," Raymond Krugell explained after the war, "[every-one] including the guides found out that we had a doctor and a priest in our group."

At 8:00 a.m. the next day, the group started out again. The guides warned the party that bad weather was on the way. Most of the food rations had already run out. Back in Paris, escape line help-ers had told Paul Louis the climb over the Pyrenees would only take eight hours. Not sure whether to trust the information, he nonetheless carried with him enough food to last several days, unlike others who simply had a one-day ration supply—a loaf of bread for every five of them, according to Second Lieutenant Drollinger. The fugitives trudged through snow up to their waists or, in some places, even to their armpits, but all through it the mood remained upbeat. PO Bill Taylor kept everyone entertained with his jokes and singing.

Although some people say he's just a crazy guy
To me he means a million other things
For he's the one who taught this happy heart of mine to fly
He wears a pair of silver wings

And though it's pretty tough, the job he does above
I wouldn't have him change it for a king
An ordinary fellow in a uniform I love
He wears a pair of silver wings . . .

When snow began to fall, the climbing party found itself going through "gale-force wind and swirling mist." 2LT James L. Liles summarized the second day of the climb, April 20, after they crossed another mountain range and reached the Larboust Valley, but also ran into trouble:

> We were caught in a blizzard that turned into a cold rain. After we had wandered lost for several hours, the clouds lifted and we found our way into a valley where we found shelter from the rain under trees. When the rain stopped we continued our march.[7]

On their way down, they had spotted a German patrol on the other side of the valley. In the late afternoon, having continued down the slopes, the men reached the outskirts of a village. Here, the presence of six German soldiers forced them to wait until nightfall. In single file and under the cover of darkness, they managed to skirt the village without detection. Charbonnier and one other guide had by then likely completed their part. Both left the group abruptly, leaving only the one named Georges in charge. Half a dozen armed Resistance fighters later appeared and helped the climbing party go through another, nearby village. The pace they set was too fast for the fugitives, who were by now totally exhausted. In an effort to avoid the German patrol seen earlier, the climbing party made a detour and followed the bank of a mountain stream riddled with cracks and crevices. According to Frenchman Raymond Krugell, one of the American airmen fell into a twenty-foot-deep crevice and hurt himself. Eddie Luff's account of the accident is different:

> We had to negotiate a narrow wooden bridge, spanning a deep river, running through a canyon. We were standing in single file on the slippery path leading to the bridge, where we were caught by the beam of a searchlight, flooding the whole line. Holding our breath for what seemed an age, we waited for the burst of machine gun fire.

Nothing happened, the gorge was silent. Just at that critical moment, an American lieutenant slipped and tumbled down through the bushes into the ravine. We all dashed down to help him.[8]

In his fall the American officer, 2LT James Joseph McMahon, had lost consciousness. After much shouting and running about, the rest of the party was able to find and revive him, but through all the commotion, the Germans were alerted to their presence. "We were all tired, cold, and making a lot of noise," Second Lieutenant Drollinger recalled. "Then some Germans yelled down in French 'who's down there?' I was scared to death and this guy who was leading us yelled up 'come on down and find out.'" McMahon had hurt his hip and appeared to have fractured his skull, and his left eye was also paralyzed. In spite of his injuries, he mustered enough strength to continue, with help from the others, who took turns carrying him up the slope.[9] Another member of the party collapsed in front of Drollinger. "We just got across the stream when all this was happening and this little French [Jewish refugee] . . . passed out," Drollinger remembered. "He was walking in front of me and I couldn't leave him there, so I threw him on [my] back and we went on up the mountain like that for about another half mile."

Now again accompanied by three guides including Georges, the group pressed on and climbed for another several hours up a scrub-covered slope. Along the way, they spotted distant lights flashing in the night behind them, no doubt signals being exchanged by the Germans. The rough and treacherous terrain made for slow going: "At another place there was shale and it was rough making headway: one step forward and two steps back. I had a branch and I would dig it in and hang on while making a step forward. I don't know how the other people did it but I am surprised we did not lose anybody."[10]

At times, they all had to reach for branches or grab onto rocks to pull themselves higher up. "Sometimes a stone would roll down and skim past a fellow's head," Eddie Luff would later write in his memoirs. "Given our number, the odd stone would find its mark, creating an immediate audible reaction."[11]

More accidents were bound to happen, and they did. Belgian Roger Bureau sustained some unknown injury while lifting the wounded American McMahon along the steep, rocky incline. Later, in complete darkness, Paul Louis stumbled headfirst into a tree and dropped to the ground unconscious. When he came to, he could no longer make out the others, who had pushed on unaware of what had just happened to him. After a moment of anguish, the priest heard someone whimper next to him and realized he was not alone. An American airman, perhaps injured or simply beyond exhausted, had also been separated from the group. Together the two men started climbing again. Fortunately, the others had not gone far, and the priest and the American were soon greeted by the beam of a flashlight and a voice saying, "Here comes the priest." It was now around 5:00 a.m. on April 21, and the group had reached a sort of cabin, a tool shed belonging to the French Water and Forest Administration. It was located in a place known as Gourron, below the rack railway leading up to the ski resort of Superbagnères-de-Luchon. Among themselves, the guides called it the black shed (*baraque noire* in French).

THEY ALL SLEPT, SOME of them until noon, then went outside to dry in the sun. Two guides, not three, had arrived at the shed, and they went down to a nearby "village" to get food. Before they left, they promised to the rest of the group that they would return in the evening, in time to lead them across the border, now a mere few miles away. Several members of the group later reported that a third man left as well, to go buy food in the nearby village. There were those in the climbing party who were already making contingency plans should the Germans catch up with them.

> The trail came right up the hill and made a ninety-degree turn right at the cabin and went around the mountain. I said to Archie [Barlow] "if the Germans attack we're going to go exactly ninety degrees off the trail, because all these other guys are going to go right up the trail. It will be everybody for themselves and we're just going to take off from the trail and leave everybody." We kind of had a

plan. It was about noon and the sun was shining and I was tired, so I just leaned up against the wall of the cabin and dozed off.[12]

Around 3:00 in the afternoon, a stranger was spotted near the cabin. When confronted, he explained that he lived in the area, and that he had seen someone from the party talking to a German in the village below them. Raymond Krugell later wrote that he directed two sentries be posted outside immediately. Lieutenant Liles and a fugitive named Maurice de Milleville had their turn at sentry duty begin two hours later. Within minutes, Liles came running up to the cabin and sounded the alarm, "the Germans are coming, the Germans are coming!"

As it turned out, the Germans were right behind him. Sergeant Hendrickson was one of twenty or twenty-five men who bolted out of the cabin and started up the slope heading to their left: "I was the last man in [the] line and saw the Germans coming. I called out a warning. [The] Germans began to fire. I jumped off [the] trail and ran down [the] mountain in direction of the Germans but heading to [the] right. Then shooting came from above the party. [The] Germans had cut them off from above."[13] Lieutenant Drollinger, Lieutenant Liles, Sergeant Barlow, Sergeant Cammish, and de Milleville all ran in a different direction from the rest of the group. The last two men to make it out of the cabin, Drollinger and Barlow raced a short distance up the mountain to their right, then stopped dead in their tracks as someone yelled, "Halt!" A man in their party—Frenchman Jacques Lartigue, who had retrieved a gun left behind by one of the guides—was firing back at the Germans from behind a tree. Drollinger and Barlow climbed farther up the slope and hid behind another tree. Meanwhile, Liles and de Milleville had found cover in thick bushes nearby.

When the shooting stopped, Liles saw Barlow and Drollinger continue their way up. He had taken the time earlier to study a local map carried by one of the guides, and as he ran on up the mountain, he knew the border ran north-south just east of their position. Ahead of him, Barlow and Drollinger had taken shelter in a gully, and there they hid, catching their breath. They saw SGT Stan Cammish of the RAF running down the trail, still wearing his railroad baggage handler uniform. Cammish had reacted on instinct, an inner voice telling him, "You've come too far to be stopped now." The Englishman veered course when he spotted Drollinger and Barlow in the gully. "He ran up there in the open," Drollinger later recalled, "and hid behind a little tree (about the size of a Christmas tree)." With hand gestures, Cammish urged the other two to come join him, but Drollinger and Barlow motioned back for the Englishman to come toward them instead. "If you'd have shot into the tree you would have hit him!" Drollinger remembered. "We finally got him to come over the hill. The Germans were shooting at him and shot off a branch above him. When he saw that limb fall he really turned on the coal!"[14] With Cammish, Drollinger and Barlow kept climbing away from the shooting.

Meanwhile, most of the other men were trapped on the slopes above the cabin. Within a half-hour, twenty-one of them had surrendered to the two dozen or so German mountain troopers. The fugitives were ordered to line up in one row with their hands raised. The Germans' second-in-command was a short, hunchbacked man who flew into a rage, shouting that they were all terrorists killing women and children. "Victory is ours!" he concluded, then went down the row of prisoners, greeting each one in turn with blows from his club. He went at one of the fugitives viciously, hitting him with his fists and striking him in the face with the butt of his rifle. Another *Feldwebel* set his dog loose on the same man, who all the while remained standing with his hands raised. The German commanding officer, a "Captain Schultz," initially threatened to execute Frenchman Jacques Lartigue. But he changed his mind, and instead decided to use him as a human shield as he went back down the mountain to capture any remaining fugitives inside the cabin.

The prisoners were taken downslope to a field, where they were ordered to lie down with their hands behind their heads for an hour. In single file, their hands still behind their heads, they were then marched down the mountain toward Bagnères-de-Luchon. Staff Sergeant Hendrickson, who had started down the slope toward Luchon and hid in a gully, saw the Germans and their prisoners pass him by. As night approached, thirteen men were still at large,

Hendrickson, Drollinger, Liles, Barlow, Cammish, and de Milleville, in addition to FSG Wilfred Gorman, SGT Paul C. Pearce,
2LT Robert Lindstrom, ILT Joseph E. Sutphin, and three others.
SSG Lepkowski might have been captured around that time, having nearly slipped through the German net. Like some of the others, he had not eaten or drunk anything but snow for thirty-six
hours. Hunger forced him out of his hiding place.

> The Germans passed by me all day long. [...] Finally, I decided
> to make a go of it and started for the top of the mountain, figur-
> ing the Germans would not expect me to go to the obvious. When
> I got near the top of the mountain, above the tree line, I could
> see a brick building which I didn't know was there, a ski resort,
> I believe. Immediately I started back down to the tree line, but it
> was too late, my footprints were in the snow and they captured
> me that afternoon.[15]

The building seen by Staff Sergeant Lepkowski had to be the Grand
Hotel, built two decades earlier for skiers and for special public
events at the top of the mountain of Superbagnères. Lieutenant
Liles likely also reached the Grand Hotel, although he would later
describe it only as a two-story stone building—the hotel was taller—on the mountaintop above the cabin. He ran toward and
through a crowd of "workmen" at the site of the building, and,
leaving them in his wake, he started on his way down into a valley with a mountain stream flowing through it.[16] A bridge allowed
passage across the river, but it was completely exposed to view. As
Liles pondered whether to cross the bridge, Drollinger, Barlow,
and Cammish caught up with him. The four men agreed to seek
another, more discreet passage across the river.

> [We] soon found a path at the river's edge. We followed this a short
> distance and then, just as it was getting dark, our path ended. It
> didn't actually end for we could see it start again across a twenty-
> foot wide chasm that had been cut by a small feeder creek. The
> chasm was spanned by a single pine tree that had been felled across
> it. With the branches all trimmed off it didn't appear very safe and
> none of us cared to attempt walking it. Finally Lynn [Drollinger] got

adventurous. Straddling it, with his feet locked beneath, he worked his way out several feet with no problem. Then on his next push there was a loud pop near the far end. Waiting a few moments he then moved again and received several more popping sounds. At about the log's midpoint the pops changed to a definite cracking sound and Lynn's spirit of adventure suddenly left him. He quickly crawfished his way back to the path and safety.

Giving up on trying to stay with the path, we worked our way down a steep and rocky bank to the river's edge and tested the water. It was very cold and very swift. Now in almost complete darkness we couldn't tell how wide or deep the river was there. We considered trying to cross it but discarded that idea after someone mentioned spending the night in wet clothing at freezing temperatures.[17]

The four men retraced their steps toward the bridge. Edging closer to it, they noticed that it was a cement bridge illuminated at both ends, with a large power station underneath and a sentry box at the other end. In spite of the risks, Liles decided to try out his luck and cross the bridge. Completely exhausted, he did not think he would have the energy to turn back and find another route across the valley. Walking, he reached the other side safely, and as there were no sentries to be seen, he motioned for the other three to follow him across.

Beyond the bridge, the road continued up the last mountain standing between the four evaders and Spain. They followed it for about a mile, until they spotted a light ahead in the dark. Someone had lit a small fire by the road, no doubt to stay warm. The four evaders now hesitated. Perhaps the fire belonged to a crew of woodcutters, perhaps not. Drollinger decided to go find out.

I [crawled] up [the] road on my hands and knees and I was just about ready to yell at them to come on up, there wasn't anybody around. Just about then somebody threw some wood on the fire. There were four German soldiers sitting around that fire. So I snuck back down the road again and I told these guys "we're gonna have to leave this road and go back up the hill again." It was dark and we had to crawl back up this cut. We went quite a ways back down the road again and up this cut and we headed east (I had a little tiny compass about as big as a nickel). I figured if we headed straight east we'd be all right. We had the North Star and it was starlight; it was a beautiful night out.[18]

For the next several hours Barlow, Cammish, Liles, and Drollinger climbed up the slopes of the mountain. Hungry and exhausted, they stopped to rest, but it was too cold to sleep out in the open. After an hour, they finally gathered enough strength to resume their climb and, well after midnight, found an abandoned house. They fell asleep on its dirt floor and did not awaken until after dawn. Cammish remembered he still carried some pound cake tucked away in his clothes, food for "a real emergency." As the four men ate, they felt some of their strength return. They left the cabin and resumed their climb.

At about the same time that Liles, Drollinger, Cammish, and Barlow were off again, most of the other evaders still on the loose finally ran out of luck. With two American airmen, Gorman had slipped past the German mountain troopers surrounding the cabin. Having traveled for several hours, they had reached the Lys Valley near the Ravi Bridge and they too had found an abandoned house where they had decided to spend the night. Early the next morning, Gorman was "awakened by four German guards with rifles pointing at [him] and two dogs eager to take a bite out of [him]." The two Americans with Gorman were also captured.

Later on the morning of the twenty-second, Liles, Cammish, Barlow, and Drollinger had reached the snow line, when Cammish yelled out a warning. Six German soldiers were climbing up the side of the mountain in their direction. The four fugitives were headed toward a gap between two peaks. They redoubled their efforts to reach the mountain pass ahead of the Germans. Drollinger was the first one to make it, then Barlow and Cammish. Liles was by now struggling far behind them, and when Cammish last looked over his shoulder, he saw the American pilot "lying motionless in the snow." The three servicemen started down the other side of the mountain, Drollinger ahead of Barlow and Cammish. Barlow and Cammish heard shots ring out in the distance behind them and shuddered at the thought of what had just happened to Liles. After a while, they reached a village, where a shepherd told them they were now in Spain. The two continued on to the town of Viella. In the hotel Cerano they found Drollinger, who had already arrived. To everyone's surprise, Liles stumbled in later that afternoon, having eluded the six German soldiers closing in on him.

> Two hundred yards short of the top I gave out. The others couldn't help me and struggled on. I must have slept two hours. When I awoke the Germans were 300 yards below me. They started shooting at me as soon as I moved. I had 50 yards to go before I disappeared from their sight, but I made it over the top without seeing them again. It took me all day to get down into Spain, and I had to stop often to get some sleep. When I finally reached a road, I sat there until a truck picked me up and took me to a village, where a gendarme arrested me at once and I joined the others who had reached the village earlier in the day.[19]

The four men were soon joined by Maurice de Milleville. He had run into an old farmer and offered him money in exchange for letting him hide in his hay cart. The farmer had taken his cart down into the same valley crossed by Drollinger, Barlow, Cammish, and Liles the night before. Near the bridge, de Milleville had allowed himself a quick peek from his hiding place. Several German soldiers had set up a machine gun next to the parapet, thus preventing passage across the bridge. Somehow, the thought that one of the men they were looking for could be hidden in the farmer's cart did not occur to them. One of the soldiers merely asked the farmer where he was headed, and without any attempt to search the cart, let him continue on his way.[20]

The last man to reach Viella was Hendrickson. After witnessing the group of prisoners being marched down the mountain, he left his hiding place in the gully at nightfall. While wandering through some woods, he found food and shelter in a barn, and the next day he climbed down to the edge of Bagnères-de-Luchon. In the afternoon, French children brought him food and led him to a nearby village. There they pointed the direction to the border, and off he had gone again. "I crossed [a] stream and swam a river," he would later recall, "and climbed straight up [the] mountain." Finally, he reached the mountaintop and at 3:00 a.m. on April 23 he set foot in Spain. After making his way down into Bossòst, he was taken to Viella, where he was reunited with Drollinger, Barlow, Cammish, Liles, and de Milleville. The six men had just escaped from France by the skin of their teeth. After the war, a veil of suspicion would be cast over one of them.

SEVEN

Hero or Villain?

In Viella Liles, Drollinger, Barlow, Cammish, de Milleville, and Hendrickson had free range of the town, having only to check in daily with the local Spanish police. Their next destination, they knew, would be an internment camp. But as the mountain pass just south of Viella was closed owing to snow, they were to stay put for now. From the hotel, Liles placed a call to the American embassy in Madrid. He received assurances that the consulate in Barcelona would intervene and, upon verifying their identities, obtain their release from the Spanish authorities. There was nothing left to do now but wait. How de Milleville occupied his time is unknown, but the other five visited the town and enjoyed a few drinks at the local bar. Back at the hotel they played cards and checkers. They spent hours exchanging war stories and engaging in light-hearted banter. Drollinger the fighter plane pilot, Barlow the top turret gunner of a B-24 heavy bomber, Liles the copilot of a B-17 heavy bomber, and Cammish the only RAF airman among them. They all had different combat experiences and unique perspectives that gave them much to discuss.[1]

> Jim [Liles] and I naturally argued the relative merits of B-17 and B-24 bombers, an area still in debate to this day. Jim stated the B-17 flyers always knew they would be safe from German fighters if B-24's were on the same mission because the fighter pilots were smart enough to attack only the "weaker" (B-24) formations. And I had to continuously point out the fact that there was no real reason for the B-17 flights at all since they had no capacity for a real bomb load.

Lynn [Drollinger] claimed to have lost more P-51 pilot friends to trigger-happy American bomber crews than to the enemy. Naturally Jim and I would counter with the fact that the "Glory Boys" in fighters had no better sense than to make head-on playful passes at our bomber formations before first flying alongside to let us see their "friendly" markings.[2]

During their debriefings more than a month later in Britain, Liles remembered de Milleville as a British civilian named "Morris," while Hendrickson referred to him as an RAF airman by the name of "Melville" and Barlow simply as a British intelligence officer. According to Barlow's memoirs written after the war, the story de Milleville told them all in Viella was that he was an English businessman who had lived in Paris before and during the war. And in that time in Paris, the Germans had become increasingly suspicious of his activities. De Milleville had been detained and interrogated on several occasions. Through it all, he had always denied that he was a spy, but after several beatings at the hands of the Gestapo—one during which he lost several of his front teeth—he decided to escape from France.

De Milleville was French, not British, and he could hardly be called a businessman. But the rest of his story was essentially true, beginning with the fact that he had run into trouble with the Nazis twice—the first time in Paris, where he was arrested in late March 1941 for illegal possession of a firearm. Sentenced by a German military tribunal, he spent nearly a year in prison, first in Fresnes, later in Troyes, Dijon, and Hauteville. His second arrest had taken place in Lyon on May 24, 1943, and as this time the Gestapo held him, one can hardly doubt that he was subjected to brutal interrogations. He was incarcerated in Lyon's Montluc prison until someone—his mother, by most accounts—arranged for his release on August 13, 1943, apparently after payment of a ransom to Klaus Barbie, the infamous Gestapo chief.

In a conversation with Lieutenant Liles, de Milleville revealed more of his identity. The American officer afterward reported that de Milleville—"Morris" as he knew him—had said he was the son of an English woman who ran an underground network, and that she had recently fallen into the hands of the Germans. Although by all indications Liles did not believe de Milleville, that information was also true.[3] De Milleville was indeed the son of Mary Lindell, celebrated in Britain after the war for her role in helping Allied officers stranded in France reach freedom. Just how many servicemen she succeeded in guiding back toward Britain has since become a subject of controversy. French journalist Marie-Laure Le Foulon argues in a recent book that for all her exertions, Mary Lindell accomplished very little. She goes even further when she depicts the English woman as a narcissist. According to Le Foulon, Mary Lindell did not just embellish the story of her life, she carefully reconstructed her past around true events to become the heroin she never was. Le Foulon cites various sources to support her claim that some French and British government officials held very unfavorable views of Mary Lindell, count de Milleville—portrayed as an adventurer—and their children, including Maurice. The most serious charges she levies against Mary Lindell are that having been deported to Ravensbrück in September 1944, she allegedly became the mistress of ss senior camp doctor Percival Treite, with whom she worked in the *Revier* (infirmary); and that during his trial after the war, she provided false statements to help exonerate him from war crimes.[4] In an even more recent book, biographer Peter Hore disputes some of Marie-Laure Le Foulon's claims, provides the names of additional servicemen assisted by Mary Lindell, and explains how she brought about the liberation of American and British women at Ravensbrück in April 1945.[5]

No historian disputes that Mary Lindell earned decorations for her bravery and her service as a nurse during World War I, or that she lived in Paris with Count Maurice de Milleville and their three children when war broke out in 1939. After the Armistice, the first French Red Cross society—the Société de Secours aux Blessés Militaires (ssbm)—asked her to transport children separated from their parents across the Demarcation Line. How many road expeditions she embarked on is unknown—perhaps only one, but one during which she famously smuggled cpt James Windsor-Lewis of the Welsh Guards (Special Reserve) from Paris to the Unoccupied Zone. An escaped prisoner of war, Windsor-Lewis had to play the part of Mary Lindell's French auto mechanic, despite not speaking a word of French. On their way south, they were stopped by a Luftwaffe officer who needed a ride to the town of Chateaudun. Mary Lindell had little choice but to oblige. Fortunately, the German officer did not speak any French either and he paid little attention to the mechanic who kept silent while riding in the back of the car. Later, having dropped off the Luftwaffe officer at his destination, Mary Lindell and Captain Windsor-Lewis successfully cleared the German roadblock set up at the Demarcation Line. In Limoges Mary Lindell purchased a train ticket for the Englishman, who went on his way to Marseille and later reached Spain, before returning to Britain.

A woman used to getting her own way, Mary Lindell could be outspoken and blunt to the point of rudeness. She also earned a reputation for personal bravery, which at times bordered on recklessness. According to her official biography, she was arrested in Paris in early 1941 and was court-martialed for helping British escapers and for insulting the Wehrmacht. After spending nine months in prison in Fresnes, she regained her freedom in November 1941 and chose to leave for England via Spain. "In uniform with numerous First World War decorations," Lindell reached Barcelona in July 1942. Upon her arrival in Britain, she then trained with MI9, a branch of the British intelligence services dedicated to helping servicemen evade capture or escape from POW camps. She returned to France on board a Lysander in late October 1942 and set up her own escape network named "Marie-Claire." She could count on French helpers near Ruffec in the Charentes department but for the moment did not have any passeurs to smuggle evaders across the border with Spain. Maurice, who now lived in Lyon and was officially enrolled in law school to avoid the Compulsory Work Service, was tasked by his mother to organize an escape route to Switzerland. At that time, while riding a bicycle to cross the Demarcation Line near Blois in mid-December, Mary Lindell was struck by a car. The accident left her with a severe head injury and several broken ribs. She was taken to a hospital in nearby Loches, where for a while she hovered between life and death.

On Christmas Eve 1942, Maurice returned to Lyon after visiting his mother at the hospital. Upon his arrival, he received a message from Marie-Claire operative Armand Dubreuille in Ruffec about "two important parcels of food." Maurice immediately went back to see his mother, and, following her instructions, traveled to Ruffec to look after the so-called parcels, in reality two stranded Allied servicemen. They were named MAJ Herbert G. "Blondie" Hasler and CPL Bill Sparks, two Royal Marines who had just carried out Operation Frankton, a covert attack on Bordeaux's harbor in the southwest of France. With eight other Royal Marines, they had cast off in five collapsible canvas canoes—or cockleshells—nine miles off the mouth of the Gironde River on the night of December 8. Paddling up the river during three consecutive nights, four men in two boats arrived within sight of the harbor. And on the fourth night, Hasler and Sparks in their canoe "Catfish" made for the west bank of the main docks and placed limpet mines on four ships. In the other boat "Crayfish," Corporal Laver and Marine Mills went to the east docks and attached mines on two ships. With the explosives in place, all four marines left the scene, and at dawn the two commando teams decided to split up to improve their odds of avoiding capture.[6]

Operation Frankton was a success. In the morning of December 12, the mines detonated and sank or heavily damaged all six of the ships to which they had been attached. The damage caused by the attack greatly disrupted shipping in Bordeaux's harbor.[7] But Operation Frankton had come at a heavy price for the Royal Marines who had been hand-picked and deployed to carry out the raid. Strong tidal currents in the Gironde River had claimed the lives of two Royal Marines after their canoe capsized. Two other boats capsized or sunk, resulting in the capture and later execution of four other Royal Marines. Even Laver and Mills, who had reached the target and participated in the attack, found themselves betrayed and arrested before they could reach safety. Neither of them ever returned home.

Operation Frankton had been a suicide raid all along, with little hope of survival for its commandos. Beforehand, Major Hasler and the other Royal Marine commandos had been briefed that, should they survive, they would need to head northeast and make for the town of Ruffec near the Demarcation Line. There they would find an underground organization capable of bringing them home. As they followed the plan, Hasler and Sparks did not know the name of that organization, nor even how to make contact with it once they arrived in Ruffec. As for Mary Lindell, she had no prior knowledge of Operation Frankton, nor of Marie-Claire being part of the plan for repatriating survivors. Operation Frankton was a morale booster for Britain during the war, and it captured the imagination of millions. Not surprisingly, Mary Lindell's rescue of the "Cockleshell Heroes" went a long way toward establishing her reputation. Maurice played a role in that rescue.

Having marched one hundred miles, Hasler and Sparks reached Ruffec early on December 18, 1942. The town had a population of nearly four thousand during the war, but by chance the two Englishmen found French patriots in the Toque Blanche Inn, where they stopped to eat. Two Frenchmen guided them the next day across the Demarcation Line to Armand Dubreuille's farmhouse east of Ruffec. According to Lucas Phillips's 1956 book, Hasler and Sparks stayed with the Dubreuille family until Maurice's arrival on January 6, 1943. Marie-Laure Le Foulon, however, argues in her book that Mary Lindell's son did not make his appearance at the farmhouse until perhaps January 30.

"In Lyon my chief will be awaiting you," Maurice reportedly told Hasler and Sparks when he arrived, "and we will make the necessary arrangements to get you back to England." Maurice and the two marines headed southeast on bicycles, arriving after dark in the town of Roumazières. They caught a train to Lyon, Maurice making sure to choose a coach "already half full of sleepy French travelers." They arrived at their destination without any incidents, and there Maurice took the other two men to see Mary Lindell. She was unhappy at the sight of the two Englishmen, though she did not say anything in front of them. But when left alone with her son, she scolded him for letting Major Hasler travel while still "sporting a magnificent English moustache." She then handed the officer a pair of scissors and told him to cut it off.

On February 23 Britain's War Office received a message from Marie-Claire. Hasler and Sparks were alive and well, the first the

British government had heard from them since Operation Frankton. And although Marie-Claire still lacked the means to repatriate evaders, the organization had crossover connections with other escape lines. Through Pat O'Leary Hasler and Sparks traveled to Marseille, and from there to Perpignan. On March 1 they made the journey across the Pyrenees from Ceret to Banolas, and they arrived safely at the British consulate in Barcelona. They were brought home from Gibraltar, Hasler first on April 2 by air, Sparks later by sea.

Maurice de Milleville had just turned twenty-two when he was arrested on May 24, 1943, in Lyon. Mary Lindell learned of her son's arrest while attempting to obtain funds for her organization in Switzerland. "Maurice is very ill and has been transferred to the clinic," the coded letter read. According to Mary Lindell's official biography, Maurice had been the victim of his own carelessness, befriending two Jewish girls who were under surveillance by the Gestapo. Later, de Milleville also wrote that he had been betrayed by an evader he was attempting to exfiltrate.[8] Whatever might have been the real reason, it seems the Gestapo became aware of de Milleville's true identity. During interrogations and beatings, the Gestapo reportedly tried to break him and get him to reveal Lindell's location. According to his mother, he remained silent.

Maurice was released from prison on August 13. The exact circumstances of his release—officially involving payment of a bribe to Klaus Barbie—remain unclear. Mary Lindell had him followed as he stepped out of Montluc, and as there were no signs of surveillance by the Gestapo, she went to see him. Her official biography describes Maurice stumbling into her arms and collapsing into tears. "Mary tried to lift his head and his glasses fell off. She saw for the first time the dreadful damage to his face. He went on his knees, groping for his glasses and Mary realized that he was practically blind. The Nazis had beaten him across the face with a thin, brass chain, demanding to know where his mother was to be found."[9]

During the next three months, Marie-Claire received and took care of a number of evaders. To Mary Lindell's credit, her organization this time went beyond providing those evaders with a chain of safe houses in France. It succeeded in smuggling at least four servicemen over the Pyrenees, Kenyan-born FO Mike Cooper, Australian PO Allan Frank "Mac" McSweyn, CPT R. B. "Buck" Palm, a Hurricane pilot of the South African Air Force, and RCAF FO Harry Smith.[10]

On the first attempt to reach the foothills of the Pyrenees, Mary Lindell traveled with the group of evaders by train to Toulouse. When she heard that the Germans had set up a control checkpoint before Toulouse, she had them all step off the train and together they returned to Ruffec. Maurice then went to arrange for a new journey, and ten days later, this time reaching Toulouse, they took a slow train to Pau, again accompanied by Mary Lindell. With Spanish and French guides, the four servicemen started out over the mountains in rainy weather. During the climb, Harry Smith felt pain in his chest and he soon collapsed. Palm and McSweyn came to his rescue and helped him carry on. In a valley, the group was able to rest, but as they continued on toward Spain, the weather took a turn for the worse. The French guide fell behind and died in the snow before anyone realized he was missing. The others reached a hut, where they were able to light a fire and recover from exhaustion and frostbite. Farther down in the valley, they arrived in a village. They were now in Spain.

A Greek army captain had been in the travel group that turned around before reaching Toulouse. After their return to Ruffec, he decided to part company with Mary-Claire. Later, after arriving in the UK, he delivered a stinging indictment of Mary Lindell's methods, revealing that virtually everyone in Ruffec knew about her underground activities and the van she used for transporting evaders. Mary Lindell, he also said, did not even bother hiding the nationality of her evaders. Instead she would speak to them publicly in English, a habit that no doubt some evaders found unsettling. The Germans were perhaps bound to catch up with her. They did so on November 24, 1943, three months after the release of her son, two weeks after Cooper and the others had left Ruffec.

IN JANUARY 1944 IT was Maurice de Milleville's turn to go to Geneva in neutral Switzerland. There, he crossed paths with Eddie Luff and LT Gordon Hardy—later with him in the Pyrenees—as well as with another Royal Navy officer, LT Ian McGeoch. An escaped POW, McGeoch had crossed the Swiss border from Italy on September 13, 1943. After reporting to the military attaché at the British legation in Berne, he traveled to Geneva to see a renowned eye specialist. Five months earlier in the Mediterranean Sea, the submarine under his command, the HM Submarine *Splendid*, had been heavily damaged by depth charges from a German destroyer and forced to surface.[11] Unknown to him at the time, he had sustained an eye injury that would soon threaten his vision and require urgent treatment. After having a metallic splinter removed from his eye in September 1943, McGeoch spent the following months waiting with growing frustration for his repatriation to England. Switzerland did not expel Allied servicemen who sought refuge within its borders, but neither did it allow them to leave. McGeoch had only been spared internment as a result of his eye injury and the long-term care it required. Taking advantage of his situation, he studied French at the University of Geneva and history and economics at the Graduate Institute of International Studies, and began to help out at the local British consulate. He became friends with Eddie Luff, then also a student at the Graduate Institute, who wanted to travel to Britain and enlist. The two men agreed that going through official channels for their repatriation would take too long. They decided instead to try and arrange for false French passports for themselves.

McGeoch first met Maurice de Milleville at the British consulate. "One day during the last week in January 1944, I met in the consulate a young Frenchman who was having a noisy altercation with Mr. Bloor in a passageway. 'This young man,' said Mr. Bloor, 'gives his name as Maurice de Milleville and wishes to acquire British nationality,' adding, somewhat superfluously, 'he seems rather worked up.'" McGeoch decided to defuse the situation and offered to take the Frenchman to lunch, where he listened to de Milleville tell his story.

> Maurice never stopped talking, very fast, mostly in French, but breaking now and then into well-spoken English when he realized that I had lost the drift of what he was saying. I quickly gathered

that he had just come across the frontier from occupied France. He was in an extremely nervous state and at times was almost incoherent. Aged about twenty, he was smallish, fine-featured, with pale complexion and dark hair, undernourished and clothed in a baggy suit. From time to time he looked towards the door and through the window, as if expecting to have been followed. It became obvious that we must leave the bistro. But where to go? Maurice had said that he had no papers and had entered Switzerland without permission; he was mortally afraid that he might be forced to return to France.[12]

To Lieutenant McGeoch Maurice de Milleville also expressed his astonishment at being refused a British passport, given what he said had been his and his mother's contribution to the Allied cause. He did not reveal that his mother ran an escape line, just that she was involved in helping British servicemen in France. His mother had continued in her activities even after being severely injured in her accident, but she had then been captured by the Gestapo. It was her capture, de Milleville said, that prompted him to risk crossing the border with Switzerland instead of making his way to the Pyrenees. On behalf of the British government, he and his mother owed French helpers the sum of 57,000 francs for assisting stranded servicemen.

At first McGeoch had his doubts about de Milleville, but having checked key parts of the Frenchman's story, he eventually decided to enlist his help in crossing occupied France and reaching the Pyrenees. He let him stay one night at his place in Geneva, then arranged for more permanent lodgings for the Frenchman through an American secret serviceman. During the weeks that followed, McGeoch, Luff, and de Milleville met frequently while making final arrangements for what would be their journey together. Luff and his Swiss fiancée had met Maurice and were both "strongly inclined to believe him to be genuine."

In late February 1944 the three men welcomed into their "escape committee" LT Gordon Hardy, who had served as navigator under McGeoch aboard the HM submarine *Splendid*. Like McGeoch and about half of the submarine's crew, Gordon Hardy had barely escaped with his life following the German destroyer *Hermes*'s attack on the *Splendid*. The survivors had been rescued onboard the *Hermes* and brought to the Italian coast near Naples. Hardy had later jumped off a train taking him from Italy to a POW camp in Germany and made his way across the Swiss border on September 22, 1943.[13] "Seeing Gordon again was a great bonus. Despite being somewhat of a pessimist and always openly self-critical, Gordon's contribution to any discussion was always lively, articulate and highly original. It was fortunate that both Eddie and Maurice liked Gordon and were prepared to take him along with them." The four now altered their plans. McGeoch would go first, followed by Luff, Hardy, and de Milleville. Having received his false papers, Ian McGeoch crossed the border into occupied France in early March 1944. He traveled by train to Lyon, where he immediately set out to establish contact with members of de Milleville's network. As all had gone well, he sent word back to Hardy and Luff to follow him. Gordon Hardy left Geneva next, in all likelihood accompanied by Maurice de Milleville. A few days later it was Eddie Luff's turn. "On 8th March 1944, my 21th birthday, I set off from Geneva equipped with false French papers under the name of Georges Louis Soyer, traveling wine salesman, born in Oran in 1926. This new identity had been arranged by my friend Colonel Romyko and produced by Major Strokatovsky who belonged to a top Polish network."

Eddie Luff traveled to Lyon by train. He was fortunate enough to have the help of a guardian angel, a fellow passenger.

> As we approached Lyon, a girl I had been chatting with, who worked at the Swiss Consulate, whispered to me, "At the Gare de Perrache, ask a railway official to take you to the sleeping car where you'll be able to get a sleeping compartment for the night. It's expensive but you'll avoid the very severe controls at the station." Bless her, whose name I never knew, who guessed I wasn't really a traveling wine salesman. The next day I heard that the Gestapo had bagged a lot of people at Perrache that evening.

From Perrache Eddie Luff had to walk only a short distance parallel to the Saone River to reach his destination at 1 Rue du Plat.

"I am Edmond," he said when a fifteen-year-old girl opened the door, "and come on behalf of Maurice." After she let him in, Eddie Luff met her family and had dinner with them. That same evening, he was taken to the home of the "lively and witty" Dr. Bonnier, the same dentist who had helped McGeoch days earlier. Luff stayed with her until the day a man known only as "Robert" came by. Eddie Luff was to be on his way the next day, and Robert went through all Luff's belongings to make sure he had no compromising materials whether in his suitcase or in his pockets.

Eddie Luff traveled alone by train to Saint-Sulpice-la-Pointe northeast of Toulouse, then walked to the nearby, remote village of Saint-Lieux-lès-Lavaur. He had been instructed to report to the village's teacher, a Mr. Auriol. And when he did, the Auriol family welcomed him "with open arms" and with calls of "my dear cousin," to deceive anyone who might have been curious about the new arrival. Eddie Luff remained in Saint-Lieux for about a month through the middle of April. But he was not the only fugitive sheltered in the village. Gordon Hardy was there as well.

> St Lieux was an isolated harbour for those who had to hide from the Germans: allied airmen, Jews, members of the Resistance tracked by the Gestapo. With Mr. Auriol, on dark nights, we visited the pariahs of the German Reich, starting with Gordon who was in good spirit. Others who had been hiding for several weeks were white-faced, bored but hopeful. We were all waiting for the snow to melt on the foothills of the Pyrenees.[14]

Eddie Luff's memoirs do not mention Maurice de Milleville's presence in Saint-Lieux-lès-Lavaur. He probably was there, however, as Luff, Hardy, and de Milleville later arrived as a group in Saint-Laurent / Saint-Paul.

In her book, Marie-Laure Le Foulon quotes a Ruffec resident who remembered Maurice de Milleville seventy years after the war: "The people of the department of Charentes got to know Maurice well. . . . A slacker, a joker! Not a bad person, not a traitor, but a partyer who preferred to chase after girls rather than to take care of his mother's business, which was much of a bore to him."[15] During his first stay in prison, Maurice de Milleville also left a lasting impression on Major Curie, a French Resistance fighter imprisoned with him in Hauteville in 1941. According to the French officer, Maurice was not the type to be frightened and he would likely not hesitate to take on dangerous missions. But he was also vain, and as a result talked too much, though he seemed incapable of knowingly betraying others. Perhaps there was another, more introspective side to de Milleville. According to Major Curie, Maurice seemed to have a passion for the sea and boating, and in prison, he spent all his time making hand-carved wooden boats. But according to others, Maurice also kept repeating the same falsehood that he was a member of the British Secret Intelligence Service. As for Lieutenant McGeoch, he came to realize that the Frenchman was intelligent, yet also vain and immature. De Milleville's ambitions were to acquire British nationality and join the Secret Intelligence Service, then distinguish himself during a difficult or dangerous mission, all in an effort to impress and seduce women. Like Major Curie, McGeoch believed de Milleville perfectly capable of acts of valor and heroism, but not one to be trusted for his silence. In fact, McGeoch reflected, de Milleville "must talk." It seems that, during that period of time the two men spent together in Geneva, de Milleville was also quite candid about his family background. One of the questions that later would arise among historians was whether the Count of Milleville and Mary Lindell were legally married. After all, the count had seemingly never divorced his first wife, with whom he had had several children. In front of McGeoch, Maurice de Milleville the son spoke of being an illegitimate child of mixed English and French blood. And it was this heritage that, in McGeoch's opinion, was behind the Frenchman being "unstable in personal relationships."[16]

In 1954 Maurice de Milleville wrote the following account of his involvement with Lieutenant McGeoch and Lieutenant Hardy.

Toward the end of [1943] I was able to establish contact with two Allied officers. I first took charge of them in Geneva. I had one of them, Lt Commander Ian Mc Geoch, guided across the Spanish border to Gibraltar; he got through without any mishap. Lt Gordon Hardy, the second officer left with me using the same route. We were already quite tired as a result of our difficult trip, when German soldiers chased after us near the Spanish border. They captured Lt Hardy, who was exhausted. I managed to get across the border.[17]

Once in Spain, de Milleville continued to pose as an Englishman. He knew the fate that awaited him if the Civil Guard discovered he was French. He thus avoided a long stay in an internment camp or in an overcrowded prison, and instead he let the British consulate look after him.[18]

In the Pyrenees Maurice de Milleville once again showed himself clever and resourceful. In all likelihood, he was not the traitor others after the war made him out to be, but he was also no hero. Had he managed to take LT Gordon Hardy and Eddy Luff with him across the border with Spain, he could have cemented his mother's legacy and his own place in history. Here, after all, was the dangerous mission he had craved for so long. De Milleville was exhausted from the long climb of the previous night, but so were all of the other men in his group. When his turn came to be on watch with Second Lieutenant Liles, it was not him who sounded the alarm. He could not have done so, for within a few minutes of them taking their posts, Liles saw that the Frenchman had fallen asleep.[19]

EIGHT

Aftermath of a Betrayal

I n 1994 Dutch researcher Herman van Rens interviewed Max Rens, a retired physician born to Jewish parents in 1913 on the outskirts of Amsterdam. Reflecting on his life during World War II, Dr. Rens explained that after the German invasion of the Netherlands, he left Amsterdam with his Catholic wife Maria and their two young children. Maria had grown up in Limburg, the southernmost province of the Netherlands, and there the family resettled. Persecution followed them in September 1940 when "racial Jews" were banned from holding public office and, as a result, Max Rens found himself unemployed. In Limburg, at least, he did not live under the threat of the mass roundups taking place in Amsterdam. But even that changed in August 1942, after the Nazis decided to retaliate against the Catholic bishops of Limburg for their protest of the Jews' persecution. All of the province's baptized Jews were to be arrested. Max Rens, who had converted to Catholicism when he married Maria in 1939, was no longer safe under his own roof. He left his home and went to live in secrecy with another family. He had his own spare room and remained indoors at all times during the day.[1]

Dr. Rens remained in hiding for more than eighteen months. He had been a reserve health officer in the Dutch army, and in early April 1944 a man came to visit him with a message from the Dutch government-in-exile. D-Day was drawing near, and the Dutch government was outfitting a brigade to take part in the Allied invasion of Europe. Max Rens was to make his way to London, where he would be assigned to that brigade. From Roermond Max Rens rode his bicycle across the border to Belgium. With help from Catholic priests along the way, he arrived in Antwerp, where he joined a group of some twenty-five men—Dutch, Belgian, and French civilians and Allied servicemen. The most prominent member of the group was Dutchman Gerrit Jan van Heuven Goedhart, the editor of an underground newspaper on his way to England to become the new minister of justice in the Dutch government. In Antwerp Max Rens received false identity papers in the name of Leopold Fernandez (or Fernandes). The Dutchmen traveled together through France as *Fremdarbeiter*, foreign workers. Bordeaux was their official destination, but instead they went to Toulouse, where members of Dutch-Paris were waiting for them. From Toulouse Van Heuven Goedhart followed passeur Palo Treillet (Pierre) and crossed over the Pyrenees to reach Spain, before arriving in London on July 17. Max Rens was captured in the Pyrenees on April 21 near Luchon.[2]

Fifty years later, Dr. Rens might not have remembered exactly all the events leading up to his capture. Not surprisingly given the time lapse, some details of his account—such as traveling on board a bus to Luchon—appear to be mistakes. But Max Rens also mentioned climbing in the mountains with a group accompanied by guides, being captured by soldiers with dogs, and witnessing the mistreatment of his travel companions at the hands of the Germans. The date of his arrest and some of the same details found in the story of the thirty-five leave little room for doubt. Max Rens must have been one of the two Dutchmen we know were in the group. His name also appears in a list of individuals helped by the organization Dutch-Paris in April 1944 along the Toulouse-Spain route.[3] The list was included in a report prepared after the war by Salomon Chait (aka Edmond Moreau), one of Jean Weidner's lieutenants. The other two names in the same list for the month of April 1944 are those of Dutchman "Van Gullik" and Belgian Roger Bureau.

UNTIL THE GERMANS TURNED up at the cabin, the fugitives had channeled all of their energy and determination toward reaching the border. But once capture seemed inevitable, new priorities emerged. Max Rens's wedding ring bore an inscription with his name on it. During his last moments of freedom, he removed the ring from his finger and tossed it aside. He was arrested under his false name Leopold Fernandez and later treated as a non-Jewish political prisoner, similar to the other civilians in his group. Englishman Eddie Luff tore his false French identification papers and threw the pieces on the ground. He had other papers in his possession, prepared by the British consulate in Geneva and establishing his true identity and nationality. Luff hid them in the lining of a pocket.

Eddie Luff was not Jewish, and as a British national he could expect to be treated better than the Frenchmen, the Dutchmen, and the Belgian in the group. Nonetheless he had decided to pose as a British officer, perhaps for fear that the Germans might discover his half-Belgian family lineage or his earlier association with anti-Nazi student protests in Brussels. Born in 1923 to an English father, Eddie Luff was not only half Belgian through his mother Sylvie, but he had grown up in Belgium, not in the UK. Originally from London, his grandfather George had moved to Brussels in 1888 as the representative of a firm for the Low Countries. He became involved in the import of beer, and as his business activities flourished, the family remained in Belgium, even during the First World War, when the Germans requisitioned shops and warehouses. From a small corner of Belgium holding out against Germany, George Luff carried on with his beer import, "greatly appreciated by the Allied troops and the local population, French and Belgian." Throughout that time, George's oldest sons—including Eddie's father, Charles—fought in the trenches but survived the war. Charles and Sylvie were married in 1919, one year after the end of World War I. And Eddie Luff, who was born in 1923, spent his childhood years during the interwar period, in comfort and largely unconcerned by what around him was called the "sound of marching boots."

> Our house, which bordered on "Avenue Molière," was vast and comfortable with a nice little walled garden. My sister and I would climb in a walnut tree and sit on top of the wall. The horses grazing in the field which still bordered part of the avenue, would amble towards us to beg a lump of sugar, presented in the hollow of our hand, a method recommended by our mother. [. . .] The

street where we lived was very peaceful; traffic amounted to 10 cars a day and at night only 5 cars were parked outside. Deliveries—milk, bread, ice, coal—were made by horse and cart.[4]

From his childhood days, Luff recalled the visits to the Brussels motor show, the sports events, the "sing-songs" around the piano, and the happy weekends at the seaside villa his grandfather had acquired in the small resort of Westende. But he also vividly remembered the start of the war, when "despite [Belgium's] neutral status, its reservists were called to arms." "Our street," Luff wrote, "was selected to bivouac during five days a battery of 75 guns, horse-drawn, which added fragrance to the military display." Then came the invasion of Belgium.

> On 10th May 1940, my mother, my sister and I had spent the evening at a Bach concert and returned home just before midnight. At six am, we were woken up by a loud bang in the neighborhood, followed by ack—ack guns further away. Meeting in pyjamas in the drawing room, glued to the radio, we hear: German forces have invaded Holland, Belgium and Luxemburg.
>
> I remember the confusion that reigned during the 20 days which followed, between Belgian ministers, the King, the allies, French and English. Should one withdraw to France or England, capitulate or entrench behind the River Yser as in 1914? It seemed to me that my father's hesitations were shared by all the higher Allied authorities who appeared to be influenced by what had happened 20 years ago. Because of this, in May 40, instead of going to Ostend to embark for Dover, way chosen by his younger brothers, we went to Westende, missed the last boat and finally had to cope with the German occupation.[5]

Only a few days into the occupation of Belgium, the German army came to take Eddie Luff and his father away. With some 250 other British nationals, the two men were interned at the Huy Fortress, a citadel with rampart walls built along the Meuse River. The life they led inside the fortress was reasonably comfortable. They saw little of the German guards and could communicate with family and friends, who were allowed to gather on a nearby piece of high ground outside the main gate. But the situation was only temporary, as the detainees were to leave for Germany soon. Wearing the uniform of the Belgian Red Cross, a friend of Eddie Luff came to visit him one day, and he told him that he would be able to secure his release. "If the Germans were to ask me my age," Eddie recalled his friend saying, "I should state, without hesitation, that I was born in 1925 and that I was aware of the mistake on my papers." And on the day that all the English prisoners gathered with their luggage for their transfer to Germany, Eddie was pulled from the ranks. After one last embrace with his father, he saw all the prisoners move out of the Huy Fortress. Later that day he was released.

Eddie Luff was a student at the university in Brussels when protests erupted in 1942. Not only did the *Kommandantur* order the university to shut down, but some students were arrested and then deported to Germany. "I felt I had to make myself small," Eddie Luff recalled in his memoirs. He became a probationer officer at the Luxor lightbulb factory, where he soon moved up the promotion ladder to a desk job. He already knew of the existence of escape routes to England through Spain, and he was no doubt already tempted to leave. An incident at the factory proved to be the tipping point.

> One morning I heard strange noises in the factory yard. From the window of the main office I saw gray cars and men with long coats; they entered the management bloc and came out a few minutes later with the manager, his deputy and his secretary, who were pushed into a car which took off immediately. Remained in the yard one Gestapo man and two "polizei" who started moving towards the factory. I did not wait for their arrival and, now that I knew the place, I went to hide in the packaging hall, where I knew of a well-hidden store room. After two hours, I heard the Gestapo cars going out and returned to the offices where reigned a wind of panic. I seized the opportunity to remove my file from the personnel department.

Eddie Luff had contacts with the Belgian Resistance. From the head of an escape network, he obtained false identity papers in the name of Jean-Louis Dupond. He was also told to go to Switzerland after first crossing the border into France. Having kissed his mother and his sister goodbye, he left on September 10, 1942, and three days later, at dawn, he snuck through a barbed-wire fence and set foot on Swiss soil.

HAVING CLIMBED DOWN THE Mountain of Superbagnères, the Germans and their prisoners reached Luchon in the valley below in the evening of April 21. According to nineteenth-century French author Henri Castillon d'Aspet, it was as though the hand of Providence had created the beautiful valley of Luchon and the surrounding region in a moment of joy and laughter, favoring it with sweeping views, a prodigious diversity of landforms, odd-shaped mountains, and numerous waterfalls. The town of Luchon, officially named "Bagnères-de-Luchon," was well known for its thermal waters under the Roman Empire. In the nineteenth and early twentieth centuries, it drew royalty, artists, celebrities, and wealthy tourists alike, not only for the majestic setting and the spas, but also for its large, elegant villas and the wealth of mountaineering opportunity in the region. Not that any of it mattered now to the prisoners as they set foot into the very town they had tried so hard to avoid. Together with others in the group, Eddie Luff now reflected bitterly that it had just taken them twenty minutes to climb down the mountain, when the night before they had spent many hours struggling up the same slopes to arrive at the cabin.

In Luchon all the prisoners were taken to the Hotel des Princes, headquarters of the Zollgrenzschutz. They were searched, and most of their money confiscated. In his indignation, Paul Louis went as far as asking to speak with the commanding officer of the Zollgrenzschutz. He told him that his papers were false and that he was in reality a priest.

"You gambled, and you lost," the officer said, "we will now take care of you!"

"I won the first round," Paul Louis countered, "you take the second one, but I hope to be the winner at the end."

The prisoners were then locked up in the basement of the hotel, eighteen of them in a cellar, the others in a room across from it. They coped with their grim, new reality by sharing funny memories of their trek together. Meals also helped. The prisoners had to pay for them, but they pooled their money so that everyone in the group could eat. A few beds in the cellar could sleep a total of only nine men. At 2:00 a.m., they traded places, and the ones who had not had been able to lie down yet got their chance to do so. Through it all, the injured Jim McMahon received no medical attention from the Germans.

AFTER THEIR CAPTURE IN the early morning on the twenty-second, Wilfred Gorman and the two Americans with him were brought down to Luchon and the Hotel des Princes, where they joined the others.[6] Gorman had yet to learn what treatment to expect from his captors: "I remember going into this hotel. I could see the dining room off to one side and I thought, "Oh good, they're going to give us something to eat," and I headed that way. They shouted and grabbed me and shoved me through another door, were I ended up at the bottom of a flight of stairs. I was all right though. No bones were broken."[7] On April 22 the seventeen men who declared themselves Allied servicemen were transferred to the Villa Raphaël, a three-story building with a mansard roof and dormer windows. Dubbed by some the "Villa of Torture," it served as the headquarters of the Gestapo's border police (Grenz-polizei) in Luchon. The officer in charge, Karl (Charles) Dethlefs, was only in his early thirties. A nearly six-foot-tall, blonde man already balding and wearing glasses, he had been a storekeeper earlier in Bremen.[8]

"The German Gestapo was not kind to prisoners," Sergeant Gorman later recalled, "and I was no exception." Gorman gave the Gestapo agents who interrogated him his name, rank, and serial number. He also told them that he was a crewman on a bomber shot down during a mission, and that he had bailed out. They were simply not interested. As he would not tell them the names of his helpers and places where he had stayed, they kept calling him a spy and he went through several rounds of beatings. The Gestapo was also relentless in going after Sergeant Lepkowski.

As he too remained steadfast in his silence, the American airman was treated to round after round of savage beatings that took a heavy toll on his body.

> The Gestapo were merciless, using a rubber hose to pound on my legs, punching me on the face and knocking me on the back of the neck. This went on day and night and you got so tired you no longer cared what happened. The constant pounding on my legs resulted in bruises on bruises until there were open sores and then it got to the point where I was unable to walk.
>
> A guard came in one day, told me to get up for another interrogation and I refused. He took out his gun, pointed it at me and said he would shoot me if I didn't get up. I told him to shoot and do me a favor, after which they left me alone.

The civilians in the group—Priest Paul Louis, Roger Bureau, and the others—arrived at the Gestapo headquarters one day after the Allied servicemen, on April 23. Paul Louis was placed in the same cell as three of his companions. They all felt great anxiety as they heard the whimpering of inmates being interrogated on the floor below. In the cell next to theirs, an inmate had been left crying in agony, his hands handcuffed behind his back and his backside black from all the beatings. Paul Louis prayed that he be given luck and strength for what lay in store for him. When his turn came to be interrogated in the evening, he was admittedly quite scared. Four German Gestapo agents waited for him in an office, including an interpreter. When Paul Louis stepped into the room, the agent who sat by the typewriter got up and walked up to the priest with a smile on his face.

"So, how are you?" The German asked.

"I've been better," the priest responded.

No sooner had he spoken that the Gestapo agent punched him in the face, knocking him down. Paul Louis heard yelling in German, and he received several kicks as he struggled to get back up.

"Are you a Jew?" the interpreter asked.

After Paul Louis gave them his real name and said that he was a Catholic priest, the Gestapo agents ordered him to take off his clothes. They checked whether he was circumcised and searched through his clothes and inside his shoes.

"Who gave you these false papers?"

Paul Louis made up a story about a man by the name of Narcisse, whom he said he had met in a bar in Paris. He had given Narcisse money in exchange for the man organizing his journey to Spain. The Gestapo agents looked though their directory of individuals wanted by the SD. They found his name, along with an enlarged photo of him.

"Why are our services looking for you?" the Gestapo wanted to know.

"I don't know," he responded.

The German policemen hit him again, and he told them that all he had done was give food to escaped prisoners.

"Who sent them to you?"

"It was their own idea to come see me," the priest told them. "It is normal for people in need to turn to a priest." "In two months' time," he could not resist adding, "perhaps it will be German soldiers who need that same help from me."

Getting nowhere with their interrogation, the Germans tried a different tack. "When will the Allied landings take place?" was their next question.

"Go ask Churchill!"

The response prompted another round of beating. Of the four Gestapo agents, only one had not touched Paul Louis. It was Charles Hammer, the interpreter. As the interrogation was nearly concluded, the Gestapo agents told Paul Louis to put his clothes back on. Then they showed him magazine photos of the Basilica of the Sacred Heart in Paris, which had been damaged by American bombs. "We didn't do this," one of the Germans told Paul Louis. "No," the priest responded, "but you are the ones right now torturing a priest." By then, the interpreter had turned as pale as death, and forty-five minutes after the end of the interrogation he visited Paul Louis in his cell to hand him back his cross. The interpreter said he was Catholic and asked the priest to keep him in his prayers.

THE GERMANS NOW KNEW they had captured seventeen Americans, Englishmen, Australians, and Canadians. The Allies later found a partially burned report dated April 24 and addressed by the German frontier police (the Grenzpolizei, branch of the Gestapo) to the Kommandantur der Sipo und des SD in Toulouse. The report listed the identities of the seventeen, along with their ranks, and dates and places of birth:

FSG Charles William Jackson, English, born April 27, 1922, in Cobridge, Stoke-on-Trent, Staffordshire;

U.S. SGT Paul C. Pearce (his name has been completely erased by the flames in the main body of the report, but it appears in the airman's individual arrest record);

SGT Thomas James Taylor, English, born March 13, 1924, in Stoke-on-Trent, Staffordshire;

U.S. SGT Melvin Porter, born March 11, 1923, in Owensville, Indiana;

U.S. SGT [sic] Curtis Finley, born February 9, 1914, in Schuyler, Nebraska;

FSG Wilfred Gorman, Canadian, born September 10, 1922, in South Nelson, New Brunswick, Canada;

U.S. 2LT Robert Dickson Lindstrom, born June 16, 1919, in Salem, Oregon;

U.S. SSG Stanley Lepkowski, born February 27, 1920, in Schenectady, New York;

U.S. 2LT James Joseph McMahon, born September 10, 1920, in Hoboken, New Jersey;

FSG John Ansell, Australian, born on June 21, [1922], in Sydney;

Englishman Edmond Luff (all the lettering of his name has been erased with the exception of "Edmond");

LT George Gordon Hardy, English, born March 24, 1915, in Cheadle, Cheshire;

PO William Herbert Taylor, English, born August 2, 1916, in Saint-Helens, Lancashire;

U.S. TSG Theodore Ralph Kellers, born December 8, 1915, in Akron, Ohio;

Australian FSG David-Thomas Balmanno, born October 9, 1923, in Brisbane;

Canadian SGT John Acthim, born February 21, 1924, in Redditt, Ontario; and

U.S. 1LT Joseph E. Sutphin, born November 22, 1919, in Winston-Salem, North Carolina.

Among the seventeen, Eddie Luff might have had the most at stake. According to his memoirs, he had decided to pose as a British officer. To the Gestapo, he declared that he was a second lieutenant taken prisoner in Egypt and had later escaped from a POW camp in Italy. In case his cover was blown, he intended to produce his consulate ID papers to at least prove he was British. Luck might have been on his side for the time being, or so he thought. The Gestapo did not question his story, Luff remembered, and presumably showed itself more interested in obtaining information on the help he had received on his way to the Pyrenees. Luff would later recall the interrogation as "succinct but fierce."[9] By all indications, however, the Grenzpolizei was not fooled. Their report lists Eddie Luff as a "civilian hoping to enlist after reaching Britain."

THE COMPLETE REPORT OF the Grenzpolizei might have also contained the names—most of them likely fake—of the dozen French, Belgian, and Dutch civilian fugitives captured in Gourron. If any such list existed, unfortunately it did not survive. In the hands of the Gestapo were Frenchmen Paul Louis, Raymond Krugell, Jules Lautman, Jacques Lartigue, Dr. Marcel Hulin, and Fernand Bellenger (the twenty-one-year-old son of a French army tank commander who was a prisoner of war in Germany), in addition to Belgian Roger Bureau, and—almost certainly—Dutch doctor Max Rens.[10] With those names added to the six who reached Spain and the seventeen captured Americans, British, Australians, and Canadians, only four men in the group remain unidentified, three of whom at least were also arrested. One of them was Dutch, perhaps named Van Gullik (or Van Gulik). According to

Paul Louis, the other three would have been French. Perhaps one of them was named Jacques Liddell.

Less than two weeks after the raid on the black shed, on the evening of May 2, 1944, Robert and Marie Liddell picked up their mail, to find a letter from their son Jacques. The letter simply read: "Luchon, 25 April 1944. Dear parents, I nearly made it but not quite. All is well, however, so don't worry. Kind regards. J." It had taken a week for the letter to reach the Liddells in the small village of Badefols d'Ans in southwestern France. The envelope bearing a Marshal Petain postage stamp was postmarked April 26, 1944, at Toulouse's train station.

Born in December 1918 to an English father and a French mother, Jacques Liddell was a teacher at the same time that he pursued higher studies in philosophy. He had taught at a high school in Toulouse during the 1942–1943 school year. In the fall of 1943, he had moved on to his next teaching post, a high school in Paris. In April 1944, however, Jacques Liddell made the decision to leave Paris, apparently for fear of being arrested by the Gestapo. Back in Toulouse, he visited with two of his ex-colleagues, professors Gustave Cassan and Pierre Marty, telling them that he was about to climb over the Pyrenees in an effort to reach Spain. He left Toulouse accompanied by a woman who was to hand him over to passeurs for the journey over the mountains.[11]

The letter Jacques Liddell wrote to his parents on April 25 does not mention him being arrested, and yet that is likely what happened. According to Paul Louis, some or all of the prisoners from the climbing party left Luchon for Toulouse in the afternoon of Wednesday, April 26, the day that Liddell's letter was postmarked. The transfer took place by rail, and evidently the vigilance of the guards was less than strict. Paul Louis mentions that at the train station in Toulouse he missed his chance to escape. And earlier, in Montréjeau, he had found himself walking around the train station in search of cigarettes. "I manage to find tobacco," he wrote, "and the other thing too: get the word out that I have been captured." Paul Louis's account suggests the following storyline. Jacques Liddell wrote a secret letter to his parents on the last day of his imprisonment in Luchon. It was not until the following day that he was able to slip it unnoticed to someone in a crowd, at the Toulouse-Matabiau train station or earlier, during the train ride from Luchon.[12]

The report of the Grenzpolizei identifies three of the passeurs who accompanied the climbing party. According to the report, Georges Capcarrère from Jurvielle guided the thirty-five fugitives to Saint-Paul-d'Oueil. There, two new guides took over, Jean Ferret from Luchon and Jean-Louis Pène from Montauban-de-Luchon. With Ferret and Pène, the group climbed to the cabin on the mountain of Superbagnères, near the hamlet of Gourron. Charbonnier is not mentioned in the report. Both Ferret and Pène were arrested, but twenty-four-year-old Georges Capcarrère remained at large. The Grenzpolizei's information was largely correct. Capcarrère lived in Jurvielle in the Larboust Valley just west of Luchon. His family was originally from the nearby Louron Valley, and his father had owned slate quarries on the mountain pass known as the Col de Peyresourde. After Georges's father passed away in 1918 during the First World War, his wife had had to sell the quarries but received financial assistance from the French government. A carpenter by trade, Georges Capcarrère had anarchist and communist sympathies, and Paul Louis later remembered that in April 1944 the passeur was engaged. Late on April 20, as the thirty-five and their guides found their way again after the storm, Capcarrère had mentioned his fiancée to the priest. He had also told Paul Louis he was exhausted and hoped not to have to make the climb to the cabin.

At the time of his arrest on April 21, 1944, thirty-nine-year-old Jean-Louis (Louis) Pène was a plasterer, not in Montauban-de-Luchon but in Juzet-de-Luchon. In February 1954 Louis Pène gave the French Gendarmerie the following signed deposition:

> In 1943, when I learned that patriots were present around Gourron, municipality of Saint-Aventin, I offered to bring them food and help them reach Spain. My activities were carried out together with Mr. Ferret, who was Water and Forestry district ranger and owned a motorcycle.
>
> We continued our activities until April 21, 1944, when we were arrested by the Germans in Gourron-Saint-Aventin. The Germans

took us to Luchon and locked us up at the Hotel d'Angleterre. The following day I was interrogated by the Gestapo at the Villa Raphaël. Eight days later, I was transferred to the Saint-Michel prison in Toulouse. There I stayed eight, or perhaps up to 10 days. Then I was shipped to Neuengamme (Germany).[13]

As for thirty-eight-year-old Jean Charles (Jean) Ferret, he was indeed a Luchon resident and worked for the Water and Forest Administration, a French federal agency. After they had been caught at the black shed, some of the men in the party blamed the guides. "Captured on the 21st of April 1944 one mile from the Spanish border in the mountains around the town of Luchon," John Acthim wrote afterward in his diary. "Believed to have been betrayed by one of the guides." Several years after the war, however, Ferret gave the French Gendarmerie a signed deposition, in which he stated that an informant had tipped off the Germans.[14] By then, in fact, the suspected local informant had long been tried and convicted, on the basis of several testimonies seemingly establishing his guilt. But there were also references made after the war to a possible betrayal in Toulouse, and in particular to an apparent attempt by the Germans to infiltrate the Françoise escape-line organization. That attempt took place in April 1944, with a young Belgian woman at the center of it all.

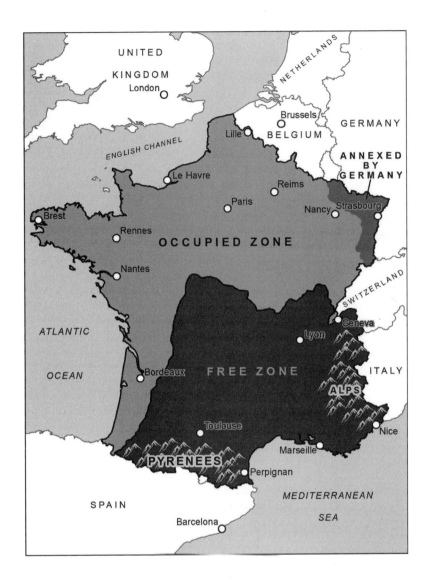

Fig. 1. Map of Occupied France, 1940–1944. The Demarcation Line separated the Free Zone in the south, under the control of Marshall Pétain's Vichy government, from the Occupied Zone in the north, ruled by a German military administration. In November 1942, the Germans crossed the Demarcation Line to occupy all of France. (© Ryan Trollinger)

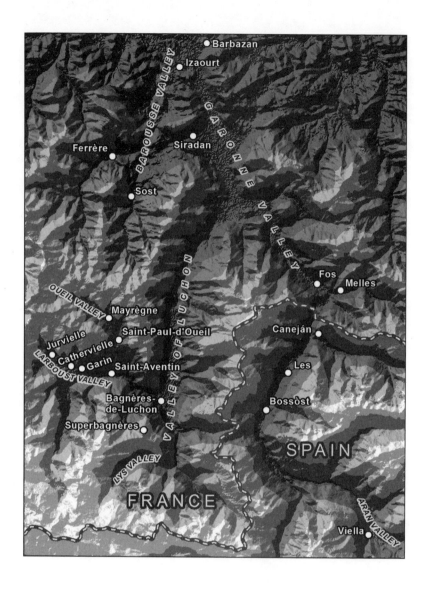

Fig. 2. Map of the central Pyrenees and the French-Spanish border near
Bagnères-de-Luchon and along Spain's Aran Valley. (© Ryan Trollinger)

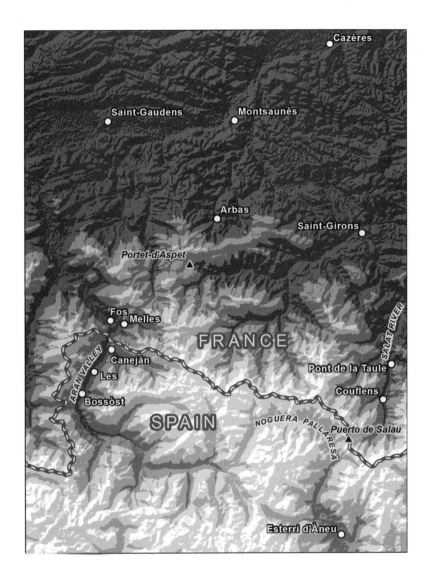

Fig. 3. Map of the central Pyrenees and the French-Spanish border along France's Ariège region—including the Couserans Valleys—east of Bagnères-de-Luchon. (© Ryan Trollinger)

Fig. 4. (*left to right*) Henri Marrot ("Mireille"), Alain Moriquant, and Palo Treillet ("Pierre"), Rue de Metz in Paris in 1943. (*Le Chemin de la Liberté*)

Fig. 5. Dutch patriots (*Engelandvaarders*) arrive in Viella, Spain, March 1944. Among them are Sam Timmers Verhoeven (*sitting, front, right*), Vic Lemmens (*sitting, second row, second from left*), and Han Langeler (*standing, back, left*). (Photographer unknown)

Fig. 6. Roger Bureau. (Directorate-General War Victims, Belgium)

Fig. 7. Belgium's national ice hockey team at the 1927 European Ice Hockey Championship in Austria. Roger Bureau is on the right. (Jan Casteels)

Fig. 8. FSG Wilfred M. Gorman, RCAF. (Philippe Connart / www.evasioncomete.org)

Fig. 9. Anselme Vierneuwe (*left*) and Charles de Hepcée. (Rose de Hepcée)

Fig. 10. Jean-Louis Bazerque ("Charbonnier"). (EGMT)

Fig. 11. Fr. Paul Louis in 1944. (Fils de la Charité)

Fig. 12. Raymond Krugell (*standing*). (Raymond Krugell)

Fig. 13. SGT Harrison "Harry" Stanley Cammish, RAF. (Harry Cammish)

Fig. 14. FSG David Thomas Balmanno, RAAF. (David Balmanno)

Fig. 15. SGT John Acthim, RCAF, in Leintrey, east of Nancy in northeastern France. (Philippe Sugg)

Fig. 16. Marie-Louise Dissard ("Françoise"). (Archives Départementales de la Haute-Garonne-Fonds Françoise 44J)

Fig. 17. 448th Bomb Group, original pilot Robert A. Martin crew (Crew 51).
Standing, from left: 2LT Joseph E. Sutphin (navigator), 2LT Joseph B. S.
Johnson Jr. (copilot), 2LT Robert A. Martin (pilot), and 2LT John E. Johnston
(bombardier); *middle row, from left*: SSG Richard G. Thalhammer (radio
operator), SGT Robert N. Metcalf (right waist gunner), SGT Earl D. Hostetter
(ball turret gunner), and SGT Melvin Porter (left waist gunner);
front: SGT Charlie Flukinger (tail gunner) (*left*) and SSG George C. Hunt
(top turret gunner and engineer). (Joe Sutphin)

Fig. 18. TSG Archie R.
Barlow Jr., USAAF.
(Lora Beth Barlow Wright)

Fig. 19. 2LT Lynn H.
Drollinger, USAAF.
(Rick Drollinger)

Fig. 20. SSG Stanley
Lepkowski, USAAF.
(Philippe Connart /
www.evasioncomete.org)

Fig. 21. TSG Theodore
R. Kellers, USAAF.
(Philippe Connart /
www.evasioncomete.org)

Fig. 22. James F. Fowler crew, 427th Bomber Squadron, in December 1943, including TSG Curtis E. Finley (*left front*). (Gary L. Moncur/www.303rdbg.com)

Fig. 23. Saint-Laurent/Saint-Paul railroad station during the 1940s. (Christophe Cathelain)

Fig. 24. Superbagnères Plateau, overlooking the Lys Valley to the south.
(Postcard in author's possession)

Fig. 25. HM submarine *Splendid* crew in 1943, with LT Ian McGeoch (*standing, front, second from right*) and RNVR LT George Gordon Hardy (*back, far right*).
(Angus McGeoch)

Fig. 26. Edmond "Eddie" Luff, 1945. (Christopher Luff)

Fig. 27. One-peseta note signed by TSG Archie Barlow, 2LT Lynn Drollinger, and SSG William Hendrickson, three of the evaders who arrived in Spain on April 22, 1944, as well as by two other evaders they joined in Spain. (Harry Cammish)

NINE

Maddy De Deken

In early April 1944 a twenty-four-year-old blonde, blue-eyed Belgian woman by the name of Marie Madeleine (Maddy) De Deken made her first appearance in Toulouse, accompanied by three American airmen, 2LT Albert W. Stravinsky, TSG Daniel F. Gilmore, and 2LT Russell E. Moriarty. After spending two or three days at the Biarritz Hotel, the group was passed on to helpers of the "Françoise" organization. Having learned of their arrival, Marie-Louise Dissard (Françoise) found out that one of the Americans, Second Lieutenant Moriarty, insisted on Maddy De Deken, his fiancée, going with them over the Pyrenees. Françoise did not know De Deken, and suspicious of the Belgian woman's motives, she refused to have any contacts with her. Accompanied by Albert Lautman, she went to see Stravinsky and Gilmore, who were staying at the home of Auguste Dauriac. Françoise had them fill out questionnaires, paid for their lodging expenses, and handed them clothes. She then directed Jacques Lartigue of her organization to pick up the two airmen on the seventh of April and take them to the train station, where they would join a group of other evaders on their way to Spain.

According to Marie-Louise Dissard, Maddy De Deken stayed a few more days in Toulouse. When the Belgian woman realized that she would not be permitted to go over to Spain, she left, stating that she was headed back to Belgium, where she intended to pick up more airmen. Russell Moriarty remained at the home of helpers Robert Cayla and his wife, but as he had a change of heart and decided to cross over the Pyrenees, Albert Lautman ("Lucien") made arrangements for him to join another party of evaders ready to leave. Having returned to Belgium, De Deken again made contact with members of the escape line she had used west of Tournai for the crossing of the French border. According to Omer Verrhoye of Hertain—who had sheltered the three airmen in March for about a week—De Deken told him upon her return "that the airmen had arrived [safely] at Barcelona and that she had married one of the three … [and that] she was to rejoin her husband before the 10th [of] May and was going to let another person know the route." To both Omer Verrhoye and Françoise Antonissen, De Deken said that "she had with her 20,000 French francs and food coupons which she had received from the American Consul at Barcelona."

Two weeks later, according to Françoise—the exact date is either April 26 or 27—De Deken returned to Toulouse and went to see the Caylas at their home. Having gone out in the evening around 9:00 p.m., she and Robert Cayla were arrested by the Gestapo on the bridge of Matabiau in front of the railroad station. Afterward, no one could find any signs of De Deken having gone to Toulouse's Saint-Michel prison. Instead the organization received reports that the Belgian woman had been seen in town on two occasions in the company of Germans. Robert Cayla was imprisoned for ten days. Even under torture, he remained silent and was eventually released by the Gestapo but kept under surveillance. A month and a half went by without the Germans learning anything further about the Françoise network. Then, on the twenty-second of June, the Gestapo arrested all the helpers who had had contacts with De Deken, except for August Dauriac and his wife, who both managed to escape just in time. Maddy De Deken was suspected of being responsible for all the arrests.[1]

BORN ON FEBRUARY 21, 1920, De Deken lived in Antwerp, where she had trained to become a nurse at the Institute of Tropical Medicine. After her older brother Guy escaped to England in May 1940 and enlisted with the RAF, the rest of the family became involved in the work of escape lines in and around Antwerp. Maddy's parents owned a house in Antwerp and a large villa in nearby Gravenwezel, and both places became safe houses for downed airmen. RCAF SGT Derek James Webb stayed with Maddy's parents in Antwerp in July 1943. From there Maddy De Deken guided the airman on his way to Brussels, where he was looked after by Comet operatives and sent on his way to Spain. In February 1944 it was RCAF FO Jacob Thurmeier's turn to stay with the De Deken family before Maddy took him to Brussels. There she safely delivered him into the care of Gaston Carolus of the "Belgian National Movement."

Both Sergeant Webb and Flying Officer Thurmeier had stayed with Elaine Delhaye-Gill at the castle of Vignée-sur-Lesse, where De Deken arrived to collect them.[2] In late February 1944, De Deken again traveled to Vignée-sur-Lesse. On that occasion, several airmen were ready for transfer. De Deken first took charge of U.S. SSG George L. Mikel and bombardier Edwin L. Vincent, taking them to Gravenwezel then to Lille in northern France. It was mid-March, and she instructed the two airmen to continue on without her to the town of Béthune, giving them the name and address of her contact in that town and telling them to wait for her there. Shortly thereafter, she returned to Vignée-sur-Lesse to collect five more airmen and bring them to Gravenwezel. In this second group were four crew of a B-17G Flying Fortress downed on March 2 during a mission to Frankfurt, navigator 2LT Edward B. Connors, radio operator TSG Daniel F. Gilmore, tail gunner SSG Verden D. Swank, and bombardier 2LT Albert W. Stravinsky. The fifth airman, Second Lieutenant Moriarty, had suffered severe burns to his left leg after his P-47 Thunderbolt fighter plane crashed on December 30, 1943, and it must have been while tending to his burns that the nurse and her pilot developed feelings for each other. From Gravenwezel, Swank and Connors struck out on their own but were both arrested just before reaching the French border. De Deken smuggled Moriarty, Stravinsky, and Gilmore into France, taking them first to Lille then Béthune. When De Deken and the three airmen arrived in Béthune, Mikel and Vincent had already left, having decided to go the rest of the way to Spain on their own.[3] From Béthune, De Deken, Moriarty, Gilmore, and Stravinsky traveled to Tours and then to Châteauroux, before finally arriving in Toulouse.

In the chain of command of her own underground organization, Maddy De Deken reported back to Gaston Carolus in Brussels. But upon her return to Belgium in April she could not find him, and later would learn that he had been killed. According to her, she left again on the twenty-second intending to go to Spain, and from there to the UK, to be reunited with Moriarty. First, however, she was to stop yet again in the area west of Tournai and show her replacement, a Belgian by the name of Frank Van Hecke, the inner workings of the new Antwerp-Tournai-Lille-Béthune-Toulouse escape line. In Lamain she introduced Van Hecke as her successor to members of the escape line.

In a statement dated November 19, 1944, De Deken wrote that she had known Van Hecke for three years and that in her eyes he was "a very ardent patriot," whom she used "to carry out some spy work" for her. On the previous day, November 18, De Deken gave her version of all that took place in a letter addressed to Russell Moriarty:

Dear Russell,

I must first make my excuses for having cut our date at Barcelona but circumstances decreed otherwise.

After leaving you I got back to Antwerp without difficulty on the 17th of April, and I tried to get into touch with my chief, but without any success for by then the Germans had killed him. I left again on the 22nd [of] April and on the 27th I arrived at Toulouse, all having gone very well, but that evening at 9 o'clock I was myself arrested by the Gestapo. The Gestapo took me to Paris and then to Brussels and as I refused to talk the beasts gave me solitary confinement for a month. On the 31st of May I was taken to the military prison at Antwerp, where I learnt that my parents and Moustique had been arrested. There I also learnt that the man who had betrayed me had been killed by Robert Comblay [sic] and as the Germans had arrested me with a P. 38 they accused me of assassinating the man in question, and I also learnt that the Gestapo had been watching me for two years. I had meanwhile not lost all hope, for the Germans had not found my dossier of reports, when in mid-July they theatrically searched our house from top to bottom and found all my reports of spying and the names of the Allied aviators I had helped.

The letter contains no admission of guilt, but it suggests that Maddy De Deken lied to Omer Verrhoye about going to Barcelona, not to mention receiving money from the American consul. But her deception went even deeper than indicated by the letter, for the three Americans she claimed she had accompanied to Barcelona did not even reach Spain. Instead, Gilmore explained to a Belgian helper in a letter dated August 4, 1945, that he and Stravinsky had been "captured in the Pyrenees by a [German] patrol."[4] In a separate attempt, Second Lieutenant Moriarty had by all appearances met a similar fate. The three airmen joined the Allied POW population of the Third Reich, Gilmore in Stalag Luft IV in Gross-Tychow, Pomerania (now Poland), Stravinsky in Stalag Luft III near the town of Sagan in the German province of Lower Silesia, and Moriarty in Stalag Luft I near Barth, Prussia. All three survived the war, though in early 1945 Technical Sergeant Gilmore and the other POWs in Gross-Tychow were forced to march 500 miles westward in cold, blizzard weather.[5] Gilmore flew back to the United States in July 1945 after spending several weeks hospitalized in Belgium and later in France. In the letter he wrote on August 4 of that year, the American airman had noteworthy news to report: "Two weeks ago, I received a letter from Antwerp announcing Lieutenant Moriarty and Maddy's wedding. As of today, they are in Antwerp, and I will give you their address. Go ahead and tell them that I am looking forward to their return to the States." Frank Van Hecke met his end on May 16, 1944. A member of the escape line in Lamain, Jean Chavalle, had grown suspicious of his activities. During a short struggle in a café in Camphin-en-Pévèle, France, Jean Chavalle gained the upper hand and pointed a gun at Van Hecke. Avoiding German patrols, he brought the Belgian back across the border to an unoccupied house in Lamain. Another member of the escape line, Albert Comblez, went through Van Hecke's papers and found *Ausweis* cards for travel through Europe and for carrying a gun, in addition to his Waffen-ss foreign volunteer ID. Comblez told Van Hecke that "the game was up." Van Hecke confessed to being a member of the Geheim Feldpolizei, and he even boasted of having previously dismantled the Beaumont-Chimay escape line, an operation that had resulted in more than 150 arrests. He gave the names of those who had been compromised as a result of his infiltrating the escape line originating in Antwerp, Louvain, and Tournai, with stops in Hertain, Lamain, and Camphin. Van Hecke was then executed, his dead body thrown into a well.

Maddy De Decken was set free from Antwerp's military prison on September 3 or 4, as a result of the Allies liberating the city. She had been incarcerated by the Germans for more than three months and sentenced to death. According to her letter to Second Lieutenant Moriarty, written after her release from prison, she had been interrogated thirty-seven times and "tortured horribly." Twenty-two-year-old Françoise Antonissen from Antwerp saw much of De Deken during that time in prison, as she herself had been denounced by Frank Van Hecke. Although her statement confirms that De Deken was interrogated, she alleges that the young Belgian revealed compromising information to the Germans.

> At Antwerp in prison I was put into solitary confinement for 77 days side by side with Maddy. [...] The Germans knew a lot but not everything. In the meantime I spoke but never said anything which might compromise other people. She (Maddy) was questioned and was very depressed after her questioning. [She] wanted to commit suicide, and I had a lot of trouble cheering her up. [...] I was able to find out that Frank's reports were very detailed. I saw bits of Maddy's interrogation. She said that I was a member of an Antwerp organization. [...] Miss Klerks was arrested on Maddy's [testimony].

The two young women, Maddy De Deken and Françoise Antonissen, communicated through an air duct between their two prison cells. Maddy told Françoise that she did not believe Frank had betrayed her. According to her, he had been arrested as well, though not at the bridge of Matabiau like her, but at a different location she did not name. Françoise Antonissen always made sure not to reveal any new information to De Deken, stating that "in prison D.D. was continually careless" and that "she promised to behave herself and do no more harm."[6]

Upon the liberation of Antwerp, Allied authorities treated
De Deken as one of Frank Van Hecke's many victims, rather than
his accomplice. Did Van Hecke accompany De Deken to Toulouse on her second trip there? If so, he might have ordered not
just Robert Cayla's arrest, but hers as well, after deciding he no
longer needed her. Subsequent arrests of Françoise operatives in
Toulouse might have been the result of her giving him names she
thought he would need to continue their work. But why, then, did
she lie when stating that she went to Barcelona? Did she receive
money as she said she did, and if so, from whom? Later, in 1945,
suspicions grew about her possible active involvement in German
counterevasion efforts. Aside from the lies and deception, Maddy
De Deken's story bears a striking resemblance with that of Belgian Andrée de Jongh, who also at the age of twenty-four set up
her own escape line—later known as "Comet"—in the summer of
1941. De Jongh herself escorted three evaders by train from Paris to
Bayonne, and from there on foot over the Pyrenees and across the
Spanish border, arriving in August 1941 at the British consulate in
Bilbao. As a result of this early success, MI9 decided to grant the
Belgian woman financial support for her escape line, and Andrée
de Jongh went on to make more than thirty double crossings of
the Pyrenees.[7] Had Maddy De Deken, perhaps, learned of Andrée
de Jongh, and did she aspire to the same success? Or did German
counterintelligence put her up to it without her being aware of
anything? The Germans, after all, had learned Andrée de Jongh's
whole story by then, and they might have been hoping for the
Americans to put their trust in a young Belgian woman, as MI9
had done previously with de Jongh. Following De Deken's contacts
with the Francoise organization, could the Germans have managed
to infiltrate the group of fugitives who left Toulouse on April 18?

TEN

The Woodcutter

During the German Occupation, the Pautot family earned little trust and respect from the two hundred or so residents of Saint-Aventin-de-Larboust. And when later, after the Liberation, nineteen-year-old Michel Pautot was arrested on charges of intelligence with the enemy, the investigating judge did not have to look far to obtain incriminating testimonies. According to Laurence Puente, a villager speaking under oath on November 22, 1944, "Michel Pautot spent a lot of time with the German border police at their outpost at Garin." "On several occasions," she said, "I went to Garin with friends of mine, and I noticed that Michel Pautot had very friendly relations with the Germans there." Another villager, Marius Mora, stated that Pautot often spent his evenings in Garin, returning to Saint-Aventin at all hours of the night despite the curfew. "I also observed," Mora said, "that whenever the German patrol came through Saint-Aventin and Michel Pautot's sisters went to shake the soldiers' hands, he himself shook their hands and called them by their names." Other witnesses reported Pautot accompanying German soldiers on their patrols through other villages of the Larboust and Oueil valleys, including Cazeaux and Castillon. In Cathervielle above Garin, Pautot was even spotted wearing a German military cap. After a while, the majority of the population suspected him of being an informant for the Germans and they simply avoided him.

Michel Pautot's older sister Naïda did not fare much better in the eyes of Saint-Aventin's villagers. She had moved to nearby Luchon, where she worked in a laundry and rented a room on the second floor of François Baylac's house. According to Baylac, she went out at all hours of the night, returning only in the morning.

Aventin Castex, whose family owned a café in Luchon, declared that Naida was one of the regular patrons.

> Very often, she came with two [Germans] named Alex and Alfred, close friends of "Stork Neck," whose real name I think is Boiffner [perhaps Ernst Butner]. According to Naïda herself, she slept several times with Alex and with Alfred. I heard it firsthand from her. . . .
> Naïda told me that she had spent the night in several of the premises occupied by the Germans, including the "Hotel d'Angleterre" [turned into the Kommandantur], and the Villa Raphaël, headquarters of the Gestapo.

When Michel Pautot was asked later about his sister, he had no qualms declaring that she had thrown her lot with the Germans. The gendarmes had been looking for her for questioning, and he confirmed to them that when the Germans evacuated the region, she had gone with them to Spain. According to Michel, Naïda could well have been passing information on to the Germans, as she knew everyone in Saint-Aventin.

During his trial, Michel Pautot defended himself by saying that all he did was to share moments of fun with the German soldiers, including when they attended local balls together. But some villagers also took note of troubling coincidences involving the arrest or near-arrest of known members of the local Resistance. "I had told Michel Pautot that my brother Victor Sansuc was a ‚passeur" Noël Sansuc told the French Gendarmerie. "A few days later," he added, "my brother was arrested in Luchon by agents of the Zollgrenzschutz while accompanying two Americans. Of all the people in Saint-Aventin, only [Michel Pautot] would have been in a position to denounce my brother."[1] Pierre and André Crampé from Castillon-de-Larboust both worked as passeurs for Charbonnier, and one day the older of the two brothers, Pierre, ran into trouble with the Germans. "The day that the Germans were hunting me down, I went to the village of Oô where I hid. The day after, in the evening, Michel Pautot showed up in Oô on his bicycle, and lurked around the village. The following evening, he did the same thing. I assume he went to Oô to find out where I was. Most likely Pautot denounced other Frenchmen."[2] To make matters worse, rumors also surfaced that Michel Pautot spent more money than he could possibly afford as a woodcutter earning 140 francs daily. Félix Arrey from Cazeaux-Larboust remembered that Pautot was a regular customer of cafés up and down the Larboust Valley, that he seemed to be spending a lot, and that he bragged about buying expensive cigarette packs worth one hundred francs each. In the minds of the Saint-Aventin villagers, all of it led to the unavoidable conclusion that he was receiving money from the Germans. Seventeen-year-old Marcel Brunet of Saint-Aventin even heard Michel Pautot apparently reveal his escape plan once France was liberated.

> He had also asked me if I wanted to go to Spain with him before the Germans left. He had not told me why he wanted to go [there]. My feeling is that he did not have a clean conscience and that he wanted to leave so he would not be arrested by the French authorities [after the Liberation]. On several occasions, Michel Pautot said to me that if anybody messed with him he would have him locked up right away. People were very scared of him.

One of the most serious charges brought against Michel Pautot was that he had alerted the Germans about the presence of American and English evaders on the mountain of Superbagnères on April 21, 1944. The statement of Charles Hammer, the interpreter for the Gestapo in Luchon, played an important role in Michel Pautot's conviction. His deposition took place under oath on November 17, 1944.

> The day following the arrests of the Americans and Englishmen and of passeurs Ferret and Pène, I went up to the Zollgrenzschutz outpost in Garin with Captain Schultz and Dethlefs. In the car I heard Schultz say "Finally someone who gets it. A peasant from Saint-Aventin came to inform us that Americans and Englishmen were in the area. I gave him 2,000 francs for reward.[3]
>
> After we had reached the outpost, Captain Schultz began to speak in French to Eglantine Thomas, known as Titi. I do not remember what the conversation was about. I was not involved in it as an interpreter since it was in French [and not in German]. The name

"Pautot" was pronounced ... I knew nothing of Michel Pautot. To the best of my knowledge he had no relations with the Gestapo in Luchon. However, I must say that Pautot could have been in contact with the Zollgrenzschutz, which gathered its own intelligence [independent of the Gestapo]. I had never heard of Naïda Pautot. In the morning I would see two women going back to the "Hotel d'Angleterre." One of them was named Theuze, Schultz's mistress. I don't know the name of the other one. She was heavy-set, with a very dark complexion, and seemed to be between 20 and 25 years old.[4]

On December 18, 1944, Michel Pautot was sentenced to hard labor for life. Throughout the trial, and even afterward, he always maintained his innocence. He declared that prior to June 1944 he had not had any relations with any of the soldiers at the Garin outpost. The soldiers had befriended his family the day they offered a piece of candy to his little sister outside their home in Saint-Aventin. Afterward they continued to stop by to have a drink and to bring bread and other food supplies. Maxime Alphonse Pautot attempted to appeal the decision of the Court of Justice of Toulouse against his son. He also pleaded for clemency, stating that he was the father of eleven children, four of them still under eighteen. His wife took care of the housekeeping while he alone worked. "The only child who helped me," he wrote, "is the one named Michel."[5] Michel Pautot had also joined the communist Resistance (the Francs-Tireurs et Partisans) on the day of the region's Liberation. "My son would have sacrificed his life to kill as many [Germans] as possible," Alphonse Pautot argued. "On August 26, 1944, he did not hesitate with the maquis to chase after the Germans all the way to the Spanish border and then go with the Interior French Forces to Bordeaux. He was arrested in Tarbes on the day he was to go to the battle front."

In defending his son, Michel Pautot's father seized on one detail of Charles Hammer's testimony. According to him, Michel Pautot could not have been the "peasant" who denounced the group of evaders and passeurs Ferret and Pène, all simply because he was a woodcutter instead of a peasant (farmer). Charles Hammer also changed his tune in November 1945 during a Gendarmerie hearing at the Detention Center of Eysses north of Toulouse, where he was imprisoned.

> I met Michel Pautot at the prison of Saint-Gaudens in October or November 1944. I did not know him at the time that I worked in Luchon. Pautot has nothing to do with the arrest of the 40 [sic] Englishmen and Americans by the border police in April 1944, and here is why.
>
> The day following the arrest, I went to [Garin] with my chief [Dethlefs of the Gestapo]. There I heard the chief of the Zollgrenzschutz [Captain Schultz] tell him how he had learned about the arrival of the Englishmen and Americans. A young Frenchman from the village of Garin or the village of Saint-Aventin came to let him know. I do not know the name of that peasant, but he received a reward of 2,000 francs.

Had any of the thirty-five fugitives testified during the trial of Michel Pautot, they would have been able to dispel any doubts surrounding the identity of the "peasant." Those who told the story of their trek through the Pyrenees years after the war might have forgotten all about him. But others who related those same events shortly after they happened mentioned the man they saw near the cabin on the morning of April 21. The guides had gone down into the valley, promising to obtain food for the party and to return in the evening for the border crossing. One other member of the party had accompanied them, according to Second Lieutenant Liles, Staff Sergeant Hendrickson, and Technical Sergeant Barlow. "In the morning," Raymond Krugell later wrote, "a man came lurking around our cabin. We asked him [what he was doing, and] he told us that he had seen three Germans in the village below us." Priest Paul Louis might or might not have talked to the peasant directly, but he similarly reported the group being told about the three Germans in the village, and he added that the peasant had come "to retrieve his cows, or so he said." Because Staff Sergeant Hendrickson only spoke "a little French," he might not have understood what the peasant said or what those who spoke with him related afterward. According to Hendrickson, however, the man told them he had seen the member of the party who had descended to the village talk with the Germans. And Hendrickson also remembered that the man who showed up near their cabin was a woodcutter.[6]

AT THE PORTET D'ASPET mountain pass back in February, German soldiers had been lying in ambush ready for the arrival of Pierre and Mireille's group. On the mountain of Superbagnères, however, the German raid took place nearly twelve hours after the thirty-five reached the black shed. Had the group decided not to wait for the return of the guides and, instead, struck out on its own toward the border, the German mountain troopers would have arrived too late on the scene. "We knew the Germans were close," Second Lieutenant Drollinger said, "but we were just too tired." Evidently the Germans had not known of the men beforehand. Either they were caught completely unaware of the presence of a group of fugitives in the area, or, more likely, the events of the previous night had alerted them but they could not determine where the thirty-five were headed. Ultimately the Zollgrenzschutz found tracks in the snow, or it received a late tip. Frenchman Jacques Lartigue remained convinced after the war that the group had been betrayed, not on the day of their capture at the black shed, but earlier, in Toulouse. A member of the Francoise organization, he likely was alluding to the incident involving Maddy De Deken. Perhaps Lartigue was partly right. Perhaps Captain Schultz knew about a group of fugitives having just left Toulouse. The Germans had been hard at work less than a month earlier in Bossòst and Viella, gathering as much intelligence as they could after the arrival of the two large groups of Allied evaders on the nineteenth and twenty-eighth of March. They knew that recent border crossings had taken place near Luchon. From maps given to them by the Spaniards or drawn for them by members of the two groups—perhaps in exchange for money or for help dealing with the Guardia Civil—the Germans likely even knew some of the important crossing points along the route to reach the Aran Valley. But they had not known about the obligatory stop at the black shed below Superbagnères, or else they would have been there, lying in ambush and waiting for the group to arrive.

Was Michel Pautot the informant who tipped off Captain Schultz and the German customs forces? Or was the informant a member of the climbing party? Not much is known of the third man who left the black shed on the morning of April 21. He was not one of the passeurs, who announced that they would return with mutton for everyone before the border crossing. Describing him, Second Lieutenant Drollinger only wrote that "one guy said he saw a small town in a valley and was going back to get some food. No one stopped him. He had never talked to anybody and always kept to himself. I assumed he was a German spy. Everyone else had been talking."[7]

Following his capture at the black shed, Raymond Krugell was lying on the ground in the field with his hands behind his head when he overheard the German officers congratulating themselves on their success. "*Gut, daß... sie verraten hat*" [Lucky for us that ... betrayed them], were some of the words the French-German bilingual Alsatian understood.[8] Raymond Krugell could not make out the name of the traitor but was confident afterward it was French. And listening in on more of the conversation, Krugell realized the German officers had been aware all along of the presence of a priest and a doctor in the group. Would Pautot, seen "lurking around the cabin" and asked to explain himself, have been able to learn the identities of two of the men in the cabin? The answer in short is that it is unlikely. If Pautot was the informant, he would have had to have known beforehand about some of the men in the group of fugitives.

BY THE MIDDLE OF April 1944, passeur Jean Ferret—at times accompanied by his friend, plasterer Louis Pène of Juzet-de-Luchon—had succeeded in guiding no fewer than 173 evaders in twenty-one separate trips over the mountains. As a district ranger equipped with a motorcycle, he had opportunities to scout out trails and study the schedule and routes of German patrols. Ferret was allowed to carry a gun, but never an automatic rifle, and one day that he carried magazine clips in his knapsack, he had a close call. Up in the mountains, he was rolling a cigarette when a German patrol came along. A soldier offered to hold his knapsack, which was sagging down his back. To decline the offer would have aroused suspicion, and thus Ferret had let the soldier take the knapsack from him while he finished preparing his cigarette. The knapsack supposedly carried Ferret's lunch. Noticing its heavy weight, the German soldier had exclaimed, "You eat a lot!" but he had not thought of checking its contents.[9]

Ferret reported back to Charbonnier, but he also belonged to the MUR, or United Resistance Movements, led in Saint-Gaudens and all of the Comminges region by Gabriel Gesse, known under the code name "Blanchard."[10] On one occasion Ferret had been ordered to deliver a message to the Underground in Toulouse. The message was concealed in a cigarette, which Ferret left in an ashtray inside a café bar near the train station. There was no direct contact with the agent in charge of retrieving the message. In fact, Ferret never identified that man or woman. He knew he would be recognized by his white socks pulled up over his riding breeches.

Ferret's involvement in guiding Allied evaders and other fugitives across the Spanish border took place in two stages. First, he and Pène went to the Oueil Valley to take charge of the group bound for Spain. From there the group crossed the Larboust Valley and climbed the slopes of Superbagneres to reach the black shed. The fugitives could rest at the cabin until the following evening, after Ferret and Pène returned for the last leg of the journey. In the intervening time, the two passeurs went home for the remainder of the night and for part of the next day. On April 21, Ferret had lunch at home with his family. And according to Jean Ferret's son, who was ten years old at the time, his father had also invited one of the workers helping out on a Water and Forestry project near Luchon, a young woodcutter by the name of Michel Pautot.

ELEVEN

Escapes and Hardships

P riest Paul Louis recorded some of the details of his life in Saint-
Michel, where he shared his cell with several other inmates,
including "Petit Jacques"—perhaps Jacques Lartigue—and
Fernand Bellenger, both caught with him in the Pyrenees. After
waking up at 7:00 every morning and following a quick splash of
cold water on their faces, they made their beds and swept their
cells. At 8:00 their captors provided coffee and the daily ration of
bread. Next, Louis and the others went out into the prison courtyard for ten minutes, the time allotted by the guards to wash up.
Soup arrived at noon, and after lunch was nap time until 3:00.
Four men per cell were allowed to go outside again, and following more soup for dinner, the prisoners went to bed. Priest Paul
Louis and his companions could only shave once a week, using old
razor blades that they shared. Singing and whistling were against
prison rules, and as there were no books to read and no pencils
to write with, time went by agonizingly slowly.

The group captured in Gourron had already arrived in Saint-
Michel when an Allied air raid took place over Toulouse on the
night of May 2, 1944. The raid targeted the arsenal, the gunpowder factory, a bridge over the Garonne River, several aircraft-
manufacturing plants, and the marshalling yard for the railroads.
As the first bombs exploded, the prison guards took some of the
inmates down to the basement for shelter, but not all of them, at
least not right away. "We were always the last ones they put in," Wilfred Gorman later explained, "[and] one time the guard told us if
the building was hit, the last thing he would do is throw the hand
grenade he had in among us." According to Paul Louis, a bomb
that night exploded a mere three hundred yards from the prison.

The first men transferred out of Saint-Michel were Eddie Luff and the sixteen Allied servicemen, accompanied by 2LT Albert W. Stravinsky and TSG Daniel F. Gilmore, two of the three airmen brought to Toulouse by Maddy De Deken. In what must have been early May, they all took a passenger train to Paris, where a "solid row of German soldiers" waited for them at the railroad station. They boarded tarpaulin-covered trucks, which then transported them to the prison of Fresnes. There, they were searched, deloused, showered, and placed in tiny cells. Stan Lepkowski would later write of the Fresnes prison as a "flea bitten place." Some of his companions also remembered vividly the daily threats and the executions of prisoners. "As an appetizer each morning at Fresnes with our ersatz acorn "coffee," we were told we would be shot that very day. They did shoot three Dutch colleagues. And every day in the prison courtyard they shot at least a score of Frenchmen. If you hoisted yourself up to the barred window, you could see them die. Almost all shouted "Vive La France" before the final fusillade. . . . We stopped watching."[1]

According to Paul Louis, the next transfer of inmates from Saint-Michel seemed imminent on May 9, causing wild rumors to circulate through the hallways of the prison. The Americans had landed in Barcelona, the rumors said, forcing the Germans to now evacuate prisons. The rumors proved false, however, and though some prisoners left on May 12, Paul Louis remained at Saint-Michel for another week. On May 19 he finally left, his transfer taking place onboard a freight train that carried prisoners mainly to two internment and deportation camps, Fort de Romainville on the outskirts of Paris and Royallieu-Compiègne, about forty miles north of the French capital. Having peeked at a prisoners' list at Saint-Michel, Paul Louis at first believed his destination to be Compiègne—synonymous with deportation to Germany, and he resigned himself to that fate. At a stop before Bordeaux, however, guards came and moved him to a different car. He learned that he would be imprisoned in Fresnes, which, he knew, entailed the prospect of more torture and possibly the firing squad. In his new car were fifteen other prisoners, five men and ten women. The space was also occupied by a large amount of luggage belonging to

Jewish prisoners onboard the train, two hundred of them reportedly crammed in just one car. Paul Louis attempted to make his way to the small opening that let in a bit of fresh air near the ceiling, but a German prisoner stood in his way and for the moment defended that space.

The next day, the train continued on its journey northward and made several stops, including in Nantes, then Angers. At those stops, the prisoners received some water and food from railroad workers and the Red Cross. At the Angers-Saint-Laud railroad station, many bystanders watched from a bridge as Red Cross nurses stood ready to help.

> The Red Cross nurses raised their heads when they heard someone call me "Priest"—because I was not wearing my cassock. All saw me get off the train after a soldier gave me permission to go empty the bucket with human waste. I was jostled by a German officer. [A] nurse took the bucket from me. She carried it off and emptied it while I stepped back on board my car. And it was the women who struck up the Marseillaise. The bystanders who watched and listened were crying.[2]

The train had left Angers when the same German prisoner who had pushed Paul Louis away the day before now decided to trust him.

> After prayer, one of the two Germans in our car came to shake my hand. We've struck an agreement. We will escape together tonight, in a spirit of true collaboration. [. . .] Last night, he managed to untie the wiring [that keeps the doors shut . . .] As early as 9 p.m., while the others go to bed below us, we climb on all the luggage under the pretext that we will be more comfortable sleeping. At 10:00, we wait anxiously for the right moment. On four or five occasions my partner has made it half way through the opening, but he has to get back inside the car. Finally the right moment has arrived. I give him absolution, he throws his bag outside, grabs the rope that will help him climb down [the side of the car]. The rope snaps and he falls from quite a height with a loud thud. Whatever happened to him? I hope that providence was on his side.[3]

Having just witnessed the German's accidental fall, the priest pulled his head back inside and wrapped himself in his blanket. For a moment he had second thoughts, as perhaps escaping out of the rolling train was too dangerous. But he found his courage, managed to climb outside through the opening, and saw an iron ramp. Clinging to it, Louis let himself slide slowly toward the ground. His shoes made contact, and he let go of the ramp. His head hit the ground and, seeing stars, he all but blacked out. As he picked himself up, still light-headed, he felt blood dripping down his face but knew that at least he had no broken bones. He let the train's red tail lights disappear into the night, then started walking through the countryside. Around 6:30 a.m., a "good Samaritan" took him into his home.

TWENTY-FOUR HOURS BEFORE ALLIED troops began landing in Normandy, one of the most spectacular mass escapes of political prisoners took place onboard a train bound for Neuengamme, the large concentration camp southeast of Hamburg in northern Germany. The train, which had left in the early morning on June 4 from Compiègne, carried some 2,060 political prisoners crammed into barred cattle cars. Many of the prisoners were members of Resistance organizations captured in France in the spring of 1944, among them at least seven of the men seized in the Pyrenees on April 21–22: Roger Bureau, Jules Lautman, Raymond Krugell, Fernand Bellenger, Jacques Lartigue, and passeurs Ferret and Pène, eight with Jacques Liddell included in that total. After their incarceration at Saint-Michel in Toulouse, the eight men had been transferred in May to Royallieu internment camp (Frontstalag 122) in Compiègne. Incredibly enough, not one, not two, but three of them were to join the group of prisoners—forty-five in total—who jumped off the train before dawn on June 5.

Led by Jean-Baptiste Biaggi and priest Georges Le Meur, the would-be escapees had made long preparations to carry out their plan while at Royallieu. A French prisoner by the name of Jean Martin wore a stomach girdle, and inside it he hid fragments of two saws, one metal and the other wood, in addition to a screwdriver improvised from a spoon. With those tools, Jean Martin was to cut a hole in the floor of the cattle car near the door. To reduce the risk of injury while jumping, all those chosen to make the attempt had been instructed to lie on their side on the footboard, with their feet facing forward and their heads facing back. They were to make the jump by rolling off the footboard. After landing on their backs, the impact would send them cartwheeling through the air. It had taken a lot of effort to convince every man that this was indeed the safest method to jump off the train in the darkness of night.

Just before his transfer from the Saint-Michel prison on May 12, Raymond Krugell had been able to say goodbye to his friend Paul Louis, and he had asked the priest to keep him in his prayers. One last time inside the prison, the Alsatian had played dumb when a guard barked orders at him in German. In spite of the interrogations and beatings, Gestapo agents had never discovered his true identity. They believed they had captured a man by the name of Jean Rehm, not a spy working for the Allies, not an Alsatian who understood German, but instead just a chief postal inspector from Paris with perhaps a vague connection to the French Resistance.[4] When Krugell arrived in Royallieu, he discovered a camp surrounded by a double line of barbed wire and guarded by armed German soldiers on top of watchtowers. Inside, Royallieu felt like a summer camp, especially when compared with conditions at Saint-Michel—and indeed in all prisons under German control. Aside from a few daily chores, the prisoners had complete freedom to choose their activities, whether to read books borrowed from a library inside the camp, take walks around the courtyard, play soccer, or watch boxing contests between detainees. Old friends ran into each other and exchanged news. After the long stays in prison, they were finally outdoors again, not to mention under a beautiful blue sky.

Roger Bureau, Jules Lautman, Fernand Bellenger, Jacques Lartigue, and Jacques Liddell arrived in Royallieu-Compiègne either with Raymond Krugell or in another convoy that followed about a week later. Frenchman Louis Joseph Perret was to spend the next ten months with Roger Bureau at Neuengamme and Hanover-Stöcken. He remembered first meeting the Belgian at Royallieu and listening to his new friend recount stories about his sports achievements. One of Raymond Krugell's cellmates in Toulouse, Jules Lautman, arrived in Compiègne still hiding under the false name of Julien Leclair. He likely would have had no inkling that his brother Albert Lautman, an important operative of the Françoise organization, had attempted through his contacts with the local police in Toulouse to have him escape from Saint-Michel.[5]

"At three in the morning on Monday, June 5," Jacques Lartigue later wrote, "the floor gave out and a railroad worker, prisoner with us, succeeded in sliding under the car and opening the door."[6] The train had now passed the town of Châlons-en-Champagne southeast of Reims, about halfway to the German border. Some in the car were unwilling to let others escape. Whatever their reasons for not wanting to jump off the train themselves—the fear of being caught and facing the Gestapo again, worries of getting injured during the escape, or the naïve belief that in Germany they would be treated decently—they were also afraid of reprisals once the guards discovered the escape. As no argument could win them over, the tension only escalated. "One more word, and I stick you," Jean-Baptiste Biaggi ended up saying to a man threatening to stop him from making the attempt.

Jean-Baptiste Biaggi, Georges Le Meur, and Jean Martin went first. One after the other, they lay down on their side on the footboard of the car, rolled over, and disappeared into the night. Raymond Krugell was in a group of four including Frenchmen Marcel Peltier and Maurice Coustaud. After a while, their turn came. Marcel Peltier later recalled the escape.

I had made sure to wrap my scarf and my handkerchief tight around my head and under my hat. As I got ready to jump, I saw a small bridge and then a pole. I waited a short moment and off I went! I ricocheted off the ground and was thrown into the air before landing on my head.

The shock was so violent it felt like I just had just smashed my skull. I lost consciousness for ten minutes or so. When I came to, I was at the bottom of an embankment under the cover of thick vegetation, which kept me hidden from view. The train was already long gone. I checked for broken bones. I found a gash along the side of my head with a flap of skin hanging over my right ear. My hands and legs were bleeding. My pants had been reduced to shreds and my hat was gone. Fortunately I found my handkerchief, and I pressed it over my [gaping] wound.[7]

Peltier went searching for his three companions along the railroad track and found both Raymond Krugell, who had only scratches on his hands, and Maurice Coustaud, also uninjured. Together, they kept looking for the missing escapee but found no trace of him. The three had to abandon their search around daybreak when they heard the voices of German soldiers guarding a bridge over a river. Leaving the railroad track behind them, they walked across fields and woods until they arrived on the bank of the Marne River. Peltier's wound was still bleeding, and as the three men were now near a village, they decided to ask for help. A local resident was opening his shutters. He turned out to be a retired French army major who immediately offered to take them across the river in his small boat. Having reached the opposite bank, Krugell, Peltier, and Coustaud later made their way to another village, where an older couple, the Viviers, took them in without any hesitation. The Viviers also alerted a local doctor, who made a house call around 11:00 that night and stitched up Peltier's wound. The three slept on straw in the attic and at 7:00 the next morning, they were awakened by the lady of the house coming up the stairs and shouting, "It's happened, they've landed!" They listened all morning long to radio news reports of events unfolding on the beaches of Normandy. Because Peltier knew he needed follow-up medical care, he left and went to nearby Chaumont two days later. Krugell and Maurice Coustaud stayed with the Viviers until Sunday, June 25. Five days later, they joined a maquis.[8]

According to Jacques Lartigue, the train was traveling about forty-five miles per hour when his turn came to jump. "I succeeded in jumping without hurting myself too much," Jacques Lartigue wrote, "followed by two comrades." Although Lartigue did not reveal the names of the other two, one of them was probably Fernand Bellenger. Lartigue also failed to provide details about the

next several hours following his group's escape, and instead simply indicated that they "reached Paris and Versailles." There they
hid until receiving new ID papers. On June 10 Lartigue left to join
a maquis in the Gers department west of Toulouse. Fernand Bellenger remained in the Paris area. As the weeks passed and the
Allies pushed east from Normandy, he and his Resistance organization began to prepare for the insurrection of Paris.

PAUL LOUIS, RAYMOND KRUGELL, Jacques Lartigue, and Fernand Bellenger had all regained their freedom, and so had Dr.
Marcel Hulin, who escaped while being transferred to Paris on
June 13, 1944.[9] There would be no such luck for the others captured in Gourron. Just before D-Day, most or all of the servicemen were transported in boxcars en route from Paris to Germany.
They arrived in handcuffs at a large prison in bomb-gutted Frankfurt, and there they spent their first night in a room with "no ven-
tilation and no room to lie down." "When the guards opened the
door [in the morning]," Wilfred Gorman remembered, "they fell
back with the stench," adding that he and his companions had
barely survived the night. They were then transferred to five-foot
by seven-foot cages in the prison's cellar, what Daniel Gilmore
later referred to as the "pigeon coop." There was not enough space
to walk around, and during the day no place to sit or lie down,
as the floor was cold and damp and the bunk had to be hooked
up to the side of the cage. The prisoners had one opportunity per
day for exercise, when they were allowed to refill one bucket with
fresh water and empty the other used as a toilet. Wilfred Gorman
and Daniel Gilmore were among the prisoners in the "pigeon
coop," and Eddie Luff, also present, recorded the names of some
of their other companions: McMahon, who had evidently survived his head injury, Sutphin, Lindstrom, PO William Taylor, SGT
Tilly Taylor, Ansell, Balmanno, and Acthim, in addition to Stravinsky and WO Vic Thompson. Most of all, Luff remembered the
servicemen's strength of character, their easy laughs, high spirits,
and willingness to help one another. Despite their miserable living conditions, the men managed to keep each other entertained,
at least for a while.

We were among friends and passed the time away by telling stories, in particular, description of life in Australia or in Canada or
in Richmond, USA. All these stories contained a gastronomic ele-
ment. The favorite dishes of the narrator with recipe and other
juicy details. Very juicy indeed as they made our mouth water like
Pavlov dogs; poor us who survived with a daily diet of a slice of
brown bread and a liquid soup tasting of slops.

They had all thought that interrogations were behind them, but
in Frankfurt the questioning resumed, some of it accompanied
by violence. The interrogators knew a lot about their prisoners. "I
don't know why you Canadians are so stubborn you won't answer
questions," a German told Gorman. "We don't have to ask you
these questions," he added, brandishing papers with a list of information about him, "here's where you're from, here's your commander, here's your crew." A Gestapo agent who spoke English told
Eddie Luff that he did not believe he was a serviceman. "You are
a spy," the Gestapo agent said with a smile on his face, "and spies
are shot." Despite their best efforts, the prisoners grew increasingly
silent and gloomy in their cages. On June 7, despite being cut off
from the outside world, they learned about D-Day.

On the morning of June 7, a Polish prisoner who cleaned the slops
out of the cages came down with the daily ration of toilet paper—
meticulously cut, 6-inch squares of newsprint from German dai-
lies. That day, the Pole excitedly pushed a quadruple ration through
the meshed wire of the cell to my right. The American sergeant
there, who read German, got down on the floor and put the squares
together like a jigsaw puzzle. It was the front page of a Frankfurt
morning newspaper. Right there, in the bottom of the left-hand
corner was a boxed communique of the German High Command:
"Enemy troops landed yesterday on the Normandy coast."[10]

The English, Australian, and Canadian servicemen left the Frankfurt prison to go to POW camps, followed by the Americans. The
last of their group, Eddie Luff remained in his cage several more
weeks. New prisoners were brought into the cellar, and at times
all the cells were full. On several occasions, Luff had to share his

tiny space with another detainee, often a French prisoner of war, but once instead a sick Swiss spy, and another time a German who was beyond himself with joy when he learned of the attempt made on Hitler's life on July 20. Every day Eddy Luff received more torn newspapers in place of toilet paper, and every day he attempted to read the news. One morning, he did not realize he was sick until the torn newspapers arrived.

[That day], I suffered a severe shock. [...] I was incapable to read the texts, instead of letters I only saw black lines. The next day I had a temperature and I could hardly perceive the bars of my cage; my voice was blurred and I had difficulty speaking. I managed, however, to tell the warden "ich bin krank." Two days after I was taken to the sick bay, where a doctor made me swallow a red pill and wrote beside my name "100% krank." For a few days I remained stretched out on my sleeping board, unable to eat much; I had diphtheria but was unaware of it.

Luff survived his bout with diphtheria, and soon thereafter, during a strip search, the prison guards tore the lining of his clothes. They discovered fragments of the ID papers he had acquired in Geneva, proof that he was English. It was enough to convince the Gestapo, and a few days later Eddie Luff finally departed from the prison in Frankfurt. When he later arrived at the English prison camp in Kreuzburg in Upper Silesia, he weighed only one hundred pounds.

TWELVE

The Road Blockade

After the raid by the Germans on the black shed, the Françoise organization did not stop smuggling fugitives over the central Pyrenees—far from it. The next group left Toulouse around May 5, first traveling by train to Lez, northeast of Luchon. It then started south into the mountains, with two guides, including a Frenchman named Etienne. The group was headed to Canején on the other side of the border, but almost from the get-go it ran into trouble. A woman bound for Algiers fell ill and could not keep pace with the rest of the group, and the guides got lost during a snowstorm on the way to the first mountain pass. When the woman, apparently at death's door, stayed in a cabin with a Dutchman trying to help her, the guides decided to go back for her. The American and British evaders continued on their own and climbed down into the Garonne River Valley between the villages of Melles and Fos, only a mile or so from the Spanish border. Here they split into two groups, as they could not agree on the safest route to follow. U.S. 1LT Robert A. Martin remained down in the valley with five other Americans: 2LT Lawson D. Campbell, SSG Marvin Bradford Alford, TSG Rex Hayes, SGT Robert Henry, and TSG Tollic G. Berry. To stay out of sight, they went down into a ditch while continuing their way south. Martin led the way, the others behind him. When he heard a German patrol making its way down the side of a hill by the ditch, Martin signaled to the others to duck, and he himself lay down flat in the mud. He soon heard a rifle bolt click and voices behind him, and as he turned his head, he saw that all five of his companions had been captured. Martin reached Spain on May 9, and so did U.S. 2LT John Betolatti, RAF SGT Raymond Hindle, and RAF FSG Fred

Franklin, who had chosen to keep some distance between them and the highway along the Garonne River, and by going up some little way up a slope had managed to skirt the valley.[1]

The Françoise organization apparently went back to Charbonnier for the next party of evaders. In Toulouse U.S. SGT Arden N. Brenden and U.S. SGT Wallace A. Trinder met Frenchman Maurice Lejeune, who told them their journey over the Pyrenees would be arranged by "Dutch-Paris." Instead they were both passed on to "Françoise" and taken to Saint-Gaudens, where they spent six days in a farmhouse. During that time they received the visit of "Frisco," and it was the American expatriate who came to pick them up in his truck at the end of their stay in Saint-Gaudens. With U.S. SGT Herman F. Hermanson plus two Englishmen and seven Frenchmen (including the guides), the party of twelve crossed the Spanish border early on May 12, but not without a late scare. They had reached a high cliff less than half a mile from the border when German soldiers spotted them and opened fire. While a guide was firing back at the Germans, the evaders scattered and ran for the edge of the cliff, and a bullet snapped Brenden's walking stick in two. The German mountain troopers set their dogs after the evaders, who "beat them off with clubs." With the Germans still in hot pursuit, the evaders climbed down the side of the cliff, where they found cover among boulders. The guide then started firing on the Germans above them with a machine gun, driving them off. A hailstorm came along, helping the evaders to reach the border after nightfall without any further trouble. After parting company with their passeur, the evaders spent most of the night climbing down into Spain's Aran Valley to arrive in Les.[2]

During the same month of May, two more groups might have been entrusted to Charbonnier and his men, including one with U.S. LTC Robert Montgomery, U.S. 2LT Walter A. Meldrich, FO Milton H. Ramsey, and RAF FSG Fred Greenwell, who left Toulouse on May 12 and reached Spain three days later. An old Jewish man and his wife had joined the party, but they were left behind when both gave out in the mountains. The rest of the climb over the Pyrenees took place without any major incidents. One of the passeurs might have been Georges Capcarrère, and the route over the Pyrenees seemingly involved a stop in Jurvielle in the Larboust Valley. After the war, Capcarrère told his family that he once brought a party of Allied airmen to Jurvielle, where they spent the night in a barn at his brother's farm. Among the evaders, the story continued, was the "son of General Montgomery," clearly a reference—ill-founded, as it turns out—to the presence of the high-ranking officer bearing the same name as the illustrious British officer.[3] And just as the presence of Georges Capcarrère with a party of evaders would suggest Charbonnier's involvement, so would any mention of Frisco. The evaders who left Toulouse around May 22 later reported having met Frisco. Charbonnier is even mentioned by name in the debriefing reports of evaders who arrived in Spain in June. Based on those reports, Charbonnier was getting ready to lead a new group over the Pyrenees, but he never finished his preparations.

ON THE MORNING OF June 13, 1944, the daily routines of life went on as usual in the small village of Larroque, located along the Save River in the Haute-Garonne department, only about seven miles northwest of Saint-Gaudens. The Allies had landed on Normandy's beaches a week earlier. Bombing raids had taken place within the last month or two on the French cities of Marseille, Lyon, Avignon, and Saint-Etienne, and even Toulouse had not been spared during the night of May 2. For now, however, Larroque remained far removed from the sounds of battle and the wailing of sirens. The school year had not yet ended, and as the children were enjoying their midmorning recess, their laughter could be heard echoing around the schoolyard. The peace and quiet were suddenly interrupted when trucks carrying German troops came roaring into the village. The local residents were shocked at the sight of the German detachment arriving in Larroque. Shock soon turned into fear as seventy-five soldiers armed with rifles took up positions around the center of the village. Three days earlier, the 2nd Waffen–ss Panzer Division "Das Reich" had nearly wiped out the entire population of Ouradour-sur-Glane near Limoges, killing 642 men, women, and children. Rumors of the massacre already circulated in France, and some of them had reached Larroque.

But probably fanning the fears of Larroque residents even more was the raid on a small village in their own neighborhood. On June 10 the same division, Das Reich, had stormed Marsoulas, east of Saint-Gaudens, and killed a third of its population, including six women and twelve children. In the evening, the subprefect in Saint-Gaudens had gone to Marsoulas and taken photographs of the victims. No doubt reports of the massacre had been heard in Larroque.

With their fingers on the trigger, the German soldiers remained at their posts when, coming from the south in the direction of Saint-Gaudens, a Salmson car appeared around a turn in the road. The soldier guarding the road motioned for the driver to stop. As the Salmson slowed down, its occupants pushed the doors open and unleashed a few bursts of fire from their guns. None of the bullets hit the soldier, and as the Salmson picked up speed again, it was caught in a hail of automatic fire. The driver managed to get across the bridge over the Save River. At the three-way intersection just on the other side of the bridge, the car began to turn left but then veered off the road. It careened down the riverbank between two poplar trees and splashed into the water. One man managed to escape from the car and attempted to run. He did not go far. Hit by German bullets and fatally wounded, he collapsed to the ground under the right arch of the bridge. Already the other two occupants of the Salmson were dead. The car had caught on fire, and soon their bodies were consumed by the flames.

Thus perished passeur Jean-Louis Bazerque, aka Charbonnier, Joseph (Joe) Barrère, better known as "Frisco," and twenty-nine-year-old Pierre Sabadie from Moncaup, southwest of Aspet. After the fatal clash, which had lasted only a few minutes, the Germans left the charred bodies of Frisco and Sabadie untouched, but they used a cable to lift Charbonnier from under the bridge. They stretched his body out on the parapet and, having searched it for documents, threw it down into the river. Fortunately for the six hundred residents of Larroque, the Germans did not carry out any reprisals other than spraying buildings and trees with bullets as they left the village. Later, after the Germans had gone, the mayor of Larroque had the bodies of Charbonnier, Frisco, and Sabadie retrieved and brought to the town hall. The three men were buried the next day in the village cemetery. Few attended the short ceremony.[4]

It took less than forty-eight hours for news of the deaths of Charbonnier and Frisco to reach Arbon near Aspet. On the night of June 14, U.S. 1LT Joel W. McPherson heard that the two men had been killed while running a German blockade. Together with U.S. 2LT Gilbert M. Stonebarger and three other evaders, he had been waiting in Arbon for the return of Charbonnier, who had left them on the twelfth telling them that he would soon return. On the night of the fourteenth, in fact, they were to start out with Charbonnier on their climb over the Pyrenees. Three days later, a Frenchman by the name of Jean Duval (Willie) joined the party, having found a new guide to take them over the mountains. The guide left them just a few miles short of the border with Spain, and Jean Duval led the party the rest of the way to arrive on the eighteenth in Canejan. Later, through the American consulate in Barcelona, Second Lieutenant Stonebarger sent a message to Joe Barrère's parents, notifying them of their son's death. And it was Stonebarger who perhaps provided the last recorded memory of Frisco, that of the Californian honking at goats on the road while transporting evaders into the mountains.[5]

Apparently there had been no ambush, and instead, Charbonnier, Frisco, and Sabadie had simply run out of luck. The German detachment had come to Larroque to retrieve a truck belonging to a French oil and gas company. For the previous three days, the truck had been parked by the local bakery. An act of sabotage prevented the Germans from driving the truck away, and the detachment had been waiting for towing equipment when the three Resistance fighters arrived. Two months earlier, Frisco had told Eddie Luff and other evaders to be prepared to use their guns if they encountered a roadblock. "We'll have to shoot it out," he had said. Frisco had truly meant those words.

After the liberation of Toulouse and the Midi-Pyrenees region in August 1944, the U.S. Military Intelligence (MIS) investigated the contribution made by Charbonnier to the Allied cause. During the course of that investigation, MIS discovered that Charbonnier had become somewhat of a legend in Toulouse, Saint-Gaudens, and Aspet, with newspaper claims that the Frenchman had smuggled between two thousand and four thousand people across the Pyrenees to Spain. Many of those who had worked with Charbonnier were full of admiration for him. A maquis chief from Aspet, a schoolteacher by the name of Fauroux, as well as Captain Gesse and Colonel Marty of the Armée Secrete, regarded him as a hero. Jean Weidner declared that Jean-Louis Bazerque was "a guide-passeur—of exceptional merit," while according to Salomon Chait (also of the Dutch-Paris organization) "[Charbonnier] was amazing and . . . 2,000 people was a conservative estimate of the number he passed." By MIS's own estimate, Charbonnier (also known under the aliases of "Sanglier," "Lebrun," "Aigle," and "Julien") had smuggled 150 or so American and British servicemen to Spain, in addition to vast numbers of French, Belgian, and Dutch patriots. Marie-Louise Dissard ("Françoise") had compiled a list of thirty servicemen that Charbonnier had taken across the Pyrenees for her organization. Although she complained that he had "made a small fortune" from payments received from her, she apparently also "spoke very highly of him."[6] In May 1946 MIS-X recommended that Jean-Louis Bazerque be awarded the Medal of Freedom posthumously.

At the same time, "Françoise" evidently disapproved of the request made after the Liberation by Jean-Louis Bazerque's mother that she and her husband be reimbursed by the American government the sum of 50,000 francs. That sum, Hélène-Marie Bazerque claimed, corresponded to the amount that her son had borrowed from them in order for him to support his covert activities. Françoise's opinion on the matter was documented by MIS.

> As for the compensation you are thinking of giving to his mother, it seems to me rather inappropriate. Charbonnier received handsome payments for every group of Americans and British he guided [to Spain]. His mother lives in Aucamville, a nice enough town. She does not seem to have fallen on hard times. She has another son, René Bazerque, born on September 8, 1907, a civil servant in the Dordogne department.[7]

In 1947 Hélène-Marie Bazerque received two checks from the American government, one for herself, the other for her husband who had passed away in the intervening time. As stated by MIS internally, it was not possible to verify that Jean-Louis Bazerque had indeed borrowed money from his parents, or that any such loans had been for the benefit of helping evaders. According to Gabriel Nahas, who had known Charbonnier better than Françoise, the French passeur did not keep any money for himself. However, he was adamant that the guides he used be paid, and he was easily offended if anyone challenged him on the issue of price.[8]

Charbonnier was awarded the Medal of Freedom with Silver Palm (posthumously). "For exceptionally meritorious achievement," the citation read in part, "which aided the United States in the prosecution of the war against the enemy from 7 December 1941 to June 1944. Throughout this period he displayed exceptional patriotism, heroism, and determination in carrying out perilous missions. Completely disregarding his personal safety he exerted every effort to aid in the evasion of Allied flyers by convoying at least one hundred and fifty of them over the Pyrenees to Spain." The latter part of the citation, however, inevitably raises an eyebrow, because it is not based on facts.

> In June 1944 he was in charge of a convoy of 30 to 40 evaders which was caught in a German ambush in the foothills of the Pyrenees. Mindful only of the patriotic task which he had undertaken, Jean Bazerque preferred to cover the escape of the fliers and shoot it out with the Germans, knowing full well the penalty he would pay in the event of his capture. He was shot and killed during the short battle; the greater part of the convoy escaped capture, however, and managed to reach Spain.[9]

Not all the evaders who got to know Charbonnier approved of him. After the war, Stan Lepkowski recalled the morning of April 19, 1944, when his group set out toward the Pyrenees. The passeur "immediately had us walk through a plowed field on the way to the mountain," he wrote, "the footprints of thirty people were quite visible and I lost faith in him immediately."[10] In early June, First Lieutenant McPherson had to wait while Charbonnier "vanished for nine days," two of which were spent by the American at a hotel in Boulogne-sur-Gesse where Gestapo agents were also staying.

Charbonnier had left telling McPherson that he would be back in twenty minutes, and when he finally returned his only comment was that he "had been busy hauling maquis."[11]

Evaders might not always have understood Charbonnier or fully appreciated the risks he took. But as seen already, those who knew him best were unanimous in their admiration for the passeur, and one might hope that even if the true circumstances of his death had been known, Charbonnier would still have received his Medal of Freedom. Ironically, some of the text in the original citation—text that was later removed—might have drawn attention to the set of skills Charbonnier brought. "For four years," that text had read, "he devoted his organizational genius, his foresight and resourcefulness to saving patriots and Allied airmen from arrest by the German authorities."

THIRTEEN

Separate Fates

After his escape over the Pyrenees, Archie Roland Barlow Jr. spent less than three weeks in the UK before returning to the United States on June 19, 1944. Back in his hometown of Hattiesburg, Mississippi, he enjoyed a twenty-one-day leave, during which he wasted no time to marry "the girl of [his] dreams." "We were married five days after my return from overseas in June 1944," he wrote in his memoirs, "and have been re-enlisting ever since." He had a long career in the U.S. Air Force, retiring as senior master sergeant after twenty-two years of service. Barlow then worked as a civilian for the state of Mississippi for another fifteen years. Throughout that time, he viewed his contribution to the Allied victory with humor and humility. "So, that is how I practically won World War II single handedly," he wrote in conclusion of his World War II memoirs, "without harming the enemy and with only the help of 15 million American GIs, forty Allied countries, and a handful of French Patriots." Archie Barlow died in Rome, Georgia on April 23, 2000.

Archie Barlow and Jim Liles had flown back from Gibraltar to the UK at the end of May 1944. Lynn H. Drollinger and William B. Hendrickson followed them just over a week later, arriving on June 8. Drollinger went back to his old squadron at Leiston. It was not long before he was asked to give lectures on escape and evasion, a topic he now knew firsthand.

> They gave me an AT6 to fly around. So I flew around [...] bases in England and had to tell them some of my stories about how I got out of Europe so they could look at me as living proof that it could be done. I wasn't a very big guy anyway so they figured if

I could do it, they could get out if something happened to them. The first time I had to talk to a bunch of them (there was probably four or five hundred) I was about scared to death. I was as scared as I was anytime on my whole trip.[1]

After the war, Lynn Drollinger served in the U.S. Air Force Reserve, and during the Korean War he was again stationed in England. He reached the rank of major before retiring from the military. He started a concrete business with his father and brother in Sunnyside, Washington. Drollinger had nearly completed a bachelor of science in mechanical engineering before the war called him. He successfully applied his knowledge to designing and building almost all of the sand, gravel, and concrete ready-mix processing equipment. After a successful career with his family business, he retired at fifty-five but built a couple more concrete plants for other companies. He then started building airplanes—and almost killed himself on a few occasions when a detail in the building of the plane did not quite work as he had imagined. His piloting skills saved him once when his ailerons stopped working but he managed to land safely. Drollinger died on New Year's Eve at the age of sixty-nine.

Following his own return to the UK, Harry Cammish became an instructor at Fighter Commands High Ercall, Shropshire Headquarters, lecturing pilots on "the finer points of Merlin engines." Promoted to the rank of warrant officer, he later served as "shutdown" air traffic controller during the time that the RAF was closing many of its airfields. He retired from the RAF in 1946 and returned to the construction business. Together with his wife Betty and their two children, he immigrated to New Zealand in 1956. "It was a bit of a shock," he once said in an interview, "to find ourselves in a little farming and forestry town where the pub closed at 6 p.m." In 1971 the Cammish family moved to a coastal town, and thirty-six years later, a "Cammish Lane" was named in recognition of the couple's community service.[2]

EDDIE LUFF WAS HELD captive in an *Internierungslager* (*Ilag*) in Kreuzburg, Upper Silesia for several months.[3] During the winter months, the temperature dropped as low as -40° Celsius. "Some nights," Luff even wrote, "one had to dress up to go to bed." Kreuz-burg was evacuated by the Germans on the same day as Bankau, January 19, 1945. The prisoners were shipped by rail to another camp in Austria. Luff never forgot the train ride, which could well have been fatal to him.

> Three of us volunteered to stand guard over our Red Cross par-cels, unaware that this meant travelling on a flat car, open to all the Siberian winds, by -25° Celsius. To survive, we built a sort of igloo with the Red Cross parcels and other camp boxes. This shel-ter could only accommodate two men, the third had to freeze but was relieved every half hour. On the other hand, we were almost better off than our comrades who were piled up at 80 in each of the 4 railway vans; and we had a better view of the countryside.[4]

The rest of Luff's captivity proved easier. Liberated after the Ger-man forces in northern Italy and southern Austria capitulated in early May, Luff made his way to Italy and shipped out from Naples on May 31, arriving in Scotland nine days later. He then joined the British occupation forces in Berlin, reaching the rank of army major. He went on to work for NATO, first in Paris and later at the alliance's headquarters in Brussels, where he was a senior official and for many years chef de cabinet to NATO's secretary general. While in captivity, he had asked his Swiss fiancée Yolanda to marry him. They enjoyed a long and happy marriage, and after his retire-ment, they lived in their manor house in France's Loire Valley.

Maurice de Milleville left Gibraltar for the UK at the end of July 1944. In October he became an officer working for Free France's Central Bureau of Intelligence and Operations (BCRA) in London. His superiors quickly formed an unfavorable opinion of the young second lieutenant, to the point that in November they sent him back to France. A note by British services included the following assessment of de Milleville's conduct during that time. "[Mary Lin-dell's] son, Maurice, is of very weak character. He tends to belittle his mother's activities, is jealous, lies incessantly, and with his line shooting grossly exaggerates whatever his contribution to the war effort was. Since the Liberation he has claimed in turn to be a Brit-ish lieutenant, a British captain, has "played" the British, French, and Americans."[5] After the war, Maurice de Milleville's role in the French Resistance remained a contentious topic. In 1949 he was excluded from the official list of "Marie-Odile" / "Marie-Claire" operatives, the officer in charge of the accreditation process going as far as describing him "as a spy working for Germany, not for Free France." De Milleville fought long and hard to earn recognition and in 1981, at sixty, he succeeded in being appointed Knight of the Legion of Honor.

FOLLOWING HIS ESCAPE ON June 13, 1944, Marcel Hulin served for three months as a surgeon in a maquis in the Ardèche department south of Lyon, and after the war, he started a medical practice northeast of Paris. Jacques Lartigue had escaped with Raymond Krugell and Fernand Bellenger as their train convoy with more than two thousand political prisoners was headed for the concentration camp of Neuengamme. Having left Paris on June 10, 1944, Lartigue joined a maquis of the Pommiès Free Corps—an army of volunteer fighters under the command of a career officer, André Pommiès—in the Gers department in southwestern France. Having fought in several battles and participated in the liberation of the Pyrenees, Lartigue followed elements of the Pommiès Free Corps headed to northeastern France on September 6, 1944, to reinforce General de Lattre de Tassigny's army. De Lattre de Tassigny liberated Autun on September 9. Less than two weeks later, the Pommiès Free Corps became part of the French First Army and Jacques Lartigue enlisted. "[On] November 11," he wrote two months later, "we attacked [the Germans at] Le Thillot, which we took and continued our advance into Alsace." After participating in the liberation of Alsace, he saw action in Germany until, on September 29, 1945, his unit was demobilized.

Prior to his capture on April 21, 1944, Jacques Lartigue escorted some 150 Allied airmen either from Paris to Toulouse or from Toulouse to the foothills of the Pyrenees, and some of them even lodged in his apartment in Toulouse. As compensation for the two months he spent in the hands of the Nazis, the American government paid Lartigue the sum of five thousand French francs. In September 1946, and now in Mont-de-Marsan where he was starting a woodcutting business, Jacques Lartigue wrote a letter to an I.S.9 British officer, asking him for assistance in obtaining a U.S. Army cargo truck for hauling trees. Lartigue's file at the U.S. National Archives does not reveal whether Lartigue was successful in obtaining the truck.

FERNAND BELLENGER DIED LESS than two and a half months after his escape from the train taking him to Germany. Together with thirty-four young French patriots belonging to various Resistance organizations, he was executed on August 16, 1944, on the eve of the liberation of Paris. The French Resistance was looking for more firearms to launch its insurrection against the German forces occupying the city. Karl Rehbein, an Abwehr agent posing as an operative of the British Intelligence Service, promised to supply the Young Christian Fighters (JCC) organization with a large quantity of guns. Other organizations were invited to participate in taking delivery of the weapons. On the morning of August 16, the thirty-five young Resistance fighters arrived at the rendezvous point at the Place des Ternes in Paris. They climbed onboard a tarpaulin-covered truck, which, they were told, would take them to the delivery spot. At the next stop, however, the truck was surrounded by German soldiers. The French patriots were all arrested and taken to the Gestapo headquarters, where they were interrogated until about 10:00 p.m. Afterward they were transported to the Bois de Boulogne along the western edge of Paris' sixteenth arrondissement. Sounds of machine-gun fire and grenade explosions were later heard. The first witnesses to arrive on the scene the next day found the thirty-five bodies heaped together. Reports stated that the French Gestapo had participated in the massacre. Bellenger, only twenty-one years old, had been the military leader of the JCC for the Paris region.[6]

JULES LAUTMAN'S DEATH IN February 1946 was all the more unfortunate because it could have easily been prevented. Lautman had survived Neuengamme, where the SS and Kapos never found out he was Jewish. Like Raymond Krugell, he spoke and understood German, and as a result he had been assigned to an administrative service, where surviving was easier than in the other barracks. Following his liberation, he recovered quickly and returned as the commercial attaché at the French embassy in Copenhagen. After undergoing surgery for intestinal polyps, he developed an infection that could have been treated by penicillin. Unfortu- nately, the Danish clinic did not have a supply of the antibiotic. Although Jules Lautman's sister sent penicillin from Paris, the package arrived too late.

Dr. Max Rens, Roger Bureau, Jacques Liddell, and passeurs Jean Ferret and Louis Pène also experienced the horrors of the Nazi concentration camps. Of the five men, only three came home. Max Rens left Toulouse on July 3, 1944, onboard a freight train carrying more than five hundred political prisoners, and arrived at Dachau after a fifty-nine-day odyssey.[7] He was liberated eight months later, on May 3, 1945, by the French army at Aussenlager Obernsdorf an der Iller, one of Dachau's subcamps.[8] After their arrival at Neuengamme on June 7, 1944, Jean Ferret and Louis Pène were both transferred to Sachsenhausen-Oranienburg. Jean Ferret was liberated on May 2, 1945, at Schwerin by the American Eighth Infantry Division, Louis Pène sometime later. When Ferret arrived in Luchon after his liberation, his younger son at first could not recognize him. Jacques Liddell died from a typhus epidemic in the Bergen-Belsen concentration camp toward the middle of April 1945, on the eve of the camp's liberation by British forces. His nephews later laid a memorial plaque in Bergen-Belsen with the inscription, "to our uncle Jacques Douglas Liddell known as 'Jacques the Philosopher.' Member of the French Resistance, freedom fighter. Born in Paris on 16 December 1918. Died at Bergen-Belsen in April 1945." Like Jacques Liddell, Roger Bureau spent nine months in Hannover-Stöcken, a slave labor camp where inmates manufactured accumulators for submarine batteries. They worked with molten lead without any protection and were continuously subjected to beatings at the hands of the Kapos. Roger Bureau served as an interpreter for his French comrades and was mistreated each time they did not obey the Kapos' orders quickly enough. His last sign of life was a letter sent to his parents by a French prisoner of war with whom he crossed paths in the evening of April 11, 1945, just hours before the ss locked more than one thousand political prisoners in a barn and set it on fire.[9]

Like Jacques Lartigue and Fernand Bellenger, Raymond Krugell had escaped from the convoy of prisoners bound for Neuengamme. In the summer of 1944, the Alsatian took command of a group of maquis southeast of Reims. As the U.S. Third Army tore through northern France, the region's maquis fighters were integrated into regular French army units, and LT Raymond Krugell (code name "Pierre") was given command of his own company consisting of more than two hundred men. During the liberation of the Haute-Marne department, "Pierre's Company"—as it came to be known—delivered critical intelligence on enemy defenses to the Third Army's general staff, either directly or through Krugell's commanding officer, CPT Jacques Taschereau from Saskatchewan, Canada. Krugell was promoted to the rank of captain before the war's end, and afterward he returned to his civilian life and to teaching. For a while he was posted in Berlin, where the French military government had opened schools for the families of soldiers serving in the occupation forces. During that time, Krugell was asked to testify in the trial of Karl Dethlefs, the chief of the Grenzpolizei in Luchon in 1944. A military tribunal in Bordeaux had charged Dethlefs with war crimes, and a rogatory commission came to Berlin to hear Krugell. Afterward, the Alsatian penned a letter to his friend Paul Louis mentioning Karl Dethlefs, "the bastard who beat you so brutally." "I cite you [in my statement," Krugell wrote, "But you probably would not recognize him on his picture, as he is not wearing his glasses." Dethlefs was sentenced to death on July 12, 1950, in Bordeaux, and Jean Ferret, who was present at the trial, even volunteered to serve on the firing squad. But the verdict was overruled in November 1950, and the case sent this time to a military tribunal in Paris. The mood was perceptibly different at Dethlefs's second trial, more focused on turning the page than punishing Nazi criminals who seemingly followed their superiors' orders. Ferret testified about the twenty-two rounds of beatings he had been subjected to by the Gestapo. Dethlefs and his men had pulled out some of his hair, Ferret at one point told the judge. "My poor man," the judge reportedly answered, "you still have hair on your head!" On January 19, 1951, Dethlefs received a sentence of a mere five-year imprisonment.[10]

PRIEST PAUL LOUIS WAS fifty-five when he died in June 1962. As the years passed after the war, he never fully recovered from the savage beatings and torture at the hands of the Gestapo. The flesh on the soles of his feet remained permanently exposed, the open wounds on his lower abdomen never healed, and he suffered from a chronic ear infection affecting his sense of balance and causing him excruciating pain. "I never once saw someone suffer physically as much as he did," the nun who treated him said. Priest Paul Louis himself was aware of his deteriorating state and he would whisper, "There is nothing beautiful about the dying." He bore the pain stoically and found solace in his faith. "Oh, how much Christ must have suffered," he would say, "I hurt, but I am with him."

Before Paul Louis's old wounds caught up with him, he had enough time to make a difference in the lives of the disenfranchised Travelers and Romani. As their chaplain in the Paris region, he rapidly gained their confidence, so much so that they soon considered him one of their own. A recipient of the Medal of Freedom and the French Legion of Honor, Paul Louis kept in touch with his friend Raymond Krugell, and on August 21, 1946, he also reached out to a close friend of Roger Bureau.[11]

> While passing through Brussels six days ago, I tried to obtain the address of the wife of Mr. Bureau from Antwerp, arrested with me on April 21, 1944, near the Spanish border. I was given your address and told you were a very close friend of Mr. Bureau. I would be grateful to you if you could confirm whether Mr. Bureau died in Germany and if so, also give me the address of his wife. It would be to talk to her about her husband, whom I got to know really well, and to let her know all that he felt for her.
>
> I only knew Mr. Bureau for a short period of time, in April 1944. If, however, Mrs. Bureau would like to hear about those days I spent with him, I would consider it my duty to tell her.[12]

THE ALLIED SERVICEMEN CAPTURED on the mountain of Superb-agnères and at the Ravi Bridge were all held in POW camps for the remainder of the war. 2LT James J. McMahon evidently survived the war, based on accounts of him being briefly reunited in May 1945 with some of his old crew members—including top turret gunner and engineer TSG Robert F. Stahlut—at Camp Lucky Strike near Le Havre.[13] Ted Kellers and Stan Lepkowski spent some of their captivity at Stalag Luft IV in Gross Tychow, Pomerania. Kellers is mentioned in the memoirs of Robert D. Davis, who was also held in that POW camp. "Ted Kellers was a little older," Davis wrote, "at least he looked older." The past weeks and months had evidently taken a toll on the American airman. "More gaunt than most of us [and] sallow complexion," Davis continued, "Didn't laugh or smile much."[14] As for Lepkowski, his leg sores had been treated and he could walk normally again. Owing to his weakened state, however, he escaped the infamous "Black March." Along with other, weaker POWs, he was evacuated from Stalag Luft IV in a train convoy consisting of boxcars. The journey to Stettin lasted fourteen days, during which, as Lepkowski explained, "[they] had so little room that one could not squat down or anything." Afterward Lepkowski was taken to Barth (Stalag Luft I), where he was liberated by the Russians in May 1945. He returned home in August 1945.[15]

With Tilly Taylor, Tom Balmanno, John Ansell, Wilfred Gorman, and Charles Jackson, Canadian John Acthim reached Stalag Luft VII on July 7, 1944. Located in Bankau, Silesia, the Luftwaffe prison camp offered poor living conditions. Some of the British POWs arrived a month earlier had immediately dubbed Stalag Luft VII a "chicken farm" and the tiny huts they moved in "dog kennels" and "chicken huts."[16] For more than three months, the six servicemen shared one of the huts, only eighteen feet by seven feet, six inches and made of stiff cardboard. "Apart from the inevitable squabbles," Acthim wrote in his diary, "we got along fairly well." They even found humor in their situation, as when "Wilf and Tilly provided [them] a laugh for a week by having their hair all cut off and then followed a moustache craze." On October 13, they moved to a new compound with thirteen barracks, eight of them serving as living quarters, the others turned into facilities including a hospital and a cookhouse.[17] Compared to the "dog kennels" of the other compound, Acthim wrote, the barracks in their new camp were "bang on." The six managed to stay together, occupying one room with two other NCOs, one from Belgium, the other one another Englishman. On January 19, 1945, the Germans evacuated the camp, now within reach of the rapidly advancing Red Army. "It was the start of our long and momentous journey," Acthim wrote, "the Russians were very near us many times." First came a march of 150 miles that took two weeks, and during which, according to Wilfred Gorman, time "passed in a painful, exhausted blur."

> It was the dead of winter and we had only the few items of clothing the Red Cross gave us and a small amount of food. In the group I started off with there were about 2,000 prisoners. A number of them didn't make it. They told us when we started that anyone who couldn't make it would be shot. We were told if we moved more than three steps out of the column it would be considered that we were trying to escape, and we would be shot.[18]

In the German town of Goldberg, Gorman, Acthim, and the others were loaded onboard boxcars and transported by rail to Stalag IIIA at Luckenwalde, about thirty miles south of Berlin. During the train ride, which lasted three days, the prisoners received no food. The journey took its toll on the health of Wilfred Gorman, who arrived "barely able to stand up and walk." Luckenwalde was a large camp with several adjoining compounds and flea-infested barracks, and in the absence of beds and bunks, the prisoners slept on the floor. As small consolation, Acthim learned during his captivity at Luckenwalde, that he had been promoted to the rank of pilot officer. "It certainly is hard to wait for the day we will be free," he nonetheless commented in his diary as the war drew to a close and as the prisoners watched Allied air raids in the skies above them. On April 21, finally, the Germans abandoned the camp. The next day, a Russian tank entered Luckenwalde around 6:00 a.m. amid wild cheering from the prisoners. "[The Russians] told us to pick up a rifle and [go] with them," Gorman recalled, "but we weren't in any condition to join them." All six men eventually made it back home, although Gorman at least spent another week in the now-liberated camp. He then traveled for three days, mostly walking, at one point riding in the back of a Russian truck, until finally he stumbled on to two American soldiers driving a scouting vehicle. Like Acthim, Gorman was promoted to pilot officer, but in his case the promotion was delayed for a while because he had been presumed dead since the day he was shot down seven months earlier. The bonds formed among the six men in some cases lasted for several decades. The Australian Tom Balmanno traveled with his wife on at least three occasions to Winnipeg, Canada to catch up with John Acthim. For a long time, Balmanno, a much-loved and respected teacher, never spoke of the war, and he remained steadfast in his refusal to eat turnips ever again.

APPENDIX 1

Allied Evaders, Escapers, Resistance Fighters,
and *Engelandvaarders* who attempted to Cross the
Pyrenees into Spain, April 19–22, 1944

American, British, and British Commonwealth Servicemen*

SGT John Acthim, RCAF
FSG John Ansell, RAAF
FSG David Thomas Balmanno, RAAF
TSG Archie R. Barlow Jr., USAAF
SGT Harrison (Harry) Stanley Cammish, RAF
2LT Lynn H. Drollinger, USAAF
TSG Curtis Finley, USAAF
FSG Wilfred M. Gorman, RCAF
LT George Gordon Hardy, RN
SSG William B. Hendrickson, USAAF
FSG Charles W. Jackson, RAF
TSG Theodore R. Kellers, USAAF
SSG Stanley Lepkowski, USAAF
2LT James L. Liles, USAAF
2LT Robert Dixon Lindstrom, USAAF
2LT James J. McMahon, USAAF
SGT Paul C. Pearce, USAAF
SGT Melvin Porter, USAAF
1LT Joseph E. Sutphin, USAAF
SGT Thomas James Taylor, RAF
PO William Herbert Taylor, RAF

Civilians**

Fernand Bellenger (FR)
Roger Bureau (BEL)
Maurice de Milleville (FR)
Dr. Marcel Hulin (FR)
Raymond Krugell (FR)
Jacques Lartigue (FR)
Edmond (Eddie) Luff (UK)
Jules Lautman (FR)
Jacques Liddell (FR) ?
Paul Louis (FR)
Dr. Max Rens (NL)

*All of the servicemen except one were evaders; LT George Hardy had escaped from captivity.

**Three of the civilians remain unidentified.

APPENDIX 2

The Escape-Line Organizations

Jewish refugees, Resistance fighters on the run, Dutch and Belgian patriots bound for England (*Engelandvaarders*), escaped prisoners of war, downed Allied airmen ... During World War II, tens of thousands of fugitives escaped out of Nazi-occupied western Europe by climbing over the Pyrenees mountains marking the border between France and "neutral" Spain. At great risk to their own lives, men and women of the Dutch, Belgian, and French Underground organized escape routes and helped the fugitives, sheltering them in their homes and escorting them in their travels toward freedom. Some escape-line organizations were independent, others set up or assisted by the intelligence and secret services of Allied governments. Escape lines could become congested; some stopped well short of the Pyrenees region. Fortunately, contacts often existed between escape lines, making it possible to hand over a group of fugitives for their continued travel farther south.

Listed below are some of the escape lines that helped the thirty-five fugitives featured in this volume reach the foothills of the Pyrenees on the French side of the border. Run by Marie-Louise Dissard, the escape-line organization Françoise assembled most of the climbing party in Toulouse, then handed it over to Gabriel Nahas ("Georges") and passeur Jean-Louis Bazerque ("Charbonnier") for the dangerous crossing of the mountains.

Comet

The "Comet" line operated in Belgium and France and specialized in helping Allied servicemen reach Spain via the western Pyrenees. The escape line was started in 1941 by Andrée de Jongh ("Dédée"), a twenty-four-year-old Belgian woman and Red Cross nurse volunteer in Brussels. In total Comet helped nearly seven hundred Allied servicemen escape from occupied western Europe, including 118 who were personally escorted by Dédée across the Spanish border. Andrée de Jongh was arrested on January 15, 1943, and was succeeded by fellow Belgian Jean-François Nothomb ("Franco"). Both Dédée and Jean-François Nothomb, who was arrested in January 1944, survived Germany's concentration camps. Notable Comet helpers include Anne Brusselmans, who sheltered Staff Sergeant Lepkowski in Brussels, and Amanda Stassart, who guided Kellers and Lepkowski across the French border to Paris via Lille in early November 1943. While in Belgium, Flight Sergeant Gorman was also helped by the Comet Line.

Dutch-Paris

Beginning in 1941, Dutchman Johan (Jean) Hendrik Weidner ran an escape line from his base of operation in Lyon, France. After joining forces with Dutch diplomat Herman Laatsman in late 1943, the expanded network became known as "Dutch-Paris." It operated in the Netherlands, Belgium, and France, rescuing hundreds of Dutch Jews and Engelandvaarders, as well as more than one hundred downed airmen. Initially, Dutch-Paris funneled fugitives and refugees into neutral Switzerland. It later also brought them to Toulouse for the crossing of the Pyrenees. Dutch-Paris collaborated with Gabriel Nahas (referred to as the middleman by historian Megan Koreman) and his network of passeurs. It was Jacques Rens, one of Jean Weidner's trusted lieutenants, who escorted Belgian Roger Bureau and a group of Allied evaders to Toulouse in early February 1944. Other notable Dutch-Paris agents include Salomon Chait ("Edmond Moreau"), Paul Veerman, and Suzy Kraay. Many Dutch-Paris agents were arrested as a direct result of Suzy Kraay's arrest in early February 1944. Afterward, the network continued to operate, but at reduced capacity. According to Weidner, Nahas arranged for about half of Dutch-Paris's passages to Spain. These passages only involved civilians in 1943 but also included airmen in early 1944. After Nahas began working for Marie-Louise Dissard's Françoise, he no longer organized whole convoys strictly for Dutch-Paris. However, he continued to help Dutch-Paris by making arrangements for the placement of fugitives in mixed convoys.

Jean-Marie ("Donkeyman" in London)

French architect Henri Frager was the second-in-command of the Resistance network Carte before he created his own network, known as Jean-Marie and, in London, as Donkeyman, his code name. Frager, an SOE agent, made several trips to London. From Paris his network sent as many as six groups of Allied evaders to the organization Françoise in Toulouse, all between February 10 and early June 1944. Sergeant Acthim, Flight Sergeant Ansell, Flight Sergeant Balmanno, Sergeant Cammish, Flight Sergeant Jackson, Second Lieutenant Liles, Second Lieutenant Lindstrom, Second Lieutenant McMahon, Sergeant T. J. Taylor, and Pilot Officer W. H. Taylor all stayed in the homes of Jean-Marie helpers in mid-April 1944 in Paris. Henri Frager sheltered Second Lieutenant Liles in his home on Boulevard-du-Montparnasse. The escape line was infiltrated and Henri Frager arrested. He was transported to Buchenwald and died in October 1944.

Marie-Claire

The Marie-Claire line was created in late 1942 by Englishwoman Mary Lindell, who set up her base of operation at the Hotel de France in Ruffec along the Demarcation Line. It specialized in helping British and British Commonwealth servicemen stranded behind enemy lines in France. The Marie-Claire line was beset by multiple problems, including the lack of a radio operator and the arrest of Mary Lindell's son in May 1943. Mary Lindell herself was hit by a car and seriously injured near the Demarcation Line shortly before Christmas 1942. She was then arrested in November 1943 in Pau and later sent to Ravensbrück, a concentration camp for women. Both Mary Lindell and her son survived the war, but the impact of the Marie-Claire line might have been grossly exaggerated afterward, not to mention the suspicious nature of some of the family's connections with Germans. Lieutenant Hardy and Eddie Luff left Switzerland in early March 1944 and used Marie-Claire safe houses to reach Toulouse; Lieutenant Hardy was accompanied by Mary Lindell's son. Marie-Claire helpers mentioned in this volume include Armand Dubreuille in Ruffec, Dr. Bonnier in Lyon, and a "Mr Auriol" in Saint-Lieux-lès-Lavaur.

Marie-Odile

"Marie-Odile" was run by Pauline Barré de Saint Venant (code name "Marie-Odile Laroche"), born on April 9, 1895. Technical Sergeant Barlow, Second Lieutenant Drollinger, Technical Sergeant Finley, Staff Sergeant Hendrickson, Technical Sergeant Kellers, Staff Sergeant Lepkowski, and Sergeant Pearce were all in the care of Marie-Odile as they traveled from Paris to Toulouse, to be handed over to Françoise. Notable Marie-Odile helpers include Simone Rossenu, who with her parents and her sister sheltered Technical Sergeant Barlow and Second Lieutenant Drollinger in Paris. Arrested on May 4, 1944, Saint Venant was deported to Ravensbrück, where she died on March 23, 1945.

Françoise (replaced Pat O'Leary after Albert Guérisse's arrest)

Marie-Louise Dissard ("Françoise") was a member of the Pat O'Leary line (Pat Line) run by Belgian doctor Albert Guérisse. Initially, the Pat line assisted Allied evaders and escapers in traveling south to Perpignan via Marseille. The evaders and escapers were then smuggled over the eastern Pyrenees into Spain. In early 1943, Pat O' Leary had to move his base of operation to Toulouse. In March of that year, Albert Guérisse was arrested by the Germans. Marie-Louise Dissard resumed the work of the escape line under her own code name, Françoise. Allied servicemen continued to be sent over the eastern Pyrenees from Perpignan, but in early 1944 circumstances forced Marie-Louise Dissard to use escape routes over the central Pyrenees instead. To that end, she enlisted the help of Gabriel Nahas and his network of passeurs, chief among them Jean-Louis Bazerque ("Charbonnier"). In 1944 Françoise received Allied evaders from various other Resistance organizations, namely Jean-Marie, Marie-Odile (once), the United Resistance Movements (MUR in French), and several maquis. Names of Francoise helpers: René Lamy ("Copain"; collected First Lieutenant Sutphin and Sergeant Porter in Perigueux and brought them to Toulouse), Jacques Lartigue, Olga Baudot de Rouville, Robert Cayla, and Albert Lautman ("Lucien").

Possum / Mission Martin

The Possum line, or Mission Martin, was conceived jointly in London by Belgium's State Security Service and MI9. Its main objective was to rescue downed RAF airmen in the Belgian Ardennes region and bring them to safe houses near Reims in northeastern France for an air evacuation. In July 1943, Belgian agent Dominique Potier ("Martin") and his radio operator French-Canadian Conrad Lafleur parachuted into Belgium to carry out Mission Martin. Before a wave of arrests by the Germans disabled the network in 1944, eleven airmen were successfully repatriated to England by air. A secondary mission assigned to Potier had been to establish one or several escape lines toward Spain. Using safe houses in and near Paris, Possum found itself collecting airmen from the Comet line. Those airmen included Technical Sergeant Kellers and Staff Sergeant Lepkowski, sheltered for five months in the apartment of Possum helper Emile Chassagne in Gentilly, on the outskirts of the French capital. Potier committed suicide in January 1944 after being arrested and tortured.

APPENDIX 3

Known Prisoners Who Escaped from the Train Bound
for Neuengamme, June 5, 1944

List compiled from Chirol (1996) and the Fondation pour la
Mémoire de la Déportation. The escape took place between the
towns of Châlons-en-Champagne and Vitry-le-François in northeastern France. Names in bold type are those of men arrested on
April 21, 1944, in Gourron on the mountain of Superbagnères. The
list is updated with two new names (*).

Argence, Louis
Bellenger, Fernand*
Biaggi, Jean-Baptiste
Boccon-Gibod, Raymond
Burtin, Fernand
Ciocca, Pierre
Cosmao, Hervé
Coustaud, Maurice
Denègre, Pierre
Dhuy, Adolphe
Dufour, Raoul
Enjalbert, Jean
Fournié, Pierre
Galland, Georges (?)
Gardeux, Guy
Guilhem-Jouan (?), Jean
Hochart, Henri
Hounau, Léonard
Jocteur-Monrozier, Louis

Krugell, Raymond
Laborde, Armand
Lafforgue, Pierre
Lalanne, Emmanuel
Larribe, Georges
Lartigue, Jacques*
Lebelle, Michel
Le Meur, Georges
Mangès, Pierre
Marchal, Marcel
Marissal, Georges
Martin, Jean
Morange, Roger
Négol, René
Noël, Yves
Peltier, Marcel
Pfeiffer d'Osmont, Georges
Thoraval, François

APPENDIX 4

The Arrest and Deportation of Jacqueline Houry

Just before 9:00 in the morning on June 14, 1944, twenty-one-year-old Jacqueline Houry was preparing to go to mass. She lived with her parents and younger brother in an apartment in Neuilly-sur-Seine, on the western edge of Paris right next to the Bois de Boulogne. When the doorbell rang, Jacqueline called out to her parents, but thinking that the mail was being delivered, she then opened the door. She came face to face with a man who spoke French with a slight foreign accent. "Jacqueline Houry?" the man inquired. She identified herself, but for a moment the man seemed puzzled and he asked again for Jacqueline Houry. She repeated who she was several times, and finally the man believed her. "German police," he said, as two more men appeared in the doorframe. Jacqueline Houry stepped back inside the apartment, letting in the three Gestapo agents. They asked her questions and searched her room, and after giving her just enough time to pack some belongings in a bag, they took her away in a Citroën Traction Avant car. Her father Gérard, still in his pajamas, had been present throughout the scene of the arrest. The Germans had shown no interest in him.

Jacqueline Houry went straight to the Gestapo headquarters on Rue des Saussaies in Paris.

> All afternoon on that Wednesday, they kept imploring and threatening me. Toward the end of the day, they ran out of patience, seeing that I would not talk. With nothing left to say, they took me to the bathtub. The way it works is that your whole head and body are kept under water. You suffocate, you run out of air, and you struggle terribly as your survival instinct takes over. I knew I had no chance

against those four brutes, and yet I fought so hard I half succeeded in getting out of the tub several times. They pin you under water for however long they choose. Perhaps they know when they see air bubbles. Then they pull you out of the tub but continue to spray you with water, and they order you to start talking. They push you back under water, etc. . . . This whole farce went on for forty-five minutes. I can assure you that I was not feeling great afterwards. I was stumbling sideways, and seeing my reflection in the mirror frightened me. I looked like a drowned victim. They interrogated me for a while longer then placed me in a room that served as a cell, with no bed and no bucket. Thank God, I had the blanket I had taken with me from home. Once dry, in spite of all my worries, I was overpowered by fatigue and fell asleep.[1]

In August 1944 Jacqueline Houry was deported to Germany, together with her mother, arrested on June 15. After a brief stay in Ravensbrück, the mother and daughter were shipped to Holleischen near the town of Plzen, in what was then occupied Czechoslovakia. One of the larger subcamps of KZ-Flossenbürg, Holleischen mostly held female inmates of different nationalities, all used as slave labor in a nearby munitions factory complex. Both Jacqueline Houry and her mother survived their ordeal and were liberated on May 5, 1945. Nearly thirty years later, Jacqueline Houry (now Jacqueline Corbineau) received the French Legion of Honor for her contribution to the fight against Nazi Germany. Jeannette L'Herminier, who was also at Holleischen, took the opportunity to pronounce the following words of praise.

I can still picture you [two] together, with smiles on your faces, dignified, reserved, so tenderly united, one lending a hand to the other—when toiling away at the gunpowder factory hidden in the forest nearby, during work in the carpentry workshop, or while clearing the woods for the installation of a new arms factory. Optimistic and courageous, mindful of first and foremost resisting the deliberate human degradation and debasement aimed at destroying us, as crisp and tidy looking as was possible given our condition of exhausted, hungry, and louse-ridden slaves, your appearance and conduct represented an example and a comfort to all of your sisters in misery.[2]

APPENDIX 5

Evaders and Escapers Helped by the "Françoise" Organization in 1944
in Toulouse and Surrounding Area

Adapted from Marie-Louise Dissard's original list (Records of Headquarters, European Theater of Operations, United States Army [Record Group 498], Entry UD 193, French Helper files, Marie-Louise Dissard, Box 997. National Archives and Records Administration). Misspelled names have been corrected and ranks added. The date of departure given is that from Toulouse. Except where otherwise noted, the evaders in the list are USAAF personnel.

Left in February:

1LT Robert V. Krengle

FO Robert M. Davenport (RCAF)

GNR Hans E. Unger (SAAF)

CPO Henry W. Cantle (RN)

SSG David L. Butcher

1LT Dennis P. Carlson

Kenneth Benstead (?)

SSG George F. Kelley Jr.

SSG John R. Myrick

MAJ Ivan W. Eveland

2LT Stanley A. Plytynski

PVT J. S. Kennard-Davis (NZEF)

Notes: Krengle and Davenport reached the Spanish border on March 28 with Witt, Leach, Walley, Yeager, and others (see notes for March 25). Unger, Carlson, Butcher, Eveland, Kelley, and Myrick all arrived in Spain east of Andorra on February 23. Cantle, also in that same group, collapsed and had to be carried by his companions. He was left at a farmhouse on the French side of the border to rest, together with a guide and another evader. Once in Spain, the evaders spent seven days in Alp in a sheepfold being fed by their Basque guides and recovering from exhaustion, frostbite, and snow blindness. According to Major Eveland, the guides kept the evaders in the sheepfold against their will, as several of them were showing signs of gangrene and wanted to leave—they reportedly later had to have their feet amputated.

Left around March 10–13:

ssg Robert Finney
ssg Stanley J. Dymek
2lt Harold O. Freeman
2lt Rueben Fier
ssg John C. McLaughlin
ssg Levi H. Collins
ssg Alvin E. Sanderson
ssg Kenneth Carson
ssg Joseph De Franze
2lt Hugh C. Shields

Notes: American airmen Dymek, Freeman, McLaughlin, Shields, and De Franze arrived in Puigcerdà in Spain on the night of March 30, together with four Englishmen and sixteen Poles. The five Americans set out over the Pyrenees on the night of March 11 with a Spanish guide. The snow was too deep and the guide turned the group back at the first mountain pass. The group then stayed in a barn in a village and set out again on March 28, this time accompanied by the four English evaders who had arrived in the intervening time. Second Lieutenant Fier and Staff Sergeant Collins were captured.

Left on March 25:

ssg Severino J. Fernandez
1lt Francis J. Witt Jr.
ssg Kenneth Leach

2LT Omar M. Patterson

2LT Jennings B. Beck

2LT Carl T. Nall

2LT Herman I. Seidel

SSG William Malasko

SSG Travis J. Ross

SSG Kenneth M. Walley

SSG Richard C. Weiss

SGT Michael J. Negro

FO Charles E. Yeager

Notes: All thirteen evaders joined a large party, mainly Americans and Dutchmen, who traveled by train from Toulouse to Saint-Laurent / Saint-Paul on the afternoon of March 25. They likely started out from the Valley of Barousse and, after reaching the Larboust Valley, climbed up to the "black shed" on the mountain of Superbagnères. They reached Spain on March 28. Krengle and Davenport were both in that group.

Left around March 30 (date given by Françoise; in reality April 6 for 2LT Smith):

PO William E. Watkins

2LT Michael L. Smith

Notes: Watkins and Smith reached the Noguera Pallaresa Valley in Spain on April 9, accompanied by passeur Jaume Soldevila and five other Allied evaders, Staff Sergeant Creason, Staff Sergeant Pederson, First Lieutenant Lathrop, Flight Lieutenant Goldberg, and Flight Officer Crosby.

Left around April 7:

FSG Wilfred M. Gorman (RCAF)

FSG Art J. "Dick" Holden (RCAF)

WO Vic Thompson (RAF)

TSG Daniel F. Gilmore

2LT Albert W. Stravinsky

Notes: Thompson, Gilmore, and Stravinsky were all captured in the Pyrenees. Holden and Gorman were split up and returned to Toulouse separately.

Left on April 18:

PO **William H. Taylor** (**RAF**)

FSG **David Thomas Balmanno** (**RAAF**)

SGT **Thomas James Taylor** (**RAF**)

SGT **Harrison Stanley Cammish** (**RAF**)

SGT **John Acthim** (**RCAF**)

FSG **John Ansell** (**RAAF**)

2LT **James L. Liles**

2LT **Robert D. Lindstrom**

2LT **James J. McMahon**

TSG **Theodore R. Kellers**

TSG **Archie R. Barlow**

2LT **Lynn H. Drollinger**

SGT **Paul C. Pearce**

SSG **William B. Hendrickson**

SSG **Stanley Lepkowski**

TSG **Curtis Finley**

FSG **Wilfred M. Gorman** (**RCAF**)

1LT **Joseph E. Sutphin**

SGT **Melvin Porter**

Notes: Before arriving in Toulouse, Bill Taylor, Balmanno, Tilly Taylor, Cammish, Acthim, Ansell, Liles, Lindstrom, and McMahon arrived in Paris in the care of the Jean-Marie organization. Kellers, Barlow, Drollinger, Pearce, Hendrickson, Lepkowski, and Finley were handed over to Françoise by the organization Marie-Odile. Gorman was rescued in Toulouse after his return from the Pyrenees. Sutphin and Porter were brought to Toulouse by René Lamy ("Copain") of the Françoise organization. The majority of men in this group were captured on April 21–22 near Luchon.

Left around May 5:

2LT Lawson D. Campbell

1LT Robert A. Martin

SSG Marvin Bradford Alford

2LT Harold G. Garman

TSG Rex L. Hayes

SGT Robert Henry

TSG Tollie G. Berry

SGT Raymond P. Hindle (RAF)

FSG Frederick J Franklin (RAF)

2LT John Betolatti

Notes: According to Marie-Louise Dissard, Campbell, Martin, and Alford all left Toulouse around April 18, when in fact they started over the Pyrenees in the same group as Betolatti and Franklin three weeks later, having first traveled by train from Toulouse to Lez. Within the group was a woman attempting to go to Algiers to be reunited with her husband. She could not follow the pace set by the group and after a snowstorm, she sought refuge in a cabin with a Dutch attorney also in the party. When the guides decided to go back and rescue her, the American and British evaders continued on alone toward the border. Before reaching Spain, they split into two groups. Martin, with Bradford, Hayes, Berry, and Henry went down into a valley, whereas Betolatti, Franklin, and Hindle chose the route higher on a mountain slope. Hayes, Berry, Henry, Campbell, and Alford were all captured by a German patrol. Martin escaped detection and reached Spain on May 9. Second Lieutenant Garman was arrested onboard the train taking him, Alford, Campbell, and Martin to Toulouse. They were accompanied by guide René Lamy ("Copain") of the Françoise organization.

Left around May 12:

2LT Walter Meldrich

SGT Herman F. Hermanson

(Alain?) Daniel Héricault (French bomber pilot)

2LT Frederick W. West

FSG Frederick A. Greenwell (RAF)

LTC Robert Montgomery

1LT Harry E Bisher

FO Milton H. Ramsey

SGT Wallace A. Trinder

SGT Arden N. Brenden

Notes: Two groups instead of one. Trinder and Brenden left Toulouse at least one week earlier. With Hermanson, two Englishmen, and seven Frenchmen (including the guides), the group of twelve set out at 2:00 a.m. on May 11. They crossed the border early on May 12 and arrived in Les in the Aran Valley. The second group with Meldrich, Montgomery, West, Greenwell, and Ramsey arrived on May 15 in Spain.

Left around May 22:

SGT Anthony L. Mills

SGT Harold F. Maher

MAJ Roderick L. Francis

1LT Monroe J. Hotaling

TSG Howard J. Turlington

SSG W. Raymond Serafin

1LT William O. Ross

TSG Laymon M. Mahan

1LT Earl E. Woodard

CPT Arthur T. Cavanaugh

TSG Francis C. Marx

2LT Bernard L. Reed

FSG Albert V. Jackson

Notes: Crossed the Pyrenees with Lieutenant Glaze and Staff Sergeant Cole (see next group; arrived in the Aran Valley on May 29).

Left around May 26:

ILT Ivan E. Glaze
SSG Warren W. Cole

Notes: Glaze and Cole arrived in Spain on May 29 with the group that left Toulouse around May 22. Glaze's escape and evasion report mentions Frisco and gives Les as the first town they reached in Spain.

Left on May 30:

PO Ronald G. Hoare
2LT Jesse M. Hamby
FO James A. Smith (RAAF)
ILT Joel W. McPherson

Notes: With U.S. 2LT Gilbert M. Stonebarger, the four evaders were waiting in Arbon for the return of Charbonnier when they learned of his death. They left with another guide and arrived in Canején, Spain on June 18. Also in the party was Frenchman Jean Duval (Willie).

Left around June 7:

SGT Edwin Worsdale (RNZAF)
LCR William L Stephens (RNVR)
FO Adolphe André Duchesnay (RCAF)
ILT David A. Donovan
FUS Joseph Purvis (Royal Northumberland Fusiliers, British Army)

Notes: ILT David A. Donovan went to Toulouse accompanied by Jean Brégi ("Philippe") of the Françoise organization. In Toulouse he stayed first with Philippe, then with the widow of René Lamy ("Copain"). Philippe then took Donovan to Laguépie, northeast of Toulouse. After waiting a month for Philippe to return, Donovan left with an Australian-born Frenchman, and instead of making the attempt over the Pyrenees ended up joining American liberating forces toward the end of August 1944. It was also Philippe who brought Worsdale, Stephens, and Duchesnay to Toulouse on June 7. The three servicemen met Françoise then took a train to Montréjeau and walked to Loures-Barousse, where they arrived at 1:00 a.m. on June 9. They stayed for two days in Izaourt in the home of Blanche Fontagnères. No guide came to take them over the Pyrenees, but they decided to attempt the journey on their own. They arrived in Spain on June 13 (see article published by Max Lambert in 2016).

TIMELINE OF KEY EVENTS, 1944

January

January 21   Dutch-Paris sends its first group of Allied airmen from Toulouse to the Pyrenees en route to Spain.

January 25   Dutch-Paris sends its second group of Allied airmen from Toulouse to the Pyrenees.

January 27   A German agent infiltrates the Françoise escape line that convoyed fugitives over the Pyrenees from Perpignan. Francoise's operative "Sherry" is arrested with a notebook containing the address of Françoise's main safe house in Toulouse, the Villa Pamplemousse.

Late January Having crossed the border between France and Switzerland, Maurice de Milleville reaches the British consulate in Geneva.

February

February 1   Marie-Louise Dissard evacuates the Villa Pamplemousse in Toulouse. Belgian Roger Bureau leaves Antwerp after he narrowly avoids being arrested.

February 6   A German ambush at the Portet d'Aspet results in the capture of about half of the fugitives in Dutch-Paris's third convoy to Spain. From that same convoy, passeur Palo Treillet, Belgian Roger Bureau, and seven other fugitives return to the foothills of the French Pyrenees.

February 11   Suzy Kraay of the Dutch-Paris organization is arrested by the French police's Brigade d'Interpellation in Paris and handed over to the Gestapo. She carried on her a notebook with the names of Dutch-Paris underground agents and contact information. Nearly 150 Dutch-Paris operatives are arrested during the following weeks as the result of Suzy Kraay's arrest and information divulged by her during her interrogation and from her notebook.

March

March 19   A large group of Allied airmen and other fugitives (mostly assembled by Dutch-Paris) reaches Bossòst in the Aran Valley of Spain. The Guardia Civil discovers the general route followed by the fugitives in the French Pyrenees. A German spy in Bossòst is handed a drawing of the last mountain pass before Spain.

March 28   Another group of fugitives including airmen reaches the Aran Valley.

April

First week   Maddy De Deken arrives in Toulouse, accompanied by 2LT Albert W. Stravinsky, TSG Daniel F. Gilmore, and 2LT Russell E. Moriarty. On April 7, Jacques Lartigue of the Françoise organization accompanies Second Lieutenant Stravinsky and Technical Sergeant Gilmore to the train station in Toulouse. The two men join a party of evaders bound for Spain.

April 9   Led by passeur Jaume Soldevila, a group of nine Allied airmen crosses the Spanish border into the Noguera Pallaresa river valley after spending one night in a cave. Other fugitives from the same group turn back. In the foothills of the French Pyrenees, most of them are captured while attempting to cross a river, including almost certainly 2LT Albert W. Stravinsky and TSG Daniel F. Gilmore. Flight Sergeant Gorman evades capture and returns to Toulouse.

April 13   Charles de Hepcée is captured at Pont de la Taule, having just crossed the French border.

April 14   Françoise's operative Jacques Lartigue is arrested by the Gestapo and incarcerated in Biarritz.

April 16	Jacques Lartigue escapes from the Gestapo in Toulouse.
April 18	The thirty-five fugitives travel by train from Toulouse to Saint-Laurent / Saint-Paul, where they meet passeur Jean-Louis Bazerque (Charbonnier).
April 19	Day one of the attempt to climb over the Pyrenees to Spain.
April 20	Day two of the attempt. After getting lost in a snowstorm, the fugitives reach the Larboust Valley above Garin and its German customs police outpost.
April 21	Day three of the attempt. Twenty-one of the men in the party are captured at the "black shed" below the plateau of Superbagnères.
April 22	Seven or eight more fugitives are captured in the early morning. Six reach safety on the other side of the Spanish border.
April 26	Paul Louis and (all?) others are transferred to the prison of Saint-Michel in Toulouse.
April 26 or 27	Maddy De Deken is arrested in Toulouse, together with Robert Cayla (Françoise organization).

May

May 15	Françoise's operative Albert Lautman is arrested.
May 16	Enemy agent Frank Van Hecke is executed in the small Belgian village of Lamain.
May 22	Priest Paul Louis escapes off the train taking him to the prison of Fresnes.
May 29	Jean Weidner, Jacques Rens, and Paul Veerman are arrested by the French Milice in Toulouse. Gabriel Nahas, who was with them, manages to escape.

June

| June 5 | Raymond Krugell, Jacques Lartigue, and Fernand Bellenger escape by jumping off the train taking them to the concentration camp of Neuengamme in Germany. |

June 6	Allied landings in Normandy.
June 13	Jean-Louis Bazerque ("Charbonnier"), Joseph Barrère, and Pierre Sabadie are killed in Larroque; Dr. Marcel Hulin escapes from a train taking him to Paris.
June 14	Jacqueline Houry is arrested at her home by the Gestapo.

August

August 19–20	Toulouse is liberated.

December

December 18	Michel Pautot is sentenced to hard labor for life.

GLOSSARY

Abwehr: Military counterintelligence arm of the German armed forces.

Demarcation Line: boundary established in June 1940 by the Germans, separating France's Free Zone (under the authority of the Vichy government) from the Occupied Zone (controlled by the German military). The Free Zone was invaded by the Germans in November 1942 and renamed the South Zone. The Demarcation Line was opened to French citizens in March 1943.

Dirección General de Seguridad (Spanish) or DGS: General Directorate of Security, an intelligence-gathering agency within Spain's Ministry of Interior.

Engelandvaarders: Dutch patriots who, during World War II, attempted to escape from occupied Europe to join Allied forces in England.

escaper: Serviceman who has escaped from secure enemy custody (e.g., a prison camp, prison, or any guarded location).

evader: Serviceman who has never been caught but is escaping from occupied territory. Usually, evaders were airmen who had parachuted out of aircraft or paratroopers and Special Forces leaving an enemy country after a raid.

Feldwebel (German): Noncommissioned officer.

Gendarmerie (French): Branch of the French armed forces with police duties. It is tasked mainly with the policing of smaller towns and rural areas, as well as the armed forces and military installations.

Grenzpolizei (German): Frontier police, part of the Gestapo.

Guardia Civil (Spanish): Civil guard, a Spanish national, militarized police force tasked primarily with maintaining order in rural areas and patrolling the country's borders and highways.

Internierungslager (German): Internment camp for the civilians of enemy states.

maquis (French): Rural guerrilla bands of French Resistance fighters who often hid and operated in forests and mountainous areas.

Milice (French): Paramilitary organization created by the Vichy regime to help fight against the French Resistance during World War II.

Oflag (German, short for *Offizierslager*): Officer camp for prisoners of war.

passeur (French): "People smuggler," guide who, during World War II, took men and women over the Pyrenees to Spain or otherwise helped smuggle fugitives out of Nazi-occupied France.

Sicherheitsdienst des Reichsführers–ss (German) or SD: Security Service of the Reichsführer–ss. One of Nazi Germany's national security agencies, the SD gathered intelligence in its mission to detect potential enemies of the leadership.

Special Operations Executive (SOE): British World War II organization set up in the summer of 1940 to carry out missions behind enemy lines, with a dual mission of sabotage and assistance to Resistance organizations.

Stalag (German, short for *Stammlager*): Prisoner-of-war camp for enlisted personnel.

Zollgrenzschutz (German): Customs frontier police, not absorbed by the Gestapo until October 1944.

NOTES

1. A Perilous Hide-and-Seek

1. From the testimony of Sam Timmers Verhoeven, written in Algiers in September 1944 and reproduced in *De Schakel: De Geschiedenis van de Engelandvaarders*, by Frank Visser (The Hague: Ad. M.C. Stok, Forum Boekerij, 1976). Also from the debriefings of TSG Nicholas Mandell (National Archives Escape and Evasion report EE-629) and 2LT Campbell Brigman (National Archives Escape and Evasion Report EE-606). According to Technical Sergeant Mandell, the party consisted of twenty-four men plus the two guides.

2. Among those captured were four U.S. servicemen: 2LT Omar E. Roberts, SSG Clyde L. Mellen, SSG Harold A. Boyce, and 1LT Frank P. McGlinchey, in addition to Dutchmen Vic Lemmens and Han Langeler. Palo Treillet and Henri Marrot were both experienced mountain guides. The ambush set by the Germans on February 6, 1944, represented the only time these passeurs failed to smuggle fugitives across the border with Spain.

3. 2LT Campbell C. Brigman Jr., was an American pilot whose B-17 had been hit by enemy fighters during a bombing mission to Germany on December 30, 1943. The crew had not bailed out and instead Brigman had managed to crash land the plane near Wimy in northern France. Brigman received help and protection from the "Armée Blanche" and "Dutch-Paris" and was able to make his way south to the Pyrenees.

4. According to Pilot Officer McLaughlin, the group stayed not in Saint-Girons as stated by other evaders, but in the nearby village of Cazères.

5. Gijs den Besten had to have two toes amputated and remained hospitalized for several months.

6. The bus to Saint-Girons encountered a German roadblock. Sam Timmers was hidden inside a luggage trailer pulled by the bus. A German shepherd dog nearly sniffed him out but at that moment was distracted by a cat inside a small basket. From the testimony of Sam Timmers Verhoeven, written in Algiers in September 1944 and reproduced in *De Schakel: De Geschiedenis van de Engelandvaarders*, by Frank Visser (The Hague: Ad. M.C. Stok, Forum Boekerij, 1976).

7. Eight of the Americans in the evader party were members of the same crew of a B-24J shot down by enemy fighter planes on March 5, 1944, during a bombing

raid on Bergerac: copilot 2LT Carl T. Nall (EE-645), navigator 2LT Herman I. Seidel (EE-644), top turret gunner SGT William J. Gabonay (EE-659), ball turret gunner SSG Kenneth M. Walley (EE-680), waist gunner SSG William Malasko (EE-666), waist gunner SSG Richard C. Weiss (EE-681), tail gunner SSG Travis J. Ross (EE-679), and nose gunner SGT Michael J. Negro (EE-682). The other American airmen in the party included 1LT Francis J. Witt Jr. (EE-647), 1LT Robert V. Krengle (EE-646), SSG Kenneth Leach (EE-677), SSG Severino J. Fernandez (EE-698), 2LT Omar M. Patterson Jr. (EE-648), 2LT Jennings B. Beck (EE-649), and FO Charles E. Yeager (EE-660).

8. Not to be confused with RAF FLT Bram van der Stok, a Dutchman, René Alphonse Van der Stock was born on April 11, 1909, in Sint-Amandsberg, Belgium. He commanded an artillery unit at the Fort of Flémalle in May 1940 and escaped from Oflag IIA in Prenzlau on or around October 13, 1943. Sam Timmers referred to him as a Belgian aviator in the group that climbed over the Pyrenees in late March 1944. Later, in January 1945, Van der Stock joined the RAF Belgian Section, but his pilot training in the Belgian Air Force had not been completed when war broke out in 1940. Individual military records for René Van der Stock, Belgian Defense Ministry, Collection DGHR-HRA-E/N/Arch.

9. From a telephone interview of André Crampé on July 20, 2017. A letter dated September 3, 1991, from Sam Timmers Verhoeven confirms that André and Jean Crampé were the two passeurs. The group crossed the border near the mountain pass known as the "Col du Portillon."

10. The large party of fugitives who arrived in Bossòst in the Aran Valley on March 19 included seven of the men who had escaped from the ambush at the Portet d'Aspet a month and a half earlier: the two British and British Commonwealth airmen FSG George L. Watts and Pilot Officer McLaughlin, in addition to Dutchman Chris van Oosterzee and the four U.S. airmen, TSG Nicholas Mandell, SGT Norman Elkin, 2LT Campbell C. Brigman Jr, and SGT Walter R. Snyder. Among those who joined them for the climb over the Pyrenees in March were at least twelve additional U.S. airmen: 2LT Victor Ferrari (EE-607), TSG William James Miller (EE-636), SGT Loral Martin (EE-634), SGT Herman D. Morgan (EE-640), SSG Kenneth Carson (EE-632), SSG Robert Finney (EE-628), SSG Harry D. Kraft (EE-635), 1LT Elwood D. Arp (EE-604), 2LT Howard Sherman (EE-608), 2LT Edward F. Neu (EE-602), SSG Carl E. Bachmann (EE-631), and SSG Frank N. Schaeffer (EE-1369).

11. In the evader party that crossed into Spain nine days later, U.S. SSG Severino J. Fernandez had many difficulties convincing the Guardia Civil in Lleida that he was not a Spanish Republican. He remained in Lleida three weeks longer than First Lieutenant Witt and Staff Sergeant Leach and even spent one night in jail. From the National Archives Escape and Evasion Report for SSG Travis J. Ross (EE-679).

12. From an April 11, 1944, statement by Australian 420242 PO John Geoffrey McLaughlin, 609 Squadron, RAAF. Questionnaires for Repatriated Personnel; UD 151: MI9 Reports and IS9 Questionnaires, Box 606, Location 290/55/20/6.

13. From SGT Norman Elkin's National Archives Escape and Evasion Report (EE-641).

14. According to Snyder, the Czechs had traveled to Toulouse from Switzerland, and one of them had indicated having been to Spain several times. They were in the prison in Lleida when the American airmen left for Alhama de Aragón in early April. National Archives Escape and Evasion Report EE-642.

15. LT René Van der Stock was eventually released, and after more trials and tribulations he reached Glasgow on September 17, 1944. After a short training course at London's Patriotic School, he enlisted in the RAF. Individual military records for René Van der Stock, Belgian Defense Ministry, Collection DGHR-HRA-E/N/Arch.

2. For King and Country

1. About one-third of the total Belgian forces in May 1940.

2. Belgian 2LT Marcel Block was Roger Bureau's superior officer during the Battle of Belgium, also referred to as the 18 Days' Campaign. Block wrote in 1948 that SGT Roger Bureau was a model officer, energetic and dedicated. The commanding officer of the 7th Battery III/I TPA trusted him with important missions that Roger Bureau always carried out with the utmost zeal. Individual military records for Roger Bureau. Belgian Defense Ministry, Collection DGHR-HRA-E/N/Arch.

3. From the unpublished autobiography of Jack Bureau, son of Roger Bureau.

4. From the unpublished autobiography of Jack Bureau, son of Roger Bureau.

5. Eleven speed-skaters competed in the two-day event, during which four distances had to be skated, 500 meters, 1,500 meters, 5,000 meters, and 10,000 meters. Roger Bureau was one of two speed skaters from Belgium. The Finn Julius Skutnabb won the competition; the Austrian Otto Polacsek and the Finn Uuno Pietilä finished second and third, respectively.

6. Roger Bureau played ice hockey for Antwerp's local team, the CPA (In French, "Cercle des Patineurs Anversois"), which dominated Belgium's elite league in the late 1920s and early 1930s.

7. *European Ice Hockey Championship Results since 1910*, by Tomasz Malolepszy (Plymouth, UK: Scarecrow Press, 2013).

8. From the unpublished autobiography of Jack Bureau, son of Roger Bureau.

9. From the unpublished autobiography of Jack Bureau, son of Roger Bureau. It was during one of their weekends along the Belgian North Sea coast that the Bureaus felt the ground shake for several seconds. On Saturday, June 11, 1938, a strong earthquake jolted Belgium, along with the Netherlands, the southeast of England, northern France, and part of Germany. It was Belgium's most powerful earthquake of the twentieth century. Although the damage reported by the Belgian press was minor, the earthquake quite unnerved the Belgian population.

10. Born Alice Van den Abeele, Roger Bureau's mother—a woman of "good Flemish stock"—was related to the Lamonds through her cousin Marguerite

de Harven's marriage with William Lamond, originally of Aberdeen, Scotland. Helen was William and Marguerite Lamond's youngest daughter.

11. Death notice for Norbert Laude (May 24, 1888–September 22, 1974). Bulletin des Séances de l'Académie Royale des Sciences d'Outre-Mer, 1975–1.

12. Born in September 1916, Jacques Rens would have been twenty-seven years old at the time of the event. His height was just under six feet. His father Leman (Louis) Rens was originally from Amsterdam and started out in life as a wood carver. After the end of World War I, he moved to Antwerp and became wealthy through his involvement in the diamond trade. Memories of Micheline Rens-de Braey recorded by her nephew Jean-Guy Rens during an interview on March 5, 2001.

13. On March 5, 2001, Jean-Guy Rens interviewed his aunt Micheline Rens-de-Braey about her late husband Jacques Rens. The interview suggests one possible link between Dutchman Jacques Rens and Belgian Roger Bureau, both from Antwerp. Micheline Rens-de-Braey states that her husband first became involved with the Van Schelle underground organization in Antwerp before Dutch-Paris ever existed. Together with Roger Bureau, Martial van Schelle was one of the twenty-five or thirty athletes representing Belgium during the 1936 Olympic Games in Garmisch-Partenkirchen, Germany, competing in both the two-man and four-man bobsleigh events. Born on July 6, 1899, of a Belgian father and an American mother, Van Schelle was, like Roger Bureau, an outstanding athlete. He was Belgium's swimming national champion in the 100-meter freestyle event no less than ten times and represented Belgium in the hot air balloon Gordon Bennett Cup. As a businessman he opened sporting goods stores and founded a new ice hockey club in Brussels. With the application of synthetic ice, he opened new ice rinks in Antwerp and elsewhere in Belgium. From an early time, Martial van Schelle was involved in the Belgian Resistance during the German occupation of the country. The Van Schelle underground organization is said to have run an escape line toward Switzerland. Antwerp's ice rink also had many German patrons, whom owner Van Schelle befriended in order to gather military intelligence for the Allies. Jacques Rens's involvement with Van Schelle might suggest how the Dutchman met Roger Bureau. Was Roger Bureau himself working with Van Schelle? Martial van Schelle was arrested on January 15, 1943, and executed exactly two months later in Fort Breendonck, Willebroek, Belgium. See "Martial van Schelle: sportif, homme d'affaires et surtout martyr," published in March 2005 by the Cercle d'Histoire de Bruxelles.

14. Upon his arrival in Toulouse on April 3, 1944, U.S. Second Lieutenant Smith was taken in by the organization "Françoise." A few hours after his arrival, Marie-Louise Dissard (Françoise) herself stopped by the house where he was lodged, pounding on the door and crying out "Angleterre" (England). After the American officer let her in through the window, the Frenchwoman told him about arrangements being made to announce his upcoming arrival in Spain. "Geneva," she said, "would radio Barcelona." On the sixth of April, or three days after his

arrival in Toulouse, a helper took Second Lieutenant Smith to Matabiau Bridge in front of the train station. His escort for the train and bus rides to the foothills of the Pyrenees was Jacques Lartigue, a nineteen-year old described as having a prominent beard. National Archives Escape and Evasion Report EE-614

15. "Pilot Officer Wilfred Gorman," in Valerie Evans, ed., *We that are Left . . . Remember: New Brunswickers in the Air Force* (Saint John, New Brunswick: 250 RCAF [Saint John] Wing, Air Force Association of Canada, 2002), 163–72. Flight Sergeant Gorman was promoted to the rank of pilot officer after his liberation in 1945.

16. Their mission was a diversion. The main raid targeted Hanover, but they "went on to drop the markers on Brunswick to draw all the German fighters away from that area."

17. Dick Holden did learn and later remember the names of some of his helpers, a "Mr Rammaert" who lived at 29 Rue de Riga in Tourcoing, and a "Madame Perdriau," 52 Rue des Dames in Paris. In the Netherlands, however, Dick Holden did not know the names of any of the helpers.

18. Charles de Hepcée's story was later recounted in two unpublished books written by his daughters: *Le Lièvre et la Lune*, by Claire de Hepcée, ed. C. H. Haljoux, 1995; and *Itineraire d'un Retour: Charley de Hepcée, 14 mars 1911–27 juin 1944*," by Rose de Hepcée, ed. Michel Fischer Touret, 2012).

19. Second Lieutenant Smith indicated during his debriefing that in Saint-Girons, helper Jacques Lartigue had delivered him and the other evaders who had joined them on the bus to "a good Spanish guide." National Archives Escape and Evasion Report EE-614.

20. By an odd turn of events, Jaume Soldevila almost shared Charles de Hepcée's fate two and a half months later, on June 27, when the Belgian was executed by the SS in a forest near Toulouse, together with several French Resistance fighters. Jaume Soldevila himself was among those to be shot that day, after his arrest on May 15 at his home in Toulouse, followed by his incarceration in Saint-Michel's prison. He had been taken to the forest and like the other prisoners, had been given a shovel to dig his own grave. He managed to escape only after the horn of a truck distracted the German who guarded him. As he bolted, he was hit in the knee by a bullet, but kept going. After he found shelter at the home of an Italian doctor who treated him, Soldevila hid from the Germans until Toulouse was about to be liberated. From his expedition to the Noguera Pallaresa river valley, he kept the list of the seven Allied airmen whom he had helped escape to Spain.

21. The circumstances of Charles Joseph Maximilien Gueulette's (code names "Gull" and "Felix") border crossing are also quite different. According to a 1949 report archived at NARA, Gueulette left from Navarrenx, France on April 6, 1944, and he was accompanied in the Pyrenees by Antoine Le Boucher, another man by the name of "Michel," and two RAF airmen, one named "Ralph," the other a London policeman before the war. In the mountains, "Gull was threatened by a revolver as Antoine Le Boucher thought [Gull's] three-day stay in Navarrenx

was suspicious. Gull managed to pacify Le Boucher, claiming that it was not his fault that his arrival had not been advised, and after two more days in a mountain refuge, not far from Oloron, they were taken. [. . .] to Spain. [They] spent the night in prison. On the 11th they arrived in Pamplona. On the 15th Miranda, where they remained until May 5, 1944. They were then transferred to Madrid on May 6, 1944, and arrived in Gibraltar on May 21, 1944." "Charles Guellette-Brussels C," UD 171, Cases of Belgian Helpers, Box 708, Record Group 498, U.S. National Archives and Records Administration.

3. The Route Past Luchon

1. *La Filière du Rail*, by Gabriel Nahas (Paris: François-Xavier de Guibert, 1995).
2. "Charbonnier" was the maiden name of Jean-Louis Bazerque's mother.
3. "Dogged crusader against drugs." *Readers Digest*, May 1988, 102.
4. Testimony of Dr. Gabriel Nahas (aka Georges), 7 bis Rue Cujas, Toulouse, as recorded by Philippe Wolff in June 1946. National Archives of France, Comité d'Histoire de la Deuxième Guerre Mondiale: Témoignages sur la Résistance Intérieure. 72AJ / 71.
5. Nahas, for his part, developed ties with early Secret Army (Armée Secrète) units, and in 1943 adhered to the United Resistance Movements (MUR), the United Forces of the Patriotic Youth (FUJP), and Service Maquis.
6. From *Montagnards de la Liberté: Les Evasions par l'Ariège et la Haute-Garonne 1939–1945*, by Émilienne Eychenne (Toulouse: Éditions Milan, 1984), 219. After the war, Nahas mentioned the congestion along Charbonnier's Luchon route: "I established contact with Mr. [David] Lautier, Albert Bartet, and Fernand, the owner of the 'Soleil d'Or' [restaurant]. All of them were in Foix and organized crossings [over the Pyrenees]. In Saint-Girons I also met my two friends Palo and Icard, who knew [mountain] guides. Thus we created new lines [of Pyrenees crossings] to somewhat relieve [the congestion on] Charbonnier's Luchon route. One through Saint-Girons and [Mount Valier], which led to Lerida. The other, through Foix and Tarascon-sur-[Ariège] going to Andorra."
7. Civilians taken to Spain with help from Nahas included Jean Cassagneau, the son of Pierre Cassagneau, prefect of the Haute-Garonne department after the Liberation (mentioned in *La Filière du Rail*, by Gabriel Nahas [Paris: François-Xavier de Guibert, 1995]). From Spain Jean Cassagneau continued on to North Africa, where he enlisted in the First French Army and participated in the landings in Provence in August and September 1944. "La Nouvelle Action Française" 48, March 29, 1972.
8. In *RAF Evaders: The Comprehensive Story of Thousands of Escapers and their Escape Lines, Western Europe, 1940–1945* (London: Octopus Publishing Group, 2009), Oliver Clutton-Brock indicates that 2,198 RAF airmen have been identified as evaders in western Europe. The breakdown by year (1940: 91; 1941: 78; 1942: 157; 1943: 398: 1944: 1,342; and 1945: 132) shows a nearly ten-fold increase from 1942 to 1944.

9. Nahas estimated that between April and December 1943, more than one hundred Allied airmen had been funneled into Spain using one of the three general routes he and Charbonnier established: at least thirty through Barbazan and Luchon with Charbonnier, some other thirty along the Saint-Girons route with "Pierre" and "Mireille," and another forty or more using the Foix route with passeurs Albert Bartet and Fernand. All of those airmen were mixed together with Belgians, Dutchmen, and Frenchmen in groups of ten to twenty.

10. Some of these stories were recently given a new life by local historian Jackie Mansas on her blog, "Les Caps Bourrut des Pyrénées," http://capsbourrutdespyrenees.over-blog.com/.

11. From *Montagnards de la Liberté: Les Evasions par l'Ariège et la Haute-Garonne 1939–1945,* by Émilienne Eychenne (Toulouse: Éditions Milan, 1984).

12. The original article appeared in the October 9, 1964, issue of the newspaper, *La Nouvelle République.* It was published again in *Résistance,* R4 N4, June 1978.

13. From SSG Orville G. Greene's National Archives Escape and Evasion Report (EE-386). Benzedrine tablets were distributed to USAAF and RAF airmen because they supposedly produced increased confidence, energy, and initiative.

4. On the Run

1. *Un mois entre les griffes de la Gestapo,* unpublished World War II memoirs of Paul Louis completed on May 26, 1944. Archives of the religious congregation Fils de la Charité, Issy-les-Moulineaux, France.

2. After the Christmas Eve operation was aborted, fourteen of the Allied airmen were sheltered in safe houses around Douarnenez. On January 21, 1944, they boarded another boat, the *Breiz-Izel,* and sailed to Britain, where they arrived safely on January 23. The story of the aborted and successful evacuations is told in Georges Broussine's 2000 volume, *L'Évadé de la France Libre* (Paris: Éditions Tallandier). Krugell later reported walking back to Quimper with an "American engineer" named Glenn, probably SSG Glenn Blakemore from 306BG/367 BS B-17 42-5130 Sweet Pea. Evasion reports indicate that Blakemore left with a Frenchman and was later captured.

3. Article published in New Zealand's community newspaper *Hibiscus Matters* on February 27, 2010.

4. From a June 6, 1944, statement by 1624536 Sergeant Cammish, Harrison Stanley, 50 Squadron, RAF Bomber Command (M19 file, National Archives of the UK, catalog reference WO 208/3320). Also from a letter from Harry Cammish to the author, dated April 2017.

5. The story of VN-Q and its crew under PO William Herbert Taylor is told in *The Long Road: Trials and Tribulations of Airmen Prisoners from Bankau to Berlin, June 1944–May 1945,* by Oliver Clutton-Brock and Ray Crompton (London: Grub Street Publishing, 2014).

6. From *Kiwis Do Fly: New Zealanders in RAF Bomber Command,* by Peter Wheeler (Auckland: Longley Printing, 2010). On February 26, a telegram arrived

at the home of Cammish's parents in Scarborough. "Regret to inform you that your son 1624536 Sgt Harrison Stanley Cammish is missing as the result of air operations on the night of 25/26 February 1944. Stop. Letter follows. Stop. Any further information received will be immediately communicated to you."

7. 2LT James L. Liles. National Archives Escape and Evasion report EE-692. National Archives Identifier: 5555332.

8. Liles refers to the four Germans carrying Tommy guns (Thompson submachine guns), but it is likely a mistake. The Germans had their own, very efficient, submachine gun, the Schmeisser MP40 machine-pistol.

9. From Wheeler, *Kiwis Do Fly*. Known in the Resistance as "Cadoudal," Robert Durand did not survive the war. With several young French Resistance fighters from the Maquis of Ranzey, he attacked German troops in the nearby village of Sornéville on September 4, 1944. The attack failed, and the majority of the assailants, including Robert Durand, were killed. The German troops were veterans of the Russian front. Their commanding officer warned the local population that another attack on German troops would result in the destruction of the villages of Mazerulles, Moncel-sur-Seille, and Sornéville. Information communicated to the author by Jeannine Heib, daughter of Mr. and Mrs. Floerchinger, neighbors of Robert Durand during the war. The Floerchingers hid and sheltered several Frenchmen who were escaped prisoners-of-war during the Occupation.

10. In his debrief on October 12, 1945, FO William Herbert Taylor stated that he stayed with a group of twenty-four evaders in Nancy. MI9 files, National Archives of the UK, catalog reference WO 208/3339/1190.

11. Liles arrived in Paris on April 12, 1944. Cammish did not remember spending any time with other Allied airmen during his time in Nancy or Paris, but he stated that he also arrived in the French capital on April 12. The identities of the evaders who traveled with Liles to Paris seems also confirmed by Marie-Louise Dissard's list of evaders her organization helped in Toulouse. The same ten men are grouped together with the annotation "Jean-Marie" next to them. Records of Headquarters, European Theater of Operations, United States Army [Record Group 498], Entry UD 193, French Helper files, Marie-Louis Dissard, Box 997. National Archives and Records Administration.

12. Henri Frager is also mentioned in 2LT Michael L. Smith's escape and evasion report. A fighter pilot (390 Fighter Squadron, 366 Fighter Group, 9th Air Force), Smith was forced to crash land near Livarot, Normandy, after the loss of his Republic P-47 Thunderbolt's engine on March 17, 1944. At the end of March, two Jean-Marie operatives brought him to Paris. There, he stayed with a jeweler and his wife near Bastille Square. He was visited by Henri Frager himself ("Captain Jean-Marie of British Intelligence"), as well as two former pilots, and a "famous French doctor," brought in to examine his feet, damaged during the crash landing. Escape and Evasion Report EE-614.

13. The altercation between Frager and Déricourt and the infiltration of the network "Jean-Marie" by Bleicher are described in *Colonel Henri's Story: The War Memoirs of Hugo Bleicher, Former German Secret Agent*, by Hugo Ernst Bleicher, Ian Colvin, and Erich Borchers (London: William Kimber, 1954). Henri Déricourt organized the pickup and return of French SOE agents summoned to London for debriefings. Déricourt believed that Roger Bardet worked for the Germans. According to Bleicher's book, he attempted to force Bardet to climb on the plane and accompany Frager to London, but Frager refused, threatening to use his gun. Henri Déricourt had been a pilot in the French Air Force during the Battle of France in May and June 1940. It is unclear whether he himself was a double agent controlled by MI6.

5. Too Many

1. Navigator ILT Joseph E. Sutphin and waist gunner SGT Melvin Porter were members of ILT Robert A. Martin's crew. Their Liberator B-24 J bomber crash landed after being hit by flak over Cognac in western France on March 5, 1944.

2. Evader 2LT Frederick W. West (EE-748) met "Françoise" in May 1944 and spent one night in the apartment above hers. He described her overall as a "remarkable, energetic old woman," "bent over like a gnome" and bow-legged, who "talks at the top of her lungs" and "bounces right off the floor when she gets excited."

3. Records of Headquarters, European Theater of Operations, United States Army [Record Group 498], Entry UD 193, French Helper files, Marie-Louis Dissard, Box 997. National Archives and Records Administration.

4. From an article published by Christian Mouly in the March 1979 issue of the history journal *Resistance*.

5. According to Marie-Louise Dissard's later statement, she was arrested on the train between Narbonne and Perpignan with four airmen, whom she identifies as "Cleve Brown," "Lee Crabtree," "Edward Bell," and "Jack Bercham." Records of Headquarters, European Theater of Operations, United States Army [Record Group 498], Entry UD 193, French Helper files, Marie-Louis Dissard, Box 997. National Archives and Records Administration.

6. Records of Headquarters, European Theater of Operations, United States Army [Record Group 498], Entry UD 193, French Helper files, Marie-Louis Dissard, Box 997. National Archives and Records Administration. "Uncle François" was the code name for Victor Farrell, the British vice consul in Geneva.

7. Personal memoirs of Olga Baudot de Rouville Collection (Ref. YDX 207), Cumbria County Archives and Local Studies Centre, Whitehaven, Cumbria, UK.

8. Françoise's list separates out the evaders handed over to her organization by the two escape networks Jean-Marie and Marie-Odile. The names of Cammish, Balmanno, Acthim, Ansell, PO William Taylor, Sergeant Taylor, Liles, Lindstrom, and McMahon are all grouped together, and next to them is the annotation "Jean-Marie"—missing from Françoise's list is FSG Charles W. Jackson, even though he had to have traveled with the other nine. Still according to Françoise's list,

seven American evaders arrived in Toulouse having been in the care of "Marie-Odile." The seven men—2LT Lynn H. Drollinger, TSG Archie R. Barlow Jr., TSG Theodore R. Kellers, SSG Stanley Lepkowski, SGT Paul C. Pearce, TSG Curtis Finley, and SSG William B. Hendrickson—left Paris on the evening of April 17 on the overnight train to Toulouse.

9. *Escape and Evasion*, by Lynn Howard Drollinger. Unpublished memoirs. Drollinger family archives.

10. Léon Sée was the manager of Italian boxer Primero Carnera, world heavyweight champion from June 29, 1933, to June 14, 1934. "I helped him, I taught him, I made him," Léon Sée once wrote of his role in launching the Italian champion's career in a newspaper article (page 21 of the *Buffalo Evening News*, Monday January 22, 1934). Although Léon Sée stood two heads shorter than his protégé, he himself was quite the athlete. He finished first in many races as an amateur cyclist and won the weightlifting world middleweight championship at Polytechnic Club in London in 1904. He conceived and launched several magazines, including *La Boxe et les Boxeurs*, the first boxing magazine in France (in 1909) and was the first one to promote boxing contests in Paris and elsewhere in France.

11. From Archie Barlow Jr.'s unpublished memoirs, *Pursuit in the Pyrenees*. Barlow family archives.

12. National Archives Escape and Evasion report EE-687; National Archives Identifier: 5555327 (TSG Archie R. Barlow). National Archives Escape and Evasion report EE-547, National Archives Identifier: 5555187 (MAJ Leon W. Blythe). National Archives Escape and Evasion report EE-549, National Archives Identifier: 5555189 (TSG Alvin A. Rosenblatt).

13. U.S. TSG Theodore R. Kellers was the engineer and top turret gunner on a Boeing B-17F Flying Fortress nicknamed *Shack Rabbit III*, shot down on October 20, 1943, by German fighter planes. With two of its engines hit, *Shack Rabbit III* went into a "steep diving turn" followed by a long spin. The pilot, 2LT Robert Z. Grimes, ordered the crew to bail out. As the aircraft was going into its dive, Kellers continued to fire his machine gun from the aircraft's top turret, and Grimes noted that it was "typical" of his engineer—"he wanted to keep fighting." Four of the ten crew members were killed; Grimes, Kellers, and four others survived. The target of the bombing raid was Aachen, on the border between Belgium and Germany, the bombing mission described during the briefing as nothing more than a "milk run, a couple of hours' flight, easy in, drop your bombs, a couple of hours back, and it's beer time." *Shack Rabbit III* was a replacement plane on loan from another squadron. During a previous mission to Gdynia, Poland, the last B-17 flown by Grimes's crew had been hit by flak and it had sustained damage to its fuselage. Second Lieutenant Grimes's World War II bombing missions and subsequent evasion to Spain are told in *The Freedom Line: The Brave Men and Women Who Rescued Allied Airmen from the Nazis during World War II*, by Peter Eisner (New York: William Morrow, 2004).

14. The parachute drop followed the BBC announcement, "Ça ne durera pas autant que les contributions." *Entre Lac et Montagne du Chablais . . . Haut-lieu de la Résistance Française: Saint-Gingolph et sa Région Frontalière dans la Résistance, 1940–1945,* by André Zénoni.

15. *In the Footsteps of a Flying Boot,* by Art Horning (New York: Carlton Press, 1994). In his own memoirs, Lynn H. Drollinger makes a reference to an incident at Toulouse-Matabiau, though he does not mention fleeing the train station. "We got off the train," Drollinger wrote, "and everyone was excited because we didn't know what was going on, but the Germans had lined up five men from the underground the night before and shot them."

16. After the war, Marie-Louise Dissard created a list of all the operatives of the Françoise organization, with notes on what became of them. Renowned mathematical philosopher Albert Lautman was executed by the Germans, while René Lamy was killed at the Creil railroad station during a bombing raid. Among the female operatives of the organization, several were arrested and imprisoned or even deported to Germany, but only one lost her life, Rolande Ulmann, arrested in August 1943.

17. The group also likely included Dr. Hulin and the other French civilian who had traveled with the seven Americans on the overnight train from Paris.

6. April Attempt

1. From Archie Barlow Jr.'s *Pursuit in the Pyrenees.* Unpublished memoirs. Barlow family archives.

2. Assuming that Frisco took the group to Sost in the Valley of Barousse, each one-way trip covered fifteen miles.

3. National Archives and Records Administration, Record Group 498, Entry 193 French Helper Files, Jacques Lartigue, Box 1073. Some evaders described Jacques Lartigue as wearing a prominent goatee, but after escaping from the Gestapo, he shaved it off.

4. *Happy Days and Adventures of a Lucky Young Man,* by Edmund George Luff. Unpublished memoirs. Luff family archives.

5. Apparently, the target practice session was not to everyone's liking. Priest Paul Louis felt compelled to admonish them. "Where do you think you are?" he asked them, "this is no day at the fair!"

6. Told by Stan Lepkowski in Hornung, *In the Footsteps of a Flying Boot.*

7. 2LT James L. Liles. National Archives Escape and Evasion report EE-692. National Archives Identifier: 5555332.

8. Luff, *Happy Days.*

9. SGT William Hendrickson did not know the name of the American airman who fell and injured himself. However, all the evidence points to that airman being 2LT James J. McMahon, one of the members of the climbing party. 2LT James L. Liles simply remembered him as "James" from New Jersey, first pilot of a plane downed around August 1943. McMahon was born in Hoboken, New

Jersey, and he was first pilot of a B-17 Flying Fortress shot down on September 6, 1943, during a mission to Stuttgart, Germany (see ssg George J. Kemp. National Archives Escape and Evasion report EE-2177. National Archives Identifier: 5556807).

10. Told by Stan Lepkowski. Pp. 171–80 in Hornung, *In the Footsteps of a Flying Boot*.

11. Luff, *Happy Days*.

12. Drollinger, *Escape and Evasion*.

13. Debriefing of ssg William B. Hendrickson. National Archives Escape and Evasion report EE-714. National Archives Identifier: 5555354.

14. Drollinger, *Escape and Evasion*.

15. Pp. 171–80 in Hornung, *In the Footsteps of a Flying Boot*. The brick building that Stan Lepkowski saw was the Grand Hotel of Superbagnères, built between 1913 and 1922. There was no road leading up to the Plateau of Superbagnères until 1960. Access was by way of the rack railway, which no longer exists.

16. In all likelihood the Lys Valley.

17. Barlow Jr., *Pursuit in the Pyrenees*.

18. Drollinger, *Escape and Evasion*.

19. 2LT James L. Liles. National Archives Escape and Evasion report EE-692. National Archives Identifier: 5555332.

20. The story of Maurice de Milleville's escape is told in Archie Barlow Jr.'s unpublished memoirs, *Pursuit in the Pyrenees*.

7. Hero or Villain?

1. Decades after the war, Cammish was asked to share his memories of World War II. He had no recollection of his time with the other five who reached Spain with him. What he remembered instead was that he had escaped out of the cabin by himself and had not stopped climbing for several hours. When he reached the other side of the border, he was so frostbitten that he could not eat and lost consciousness for a few days, waking up in a "boarding house." After his return home, Cammish showed signs of acute posttraumatic stress disorder (PTSD). Psychiatrists treated him for three weeks for "recurring nerve problems, stress, and nightmares." In all likelihood Cammish also suffered from loss or repression of memories.

2. Barlow Jr., *Pursuit in the Pyrenees*.

3. In his debriefing, Liles reported what de Milleville revealed to him, then added "is lying bastard" seemingly in reference to the Frenchman.

4. During his trial, Percy Treite acknowledged his role in building a gas chamber at Ravensbrück: "I remember that many Polish women were killed with a bullet in the nape of the neck. This killing was done in a perfectly savage way, and it was feared that some bodies might be burned while still alive. So, under pressure of circumstances, I concerned myself with finding an appropriate killing process. It was the gas chamber." From *Nazi Mass Murder: A Documentary History of the Use of Poison Gas*, by Eugen Kogon, Hermann Langbein, and Adalbert Rueckerl, eds. (New Haven CT: Yale University Press, 1993).

5. Peter Hore, *Lindell's List* (Stroud, UK: The History Press, 2016).

6. The story of Operation Frankton and the "Cockleshell Heroes" has been described in detail in numerous books including C. E. Lucas Phillips's (1956) *Cockleshell Heroes: Epic Exploit of the War* (London: Pan Books, 1956) and Airey Neave's *The Escape Room* (New York: Tower Publications, 1969).

7. In assessing the impact of Operation Frankton, Winston Churchill would later go as far as stating that it had shortened the war by six months.

8. *Lady Mensonges: Mary Lindell, Fausse Heroïne de la Résistance*, by Marie-Laure Le Foulon (Paris: Alma Editeur, 2015).

9. *No Drums . . . No Trumpets*, by Barry Wynne (London: Mayflower Books, 1971).

10. *Shot Down and on the Run: True Stories of RAF and Commonwealth Aircrews of WWII*, by Graham Pitchfork (London: A & C Black, 2007). Kenyan-born FO Mike Cooper bailed out of his spitfire on August 16, 1943, during a bombing raid on Le Havre, France. He landed in a tree near Lisieux in Normandy. He was given shelter by a French farmer's family for two months, then taken to Paris and eventually Ruffec with two other evaders, including FO Harry Smith. Australian PO Allan Frank McSweyn had escaped in September 1943 from Stalag VIIIB in Lamsdorf. SAAF CPT R. B. "Buck" Palm was a Hurricane pilot who had crashed in North Africa during the Western Desert campaign. Taken to a POW camp in Italy, he escaped but was recaptured as he attempted to cross the Swiss border. He escaped again as he was being shipped to a POW camp in Germany.

11. Launched in January 1942, the HM Submarine *Splendid* was an S-Class submarine in the Royal Navy. It served in the Mediterranean Sea and disrupted Axis supply lanes to North Africa, sinking Italian merchants and warships, including the *Soldati*-class destroyer *Aviere*. The German destroyer *Hermes*, which attacked and damaged the Splendid, was British-built (ex-Greek destroyer *Vasilefs Georgios*). Damaged by depth charges, the *Splendid* was forced to surface. The crew scuttled the *Splendid* before the men were taken prisoner onboard the *Hermes*.

12. Ian McGeoch, *An Affair of Chances: A Submarine's Odyssey 1939–44* (London: Imperial War Museum, 1991).

13. Before jumping off the train bound for Germany on September 12, 1943, Lieutenant Hardy had participated in an unsuccessful tunnel escape attempt at Certosa di Padula, a POW camp in Italy. He had escaped from Bologna on the night of the armistice between Britain and Italy (on September 3, 1943) but been recaptured hours later by the Germans. Lieutenant Hardy's liberation report (General Questionnaire for British/American Ex-Prisoners of War). Received from Oliver Clutton-Brock.

14. Luff, *Happy Days*.

15. Le Foulon, *Lady Mensonges*.

16. Report by LCDR I. L. M. McGeoch R.N. on his capture and subsequent escape to Switzerland and thence to Spain. National Archives of the UK, TNA ADM 1/16841.

17. Quoted from Le Foulon, *Lady Mensonge*.

18. In Spain, de Milleville not only risked a lengthy internment but also perhaps being deported back to France.

19. 2LT James L. Liles. National Archives Escape and Evasion report EE-692. National Archives Identifier: 5555332.

8. Aftermath of a Betrayal

1. From Herman van Rens's notes taken during the interview of Max Rens and communicated to the author.

2. Herman van Rens m.m.v. and Annelies van Rens, *Vervolgd in Limburg: Joden en Sinti in Nederlands-Limburg tijdens de Tweede Wereldoorlog* (Hilversum, Netherlands: Uitgeverij Verloren, 2013).

3. Report by Salomon Chait on his activities from November 1942 through September 1944. National Archives at College Park, MD. Records of Headquarters, European Theater of Operations, United States Army (Record Group 498) Entry UD 193, French Helper Files. The file is: m. Salomon-Edmond Chait and is found in Box 958.

4. Luff, *Happy Days*.

5. Luff, *Happy Days*.

6. The German arrest report suggests that the two Americans who had fled with Wilfred Gorman were Sergeant Pearce and Second Lieutenant Lindstrom. The same date, time, and location are given for the capture of all three men.

7. Evans, ed., "Pilot Officer Wilfred Gorman."

8. Police report dated January 21, 1946. Deposition of Jean Ferret. *Musée Départemental de la Résistance et de la Déportation* 31–042-D. Toulouse, France. The police report ends with the description of Dethlefs by the Gestapo's interpreter, Charles Hammer.

9. Luff, *Happy Days*.

10. On March 12, 1949, Paul Louis wrote a letter to a French investigating judge. In the letter, Paul Louis stated that 28 of the 35 in the group were apprehended on April 21 and 22. He specifically named Roger Bureau, Raymond Krugell, Jules Lautman, Jacques Lartigue, Fernand Bellenger, and Marcel Hulin as having all been captured with him. Archives of the religious congregation "Fils de la Charité," Issy-les-Moulineaux, France.

11. Jacques Liddell's file (AC 21 P 478 761), The Archives of Victims of Contemporary Conflicts (Ministry of Defense /SHD), Caen, France.

12. In Paul Louis's memoirs, one of the fugitives in the climbing party is referred to simply as "*Jacques le Hollandais*" (Jacques the Dutchman). There were two Dutchmen in the group, one of whom remains unidentified though perhaps named "Van Gullik" (or Van Gulik). Frenchman Jacques Lartigue is called "Petit Jacques" by Paul Louis, but a memorial plaque unveiled after the war indicates that Jacques Liddell was known by the nickname "Jacques the Philosopher." French writer Jeanne Hyvrard, whose parents went on mountaineering expeditions with Jacques Liddell before the war, had a possible explanation for

why the young Frenchman would have been also called "Jacques the Dutchman." As a graduate student in philosophy, Jacques Liddell would have been familiar with two works of eighteenth-century French philosopher Denis Diderot, "Jacques the Fatalist and his Master" and "Voyage to Holland." Paul Louis wrote that, however brutally he was treated by the Gestapo in Luchon, it was nothing compared to what "Jacques the Dutchman" endured.

13. Jean-Louis Pène's file (AC 21 P 657 149), The Archives of Victims of Contemporary Conflicts (Ministry of Defense /SHD), Caen, France.

14. Jean Ferret's file (AC 21 P 645 157), The Archives of Victims of Contemporary Conflicts (Ministry of Defense /SHD), Caen, France.

9. Maddy De Deken

1. Robert Cayla died in March 1945 at Plömnitz-Leau, a subcamp of Buchenwald where inmates worked in salt mines to build an underground factory for aircraft parts production. Marie-Louise Dissard (Françoise) had no doubts about Maddy De Deken being an informant for the Germans. On November 21, 1950, she wrote that Robert Cayla had been "denounced by the Belgian Mady also known as de Deckens [sic], who escorted American pilots on behalf of the Germans in order to infiltrate escape networks." Affidavit signed by Marie-Louis Dissard in Robert Cayla's file (AC 21 P 434 246), The Archives of Victims of Contemporary Conflicts (Ministry of Defense /SHD), Caen, France.

2. Like Marie-Louise Dissard ("Françoise") and Andrée de Jongh ("Comète"), Elaine Delhaye-Gill was awarded the Medal of Honor by the U.S. government after the war.

3. The two airmen were arrested and sent first to Buchenwald then to Stalag Luft III in Sagan in occupied Poland.

4. The two airmen were almost certainly members of the group that left from Saint-Girons with Jaume Soldevila and another passeur and spent one night in a cave in the mountains. In that same group were U.S. 2LT Michael L. Smith, U.S. SSG Lowell Creason, U.S. SSG Arnold O. Pederson, U.S. 1LT Neil H. Lathrop, RCAF FLT David Goldberg, RAF PO William Edward Watkins, and FO Robert Gordon Crosby, all of whom reached the Spanish border with Soldevila. First Lieutenant Lathrop's Escape and Evasion report (EE-613) includes the following statement: "A bombardier and radio op turned back in Pyrenees. From same Fort. Lived together so long that fed up with each other. Came down in Belgium." Gilmore (radio operator) and Stravinsky (bombardier) would have headed back toward Saint-Girons with FSG Wilfred M. Gorman but been captured while attempting to cross a stream (see "For King and Country" in this volume). TSG Daniel F. Gilmore's letter appears in full in *Une forteresse volante s'écrase entre Haversin, Buissonville et Serinchamps,* by Amand Collard, 2004, *Revue du Cercle Historique de Rochefort.* From the prison in Foix, Gilmore was transferred first to Saint-Michel in Toulouse, then Fresnes and Frankfurt, before reaching Stalag Luft IV. Stravinsky and Gilmore probably stayed together through their incarceration

in Frankfurt. Eddie Luff mentions being imprisoned in Frankfurt with a "2nd Lieutenant Fred Stravinsky USAAF," in all likelihood 2LT Albert W. Stravinsky.

5. The advance of the Red Army prompted Adolph Hitler to decide evacuating POW camps in the east. As with the evacuation of slave labor camps, German authorities hoped to keep control of all their prisoners to leverage a peace deal with the Western Allies.

6. Françoise Antonissen Antwerp C-9, Records of Headquarters, European Theater of Operations, United States Army (Record Group 498) Entry 171, box 695. National Archives and Records Administration.

7. Andrée de Jongh was arrested in January 1943 and later sent to Ravensbrück and Mauthausen, but Comet carried on her work, helping more than seven hundred stranded Allied servicemen reach safety.

10. The Woodcutter

1. Victor Sansuc was sent to the concentration camp of Dachau as a political prisoner on July 2, 1944. He survived Dachau and later stated that he had been arrested at the Luchon railroad station while guiding two Spaniards toward the border. The date of the arrest appears to be early March 1944. According to Victor Sansuc's mother, her son worked in Toulouse. Several weeks before Easter 1944, he returned to Saint-Aventin accompanied by the two Spaniards, "who wanted to go visit their families in Spain." The three men were arrested by two German officers during an ID check at the railroad station. The two Spaniards did not carry any official papers. Victor Sansuc's file AC 21 P 670 007, The Archives of Victims of Contemporary Conflicts (Ministry of Defense /SHD), Caen, France.

2. Ruling and proceedings in the case against Michel Pautot, Court of Justice of Toulouse, France. File 31-042-D, Folder 31-042-1 ("Bagnères-de-Luchon") and File 2546 W3, #29. Musée Départemental de la Résistance et de la Déportation, Toulouse, France. The verdict and sentencing were issued on December 18, 1944, by the Court of Justice of Toulouse.

3. By the author's estimation, two thousand francs likely represented one to two months of salary for Michel Pautot. One kilogram of bread was around four francs during the war.

4. Charles Hammer's description of the second woman matches that of Naïda Pautot, who according to Aventin Castex of Luchon was about 5 ft. 5 and very heavyset, with a dark complexion, an oval face, brown eyes, light brown hair, small ears, and a scar on one of her knees.

5. In 1934 the French newspaper L'Express du Midi reported that Catherine Pautot from Saint-Aventin had earned a gold Medal of Honor of the French Family for her having ten children. Since 1920 mothers with many children had been eligible to earn a Medal of Honor of the French Family.

6. Archie Barlow stated during his debriefing that "later that morning three guides went down to a village for food and one of the Frenchmen went with them. One guard remained with the party." The "guard" was probably French-

man Jacques Lartigue, since he is the only member of the party who, we know, fired back at the Germans on the slopes near the cabin.

7. Drollinger, *Escape and Evasion.*

8. Signed statement by Raymond Krugell, October 3, 1945. Archives of the religious congregation Fils de la Charité, Issy-les-Moulineaux, France.

9. From a series of recorded telephone interviews with Christian Ferret, Jean Ferret's son, in June and August 2017.

10. Following the arrests of much of the regional leadership of the M.U.R.— nearly 110 high operatives and family members—on December 13, 1943, Gabriel Gesse himself was captured the next day after attempting to run away. He was injured during his arrest and taken to the hospital in Saint-Gaudens, where a group of Resistance fighters came and whisked him away. "Mémorial François Verdier-Forain-Libération Sud."

11. Escapes and Hardships

1. "D-Day: 40 years later: A former POW remembers," by Daniel F. Gilmore. June 2, 1984. UPI Archives.

2. Louis, *Un mois entre les griffes de la Gestapo.*

3. Louis, *Un mois entre les griffes de la Gestapo.*

4. The real Jean Rehm was a friend of Raymond Krugell, professor of physics at the University of Galatasaray in Istanbul.

5. "Aux Frontières de la Liberté," by Robert Belot (Paris: Fayard, 1998).

6. National Archives and Records Administration, Record Group 498, Entry 193 French Helper Files, Jacques Lartigue, Box 1073. In reality, Jean Martin had to abandon his plan to make an opening in the floor of the car. At nightfall, as the train finally left the Paris area and sped along the track toward Germany, he set out to saw off boards in the floor near the door. After working for several hours in near complete darkness, he discovered that the floor was reinforced by an iron bar preventing him from making the required opening. Their only hope, he realized, was to reach the locking bar and hook operating mechanism through the sliding door. It was already about two in the morning when he began to saw one of the iron boards in the gate. Fortunately, he was able to complete that task quickly. "Sur les Chemins de l'Enfer," by Jean-Marie Chirol. Published by Club Mémoires 52, 1996.

7. "Sur les Chemins de l'Enfer," by Jean-Marie Chirol. Published by Club Mémoires 52, 1996. A liaison officer in the ORA (Resistance Organization of the Army), Marcel Peltier was arrested on March 29, 1944.

8. Maurice Coustaud did not survive the war. He was arrested by a German patrol on July 20 and vanished after spending time in prison in Chaumont then Châlons. "Sur les Chemins de l'Enfer," by Jean-Marie Chirol. Published by Club Mémoires 52, 1996.

9. Statement written and signed by Marcel Hulin on July 17, 1946. Private archives of the Bureau family.

10. "D-Day: 40 years later: A former POW remembers," by Daniel F. Gilmore. June 2, 1984. UPI Archives.

12. The Road Blockade

1. National Archives and Records Administration, Record Group 498, Escape and Evasion Reports, 1942–1945, E&E 724 (ILT Robert A. Martin) and E&E 709 (2LT John Betolatti).

2. Debriefing report for SGT Arden N. Brenden. National Archives and Records Administration, Record Group 498, Escape and Evasion Reports, 194, E&E 749.

3. Details of Georges Capcarrère's family origins and life were communicated to the author by his son Léo Capcarrère. It should be noted that Field Marshal Bernard Law Montgomery ("Monty") had no children of his own. His stepson Major Richard Carver fought during World War II. He was captured and detained as a POW, and later escaped back across German lines, but his year-long four-hundred-mile trek took place entirely in Italy. Other related rumors or stories exist in escape and evasion reports. During his debriefing in the UK after escaping over the Pyrenees, U.S. 2LT Michael L. Smith (Escape and Evasion report EE-614) mentions arriving in Toulouse on April 3, 1944, and staying in the house of a Frenchwoman and her daughter Marcelle. There, he was told that "General Eisenhower's nephew and the son of a British General Wilson had just gone through." The British general in question would have been GEN Henry Maitland Wilson, who succeeded Dwight D. Eisenhower at Allied Forces Headquarters (AFHQ) as the Supreme Allied Commander in the Mediterranean on January 8, 1944.

4. "Larroque, Mardi 13 juin 1944," by Guy-Pierre Souverville. Pp. 108–12 in the 1994 issue of *Nébouzan*, published by the Société Etudes et Recherches de l'ancien Pays de Nébouzan.

5. National Archives Escape and Evasion Report EE-846, 2LT Gilbert M. Stonebarger. In that same party of evaders were ILT Joel W. McPherson, Willie (Jean Duval), Yves Attali, Bob Roby, and Poney.

6. In a confidential memo dated July 19, 1945, ILT Alfred W. Satterthwaite wrote that "Françoise doesn't think much of him," but another statement seems to correct or contradict that statement, before adding that it was "highly debatable" whether Charbonnier could have "made a small fortune."

7. National Archives and Records Administration, Record Group 498, Entry 193 French Helper Files, Jean-Louis Bazerque ("Charbonnier"), Box 922.

8. Nahas, *La Filière du Rail*. According to Nahas, Charbonnier described his passeurs as men who smuggled livestock over the border before the war, adding that the money he received all went toward feeding and clothing their families. This was not entirely the case with some of the passeurs who worked for Charbonnier in 1944, whether Jean Ferret and Jean-Louis Pène, both employed, or André Crampé, too young to have his own family.

9. Recommendation for the award of the Medal of Freedom to Jean-Louis Bazerque (posthumously), dated May 1946. National Archives and Records Admin-

istration, Record Group 498, Entry 193 French Helper Files, Jean-Louis Bazer-que ("Charbonnier"), Box 922.

10. Pp. 171–80 in Hornung, *In the Footsteps of a Flying Boot.*

11. National Archives Escape and Evasion Report EE-849, ILT Joel W. McPherson. Worthy of notice is that Larroque is located about halfway along a road leading from Saint-Gaudens to Boulogne-sur-Gesse, where on June 3 three Americans were hiding.

13. Separate Fates

1. Drollinger, *Escape and Evasion.*

2. From "Harry Cammish, local identity," an article published in New Zealand's community newspaper *Hibiscus Matters* on February 27, 2010.

3. *Internierungslager* were internment camps to hold Allied civilians caught in areas occupied by the German Army.

4. Luff, *Happy Days.*

5. Le Foulon, *Lady Mensonges.*

6. *Les fusillés de la cascade du Bois de Boulogne, 16 août 1944,* by Guy Krivopisco and Axel Porin. 2004. City of Paris. Available at http://www.fondationresistance.org/documents/cnrd/Doc00135.pdf.

7. The train convoy reached Bordeaux, then headed north toward Paris, but was forced to turn back in Angoulême. The prisoners were returned to Bordeaux, where for nearly a month the women were interned in military barracks, the men in a synagogue. On August 9, they left again, but this time the train convoy traveled east to Carcassonne and Nîmes, before it followed the length of the Rhône Valley northward. After more delays caused by the destruction of several bridges, the train reached Nancy and Metz in northeastern France, crossed the German border, and arrived at Dachau on August 28. At Bordeaux's synagogue on July 31, eleven men were extracted from the rest of the male prisoners and transferred to the Camp of Souges, where on the next day they were executed by a firing squad. Among them was Albert Lautman of the Françoise organization, arrested on May 15 in Toulouse. Albert Lautman had learned of the capture of his younger brother Jules, whom according to Gabriel Nahas he wanted to help escape from Saint-Michel's prison. Nahas, *La Filière du Rail.* Two other notable Resistance figures among the eleven included Robert Borios, a police officer in Foix, and Litman Nadler, a medical student born in Romania, expelled from the University of Toulouse in 1941 because he was Jewish. On the day he was apprehended, Albert Lautman ("Lucien") was about to meet with passeur "Ramon" (Jaume Soldevila). Jaume Soldevila was also arrested on May 15, 1944.

8. *Vervolgd in Limburg: Joden en Sinti in Nederlands-Limburg tijdens de Tweede Wereldoorlog,* by Herman van Rens m.m.v and Annelies van Rens (Hilversum, Netherlands: Uitgeverij Verloren, 2013). Herman van Rens and Max Rens are not related.

9. See Jean-Luc Cartron, *La Vie de Marcel Chichery: Résistant Poitevin disparu en Déportation* (La Crèche, France: Geste Editions, 2015).

10. From Jean Ferret's statement in January 1946, most of the beating was actually administered not by Dethlefs, but by Ernest (Ernst?) Utesch, the Gestapo's driver. Utesch was a farmer from Rostock, about 5'5", with a medium build, a red moustache, and freckles on his face. Jean Ferret's deposition is part of a police report dated January 21, 1946. Musée Départemental de la Résistance et de la Déportation 31–042-D. Toulouse, France.

11. Raymond Krugell outlived his friend Paul Louis. He died in the spring of 1974.

12. Letter from Paul Louis to an unknown friend of Roger Bureau. Archives of Roger Bureau's children and grandchildren.

13. "The Way I remember it," by Robert F. Stahlhut. 2006. Available at http://384thbombgroup.com/_content/Stories/STAHLHUT-R-F.pdf.

14. From Robert D. Davis, *Before I Forget* (Bloomington IN: AuthorHouse Publishing, 2011).

15. SGT Melvin Porter was also held for some time at Stalag Luft IV while ILT Joseph E. Sutphin was sent to Stalag Luft III. Both men died fairly young, Melvin Porter in 1970 at the age of forty-seven, Joseph Sutphin from a heart attack at forty-three, leaving behind his wife Rose, daughters Diane, Sally, and Melody, and a son Joey. After his liberation in 1945, Joseph Sutphin spent three months in a hospital in Florida. Such was his weakened state that the army would not allow his wife or any other family member to see him.

16. Clutton-Brock and Crompton, *The Long Road*.

17. In his diary, John Acthim noted on November 1, 1944, that the population of the camp numbered 1,300 prisoners, all NCOs.

18. Evans, ed., "Pilot Officer Wilfred Gorman."

Appendix 4

1. Excerpt from a letter Jacqueline Houry wrote to her godmother on August 5, 1945. Letter kept in the family archives of Jacqueline Houry's children, Bernard and Martine.

2. Text of Jeannette L'Herminier's speech during the ceremony held for awarding Jacqueline Corbineau (born Houry) the French Legion of Honor. Family archives of Jacqueline Houry's children, Bernard and Martine.

SELECTED BIBLIOGRAPHY

Belot, Robert. *Aux Frontières de la Liberté*. Paris: Fayard, 1998.

Bleicher, Hugo Ernst, Ian Colvin, and Erich Borchers. *Colonel Henri's Story: The War Memoirs of Hugo Bleicher, Former German Secret Agent*. London: William Kimber, 1954.

Broussine, Georges. *L'Évadé de la France Libre*. Paris: Éditions Tallandier, 2000.

Cartron, Jean-Luc. *La Vie de Marcel Chichery: Résistant Poitevin disparu en Déportation*. La Crèche, France: Geste, 2015.

Chirol, Jean-Marie. *Sur les Chemins de l'Enfer*. Club Mémoires 52 (1996).

Clutton-Brock, Oliver. RAF *Evaders: The Comprehensive Story of Thousands of Escapers and their Escape Lines, Western Europe, 1940–1945*. London: Bounty, 2012.

Clutton-Brock, Oliver, and Ray Crompton. *The Long Road: Trials and Tribulations of Airmen Prisoners from Bankau to Berlin, June 1944–May 1945*. London: Grub Street, 2014.

Collard, Amand. "Une forteresse volante s'écrase entre Haversin, Buissonville et Serinchamps." *Cercle Historique de Rochefort* 39 (2004).

Connart, Philippe, Michel Dricot, Édouard Renière, and Victor Schutters. "The Comet Network." Available at: http://www.evasioncomete.org/.

Davis, Robert D. *Before I Forget*. Bloomington IN: AuthorHouse, 2011.

Dyreborg, Erik. *The Young Ones: American Airmen of World War II*. Bloomington IN: iUniverse, 2003.

Eisner, Peter. *The Freedom Line: The Brave Men and Women Who Rescued Allied Airmen from the Nazis during World War II*. New York: William Morrow, 2004.

Evans, Valerie, ed. *We that are Left . . . Remember: New Brunswickers in the Air Force*. Saint John, New Brunswick, Canada: 250 RCAF (Saint John) Wing, Air Force Association of Canada, 2002.

Eychenne, Émilienne. *Montagnards de la Liberté: Les Evasions par l'Ariège et la Haute-Garonne 1939–1945*. Toulouse: Éditions Milan, 1984.

Eychenne, Émilienne. *Pyrénées de la Liberté: Les Evasions par l'Espagne 1939–1945*. Toulouse: Éditions Privat, 1998.

Hore, Peter. *Lindell's List*. Stroud, UK: The History Press, 2016.

Horning, Art. *In the Footsteps of a Flying Boot*. New York: Carlton, 1994.

Husson, Jean-Pierre. "Histoire et mémoires des réseaux." Available at http://www.cndp.fr/crdp-reims/memoire/enseigner/memoire_reseaux/menu_reseaux.htm.

James, Keith. *They came from Burgundy: A study of the Bourgogne escape line.* Leicester, UK: Troubador, 2017.

Kogon, Eugen, Hermann Langbein, and Adalbert Ruecker, eds. *Nazi Mass Murder: A Documentary History of the Use of Poison Gas.* New Haven CT: Yale University Press, 1993.

Koreman, Megan. *How the Ordinary Heroes of Dutch-Paris Resisted the Nazi Occupation of Western Europe.* New York: Oxford University Press, 2018.

Lambert, Max. "Behind Enemy Lines: Eddie Worsdale's Amazing Journey Through Occupied France." *Air Force News*, March 2016. [*Air Force News* is the official magazine of the Royal New Zealand Air Force.]

Lasseter, Don. *Their Deeds of Valor.* Bloomington IN: Xlibris, 2002.

Le Foulon, Marie-Laure. *Lady Mensonges: Mary Lindell, Fausse Heroïne de la Résistance.* Paris: Alma Editeur, 2015.

Lucas Phillips, C. E. *Cockleshell Heroes: Epic Exploit of the War.* London: Pan Books, 1956.

Malolepszy, Tomasz. *European Ice Hockey Championship Results since 1910.* Plymouth, UK: Scarecrow, 2013.

McGeoch, Ian. *An Affair of Chances: A Submarine's Odyssey 1939–44.* London: Imperial War Museum, 1991.

Nahas, Gabriel. *La Filière du Rail.* Paris: François-Xavier de Guibert, 1995.

Neave, Airey. *The Escape Room.* New York: Tower, 1969.

Pitchfork, Graham. *Shot Down and on the Run: True Stories of RAF and Commonwealth Aircrews of World War I.* London: A & C Black, 2007.

Souverville, Guy-Pierre. "Larroque, Mardi 13 juin 1944." *Nébouzan* (1994): 108–12. Boudrac, France: Société Etudes et Recherches de l'ancien Pays de Nébouzan.

Van Rens, Herman m.m.v., and Annelies van Rens. *Vervolgd in Limburg: Joden en Sinti in Nederlands-Limburg tijdens de Tweede Wereldoorlog.* Hilversum, Netherlands: Uitgeverij Verloren, 2013.

Visser, Frank. *De Schakel: De Geschiedenis van de Engelandvaarders.* The Hague: Ad. M.C. Stok, Forum Boekerij, 1976.

Wheeler, Peter. *Kiwis Do Fly: New Zealanders in RAF Bomber Command.* Auckland: Longley, 2010.

World War II Escape and Evasion Information Exchange website. Available at: http://www.conscript-heroes.com/escapelines/index.htm.

Wynne, Barry. *No Drums . . . No Trumpets.* London: Mayflower, 1971.

Zénoni, André. *Entre Lac et Montagne du Chablais . . . Haut-lieu de la Résistance Française: Saint-Gingolph et sa Région Frontalière dans la Résistance, 1940–1945.* Saint-Gingolph, Switzerland: A. Zénoni, 1994.

INDEX

Index